To Nancy Mizey
5/8/

Thanks for helping

Voices from the Global Margin

me with the literature
& focus of chapter 2.
I'm responsible for the
errors, but you
helped considerably
in shaping my ideas.

Voices from the Global Margin

CONFRONTING POVERTY AND
INVENTING NEW LIVES IN THE ANDES

by William P. Mitchell

University of Texas Press ◆ *Austin*

Requests for permission to reproduce material from this work should
be sent to:
Permissions
University of Texas Press
P.O. Box 7819
Austin, TX 78713-7819
www.utexas.edu /utpress/about / bpermission.html

⊗ The paper used in this book meets the minimum requirements of
ANSI / NISO Z39.48-1992 (R1997) (Permanence of Paper).

Library of Congress Cataloging-in-Publication Data
Mitchell, William P., 1937–
   Voices from the global margin : confronting poverty and inventing
   new lives in the Andes / by William P. Mitchell. — 1st ed.
      p.   cm.
   Includes bibliographical references and index.
   ISBN 0-292-71269-3 (cl. : alk. paper)—ISBN 0-292-71300-2
   (pbk. : alk. paper)
      1. Indians of South America—Peru—Economic conditions.
   2. Indians of South America—Peru—Social conditions.   3. Indians
   of South America—Peru—Government relations.   4. Poverty—
   Peru. 5. Peasantry—Peru.   6. Sendero Luminoso (Guerrilla group).
   7. Peru—Politics and government—1980.   8. Peru—Social
   conditions. 9. Peru—Economic conditions.   I. Title.

F3429.3.E2M58 2006   2005019191
305.898′085 — dc22

To Barbara Jaye,
compañera, wife, friend, and colleague,
who (among other things) taught me to write,

and
to Anna Saltzman Cohn, my teacher at Midwood High School
in the 1950s, who challenged me to question.

Contents

APOTHECARY: Who calls so loud?

ROMEO: Come hither, man. I see thou art poor;
Hold, there is forty ducats; let me have
A dram of poison, such soon-speeding gear
As will disperse itself through all the veins
That the life-weary taker may fall dead. . . .

APOTHECARY: Such mortal drugs I have; but Mantua's law
Is death to any he that utters them.

ROMEO: And fears't to die? famine is in thy cheeks,
Need and oppression starveth in thine eyes, . . .
The world is not thy friend nor the world's law:
The world affords no law to make thee rich;
Then be not poor, but break it, and take this.

APOTHECARY: My poverty, but not my will, consents.

ROMEO: I pay thy poverty and not thy will.

—*Romeo and Juliet,* Act V, Scene I

Acknowledgments

I have many people to thank. The people of San Pedro and San José, and especially those described in this book, occupy first place. Not only have they shared their lives with me, but I have also learned about my own as I have been with them. Yvonne Gavre, a volunteer in the Peace Corps in the 1960s, oriented me to Ayacucho and provided me with warmth and housing. I am grateful to her and to Kate Milner Wright and Peter Wright, as well as to my brother Charles Mitchell (who lived with me for a period in the 1960s), for creating a welcome community in Ayacucho. Daphna Mitchell, my former wife, accompanied me to Ayacucho in 1973 and 1974; she continues to be a friend and to provide encouragement and intellectual support.

The Monmouth University Grants and Sabbaticals Committee, the Freed Foundation, and the Wenner-Gren Foundation for Anthropological Research have funded recent research, while the Foreign Area Fellowship Program, National Institute for the Humanities Summer Stipend, the National Science Foundation, Fulbright Hays, and Monmouth University supported earlier investigations.

Wilton Martínez assisted me in Peru in 1983, and Carla Tamagno in 1997. My colleagues at Monmouth, of course, have been a constant source of encouragement and intellectual vigor; the university librarians, especially Linda Silverstein, helped provide the materials that made the book possible. I am particularly grateful to Carol Felstein-Vignet and to Gil Podorson and Myra Podorson and to the many other people who encouraged me to put more of myself in the book and who have read and commented on the manuscript.

It has been especially delightful to deal with the critiques of my sons Sean, a colleague anthropologist, and Nicholas, a consummate writer. My siblings Cathleen, Charles, and Richard Mitchell have encouraged me throughout my career; my brother Edward Mitchell reviewed the manuscript, and his concern for social justice has been an inspiration. Discussions with Barbara Price, Constance Sutton, Antonio Lauria, and Sean Mitchell have contributed greatly to my intellectual development. Conversations with Dean Arnold about artisan production, irrigation, and ecology during our early field collaboration created an important synergy that improved my intellectual understanding of the Andes. I am especially grateful to him for spurring my interest in Andean ecology and for commenting on Chapters 3 and 4. Rick Vecchio reviewed Chapter 9 and has provided me with important information and perspectives gleaned as a newspaper correspondent stationed in Lima. Shari Friedman, George Ann Potter, and Eleanor Swanson commented on the entire manuscript; Leslie Fields, the Introduction and Chapter 9; Sharry Galloway, on Chapter 6; Yvonne Gavre, Chapters 1–3; Leslie Gill, a section of Chapter 6; Charles Harmon, Chapter 1; Jim Lewis, Chapter 8; Edward Mitchell, Jr., Chapter 1; Gloria Rudolf, Chapters 2 and 9; Diana Sharpe, Chapter 9; and Johanna Foster, Nancy Mezey, Karen Schmeltzkopf, Constance Sutton, Francis Trotman, and Katie Parkin provided invaluable comments on my discussion of gender in Chapter 2. Priscilla Gac-Artigas checked some translations, and José Oriundo helped translate difficult passages throughout the book. Lola Campoy Felices reviewed my Spanish orthography. Barbara Price, my good friend and colleague, has commented on the manuscript twice, providing theoretical insights and editorial advice that aided the book's development considerably.

Jane Freed has assisted with my research over the years and provided most of the statistical work for my 1983 research. She also has edited my manuscripts, including this one, and has taught me much. As the holder of the Freed Foundation Chair in the Social Sciences, I have been provided time and other resources needed for research and writing. I would not have been able to complete the book without that assistance, for which I am most grateful. My assistant, Jo Ann Aiton, has not only entered my near-indecipherable script into the computer, but has also commented on the manuscript and ferreted out obscure reference materials. My step-daughter, Valerie Harris, transformed my color photographs into black-and-white prints and, in the process, improved their quality considerably.

Peruvian colleagues, especially Luis Millones and Teófilo Altamirano, have been consistent sources of advice and inspiration. June Nash and Orin Starn provided crucial suggestions for the manuscript. I am grateful to Theresa May at the University of Texas Press

for her support and encouragement and to Kathy Bork for her edit-
ing, which helped clean up errors and improve the clarity of my
language.

My thanks to everyone, but especially to my wife, Barbara Jaye,
who as colleague and spouse has understood the isolation required
to complete a book, has spurred my growth as a writer, and has been
a companion, a friend, and a vast source of knowledge. I would not
have been able to complete the book without that assistance.

Acknowledgments

Introduction

A PERSONAL AND INTELLECTUAL ODYSSEY

"¡Su pasaporte, Señor!"

It was 1965 and I had just landed in Lima, the capital of Peru, the first stop on my way to the Andes, where I was to live for two years among Quechua-speaking peasants to gather data for my doctorate in anthropology. Since then fierce economic and demographic forces have undermined the lives of the people I met and those of other peasants, transforming Peru from a rural to an urban country. Peruvian peasants have long been tied to the global system, forced to mine the gold and silver sent to Spain in the colonial period, then laboring in wool, cotton, and guano production, their sweat generating more recent exports. Since the mid-twentieth century, however, economic decisions made in international capitals, compounded by a rapid increase in population, have impoverished them further, fomenting profound social disruption and stark inequalities that have underlain other changes, including the brutal Shining Path war of the 1980s. Peasants and their city children have struggled against these forces, and their voices as they have done so illustrate the human dimensions of a crisis pummeling not only Peru, but most of the developing world.[1]

My flight to Peru in 1965 was my first foreign trip. Outside the Lima airport, I gawked at peddlers selling tropical fruits and barbequed beef hearts, scenes vividly different from the Irish-Catholic neighborhood of my Brooklyn childhood. Flat-roofed houses and occasional moonscapes of oil-stained car repair pits flickered past the car window as I rode to my temporary Lima home. It was early November, springtime, but the winter fog that dampened and hid Lima had not yet lifted, and I could see little beyond the nearby streets.

Peru was in the midst of enormous changes, but their scope, like the fog-enveloped city, was not yet readily apparent. Most Peruvians

1 An Andean village

lived in rural villages, the majority in high Andean valleys, where monolingual Quechua-speaking peasants grew food primarily for home consumption rather than for sale in the market. Many were peons on haciendas, large feudal estates. They dressed in homespun clothing, often walked barefoot, and most lacked electricity, potable water, and roads. I was headed to San Pedro and San José, two such towns in the Andean area of Ayacucho.

The changes have been vast, beginning in the mid-twentieth century with a rapidly expanding population confronting an economy that squeezed the peasantry, processes taking place simultaneously throughout the developing world. To defend themselves, peasant farmers turned more and more to commerce, producing crafts for cash rather than bartering them for the farm produce they lacked. Most left their rural homes to work elsewhere. Some went to the nearby tropical rain forest to produce coffee, cacao, and fruit for national and international markets, then entered the coca/cocaine trade when prices for the legal commodities fell. Others became temporary laborers, sending remittances to family back home. So many migrated permanently to Lima that the city's population had exploded from 591,000 in 1940, to some 2 million when I arrived in 1965, to 7.8 million in 2002.[2]

Some continued on to the United States, Japan, Spain, Italy, and other rich countries, looking for work and becoming part of the new global movement of labor. I have listened to Peruvian and Ecuadorian buskers, itinerant street musicians, play Andean music in New York

City, Paris, Avignon, San Malo, Amsterdam, and Venice, their beating drums and reverberant panpipes drawing large crowds. I have run across distinctive Andean pottery and sweaters in a flea market in New Jersey, sold by a man from La Paz, Bolivia. A community of Peruvians has joined other Latin American migrants near me in New Jersey, transforming my home locality as well, a few gathering once a week at a Chinese buffet to convert the clams and raw fish used for sushi into ceviche, the Peruvian national dish.

To prepare for their new lives, rural farmers learned Spanish and sent their children to school. Many flocked to Protestantism, abandoning Roman Catholicism and changing the face of public religion. In 1996 my wife and I attended a rural Pentecostal church as some thirty people struggled to read Bible passages in Quechua. Most of the elaborate Roman Catholic fiestas I attended in the 1960s are no longer celebrated, but in 1996 I joined a circle around a pyre on the outskirts of Ayacucho City, the capital of the region where I have done most of my work. The scraggly bearded men were dressed in robes and the women in long gowns and veils, looking like popular representations of the apostles and the Virgin Mary. All sang and prayed while the fire consumed a ram's head: the Israelites of the New Covenant (Israelitas del Nuevo Pacto), a new Peruvian religion, were celebrating Passover.

Introduction

Some rural migrants to Lima have succeeded economically, even selling crafts over the Web to the global market. Most, however, have found ill-paid work, high unemployment, and increased poverty. In 1970 one-half of all Peruvian families, most first- or second-generation migrants from the Andes, lived below the poverty line, and 25 percent of the nation's families were destitute, unable to feed themselves. When nearly half the population lives in a state of perpetual poverty, and many others teeter on its dark edge, the consequences are enormous. "We're going to die of hunger!" Martín Velarde (Chapter 4) exclaimed to me in 1983, as he and his family, confronting this terrible economic picture, faced one disaster after another.

Crime, violence, prostitution, drug and alcohol addiction are not caused by poverty alone, but they almost invariably accompany it. In 1987 a man toting a machine gun robbed a shoemaker down the street from me in a middle-class area of Lima. I was dismayed (the shoemaker was such a poor man), but I was not surprised. Affluent Limeños routinely employ private police to guard their streets, a practice that has spread to Ayacucho and other provincial cities.

"My sister had a grocery store in the front of her house," Valentina Rodriguez (Chapter 5) told me. "She was robbed four times, but once she barricaded the entrance with bars, the robberies stopped." Like many other small-store owners, her sister has erected a mini-fortress. Denied entrance, her customers stand in the street, ask for what they want, then conduct their transaction through a small opening in the bars.

Political violence also festered in this amalgam of rapid population increase, great poverty, visible inequality, and enormous social change. In 1980 Shining Path, a Maoist guerrilla group, began its "armed struggle," a war that terrorized Peru for more than a decade, crushing the peasantry "between the sword and the wall," between the violence of Shining Path and brutal military repression. The war ended in 1992, but the sixty-nine thousand dead and six hundred thousand to one million refugees attest to its ferocity.[3]

During forty years of work in the Andes, including six living, working, and teaching there, I have interviewed many people who have been part of these events.[4] I want to bring them to life in this book, to show real people reshaping their lives as they have confronted the economic difficulties thrown at them, to try to give "a human face to the realities of poverty and violence."[5] Like most Peruvians, the majority of the people I know became neither guerrillas nor thieves; instead, they have struggled to keep food on the table and to bring joy to themselves and to their families. They also have brought great joy to me. As they have struggled, however, they have transformed their own lives and, in the process, transformed Peru.

I chose the people portrayed in this book because I know most of them well—so I could flesh them out with the detail obtained from frequent interaction—and because their stories illustrate the ways Peruvians have coped. They are a representative sample, not a scientific one, but I have listened to many similar accounts in Lima, Ayacucho, and Huancayo. I also have given myself a voice by trying to demonstrate my joys and blunders as an anthropologist, by describing how anthropologists work and correct our mistakes as we live with others, and how we gradually develop a deeper understanding of the societies we are studying and of ourselves.

The chapters are arranged in a sequence that represents developments in the Andes since the mid-twentieth century. In Chapter 1, Pablo de la Cruz and Claudia Velarde, Quechua-speaking peasants, represent something of a baseline. Neither fit the mold of the archetypal, nonchanging peasant (the quintessential *andino,* the timeless Andean) that some anthropologists incorrectly emphasized in the past.[6] Like other Andeans, Pablo and Claudia fashioned lives different from those of their parents as they encountered new ideas and realities. Nonetheless, they remained monolingual Quechua-speaking peasants, growing food primarily for their own consumption, even though Pablo was also a muleteer trading throughout Peru. Some people have remained monolingual Quechua speakers, but their numbers dwindle each year.

In Chapter 2, Horacio Gutiérrez and Benjamina Enríquez illustrate issues of gender, race, and class, social forces that have constrained peasant choices and that underlie many of the abuses of the Shining Path war. Because I knew Horacio and Benjamina before anyone else, I also discuss my entry into the community and my developing skills as an ethnographer. I continue with the story of Horacio and Benjamina in Chapter 3, describing the economic pressures that encouraged them and other peasants to enter commerce and to migrate.

The next two chapters depict peasants who migrated from their rural homes. Chapter 4 describes Martín Velarde, who, forced by poverty to live apart rather than with his family, left his wife and children in San Pedro to seek work on the coast of Peru. Valentina Rodríguez (Chapter 5) began life as the daughter of small hacienda owners, but now lives in the United States, a relatively successful international migrant, even as she has worked as a maid cleaning houses and caring for children.

Chapters 6, 7, and 8 portray the economic devastation and violence of the 1980s through the eyes of Triga, who as a teenager was briefly a partisan of Shining Path and a participant in the cocaine trade. After escaping a massacre in which his brother was murdered by the military, he became a successful businessman selling artisanal work to the global market (Chapter 6). Commander Tiger (El Tigre), the head of San Pedro's peasant militia, had worked in extracting guano; after returning to the sierra, he became head of the peasant militia fighting Shining Path (Chapter 7). Anastasio Huamán, who, along with his family, had to flee the death threats of Shining Path, finally settled in Lima to produce crafts for international clients (Chapter 8). Chapter 9 explores the forces underlying these changes.

To many who live north of Mexico, Latin America is like the waiter at the table: essential to the meal but ignored and unnoted. To bring one small part of this wonderful world to life, I have written the book for nonanthropologists and students, as well as for professional colleagues. To facilitate this broad readership, I have avoided jargon and placed citations in endnotes; a glossary of foreign words follows the notes. I have created pseudonyms for both the towns and the people and altered a few details to further obscure identity. Otherwise, all the

Introduction

people and events are real. Quotation marks represent actual speech, as I have translated it, but dialogue without quotation marks is a summary of a larger discussion.

In the 1980s I began to tape life histories. I use these histories beginning in Chapter 4. These long narratives (and their preliminary brief quotations within the same chapter) are set off in italics. It is never easy to translate another's speech, and the italicized material is not translated word-for-word.[7] Instead, I have tried to impart the rhythm and power of the original by freely translating the narratives into colloquial English that approximates the spirit of the original, generally omitting my own comments and in some cases condensing material and altering the recorded order to create a coherent account.

Similarities to the Peruvian experience are found throughout the developing world, as poor people have struggled to manage global processes that have impoverished them. This unequal economic order does not affect all aspects of people's lives equally (the belief in the mountain god, for example), but it does affect the distribution of wealth and life opportunity, with all the consequent social disruption. I hope that this book will provide some insight into the human costs of these phenomena and foster not only compassion but also greater efforts to seek a more just world.

ONE

Pablo and Claudia

PEASANT FARMING

Settling In

"Come back tomorrow!"

I was stuck in Lima, unable to get my nonimmigrant resident visa even after three months of going to and from the Ministry of Foreign Relations. I was disheartened but spent my time improving my Spanish, associating primarily with non–English speakers in order to do so.

"They want a bribe," a congressman from Ayacucho laughed. I had met him by chance, but by waving his letter, I not only entered the ministry after hours, but was issued a visa immediately.

Visa in hand, I climbed the stairs into the propeller plane to Ayacucho City in January, 1966. Leaving the Pacific coast, we flew over the western Andes, a stark landscape of barren mountains relieved only occasionally by narrow strips of green irrigated fields in deep and rare river valleys. Crossing the Continental Divide, we descended into the Ayacucho Valley, where we were met by stands of cactus and large swaths of green fields—a difficult land but more hospitable than the desiccated west. I stepped from the plane onto a dirt runway, saw to my luggage, and, along with other passengers, climbed into a rickety American car that took me into the city.

Known locally by its colonial name of Huamanga, Ayacucho City was once a rich colonial center on the Cuzco-Lima highway and home to wealthy miners from Huancavelica. Impoverished in the nineteenth century after new roads and a railroad bypassed the department, the city looked like a down-at-the-heels aristocrat: poor but elegant. I checked into the government-run tourist hotel, then walked to the central plaza. A statue to Sucre, the general who defeated the Spanish in the Battle of Ayacucho liberating Peru from

2 Ayacucho City cathedral

colonial rule in 1832, rose majestically from the park's center, its elegance accentuated by nearby royal palms. Colonnaded arches fronting the two-story buildings surrounding the square, anchored at one corner by a reddish-brown cathedral, framed the scene. Seated on a bench, I listened to men in ponchos and women in colorful skirts speaking Quechua. I had studied the language at Cornell University, but I was baffled by their rapid speech. Dark clouds threatened rain. I felt disoriented and lonely. The high-altitude air, oddly, smelled both moist and dusty.

I stepped into the baroque interior of the cathedral and stared at the magnificent central altar of embossed silver and gold, relics of Andean wealth produced for export to Spain and the nascent global system. Leaving the cathedral, I wandered along narrow streets lined with once-grand mansions interspersed with massive colonial churches. A small door in the huge wooden portal of one of the houses revealed a decaying courtyard paved with small stones. I entered the large central market building and was jostled by crowds of women, most carrying infants, vague outlines inside the shawls on their backs. "Buy from me! ¡Cómprame!" tradeswomen in broad-brimmed fedoras called, hawking produce heaped on their stalls. Butchered meats hung from hooks. Manufactured pots, pans, and plastic household receptacles, interspersed with manufactured clothing hanging like draperies clogging the passageways, were strung on clotheslines in a large area behind the market. Dried herbs, snakeskins, amulets, and other medicines were clustered in a section inside. Mustering my courage, I bought a *suyruru,* a medicine vial containing a black-spotted red seed floating in a clear fluid. "It'll bring you good luck," the vendor claimed.

I explored the city for a few days and met a group of Peace Corps volunteers teaching weavers how to prepare fabrics for sale in the United States. Four of us became good friends, a community of expatriates where I sought refuge when lonely. "You're going to need a Primus stove," one of my friends recommended as she helped me buy provisions. Several days later, she accompanied me to San Pedro, my first field destination. I later traveled to San José, some four hours away, establishing myself in both communities.

"I know the mayor and some of the artisans" in San Pedro, my friend said. We walked to the *salida,* the departure point at Ayacucho's northeastern edge. It was dawn, but a large crowd, bundled against the early morning chill, already stood waiting for trucks and buses to shuttle them throughout the interior. The unpaved street was still damp from the night's rain. Mud spattered our shoes. City bred, I wore desert boots, inadequate for the Andes. Most trucks were going in other directions, but after nearly two hours, we caught "La Virgen de Cocharcas," a truck headed toward San Pedro. Derived from an Andean manifestation of the Virgin, the truck's name was proudly inscribed in red above a faded blue cab.

"There's no room for me," I thought, lifting my foot onto the open back of the truck and joining some twenty others sitting on the sacks and boxes occupying most of the space. I maneuvered my way to a spot by the side, seeking a railing to grab, stepping carefully to avoid a squealing pig inside a burlap bag and noisy chicks in a wooden cage.

"Make a place for yourself, gringo," a woman in a brown fedora and a long, dark skirt told me pleasantly. "Who are you? What are you doing here?" I was not offended. In Peru, "gringo" is generally not an insult, as it is in some parts of Latin America, but refers positively to someone light skinned, usually a foreigner. If she had wanted to insult me, she would have called me *"yanqui,"* an epithet I heard only rarely.

After circling several times to search for more passengers ("Where will they fit?"), we set off down the dirt highway, hurtling around the curves. Passengers pounded the cab with their fists when they wanted to leave. Others climbed on, hauling sacks of produce and supplies. We arrived in San Pedro after two hours of stopping and starting.

Located on a high shelf around 3,300 meters (10,826 feet) above sea level, San Pedro commands a breathtaking view of the Ayacucho Valley, a broken terrain lying far below. It was such a vast expanse that I found my eyes drawn first in one direction and then another, the view blocked only far to the west by the Continental Divide, the snaggletoothed ridge of high mountains dividing the continent, and tumbling rivers to either the Pacific or the Atlantic oceans. Denuded of trees, except for recently planted eucalyptus forests, the prospect recalled the high plateaus of the southwestern United States.

I never tired of the view. Standing in brilliant sunshine, on some days I could see rain falling below in the distant valley, dark streaks draining a large, inky area of an otherwise deep-blue sky. Nights in the dry season, like Christopher Marlowe's Helen of Troy (*Doctor Faustus*), were "clad in the beauty of a thousand stars," the celestial gallery for some impressionist painter. Every time I return I am impressed anew. How can any place be so beautiful?

On that first trip, my Peace Corps friend introduced me to the mayor and to the police. I presented my credentials and letters of introduction. The mayor steered me to a place to live. Through ignorance, I neglected to seek out the district governor, who happened to be a political opponent of the mayor. Every district town has a mayor responsible for municipal policy and a governor, not the exalted position a U.S. reader might assume thinking of the governor of a state, but a kind of head policeman, responsible for maintaining order.

"Maybe you're a communist," the governor conjectured when I realized my error and finally sought him out. I went out of my way to placate him, and he soon invited me to visit his farm below the town, but I was never able to eradicate my initial blunder, and though they treated me with courtesy, the governor and his allies were usually reticent with information.

I was finally living in San Pedro, but had only the vaguest notion of how to begin. Fortunately, I had arrived in February, just before Carnival. I had met the gregarious Horacio (Chapter 2), and he invited me to join a group of costumed men, some wearing capes fashioned out of cheap blue plastic and others dressed as women, all playing flutes, whistles, drums, and cowbells. I blew a whistle and rang a cowbell, not being very good at much else. We roamed the countryside looking for scattered household fiestas, stumbling over muddy mountain trails, shooting off firecrackers, eating meals, and drinking *chicha,* the local maize beer. We danced and coated the faces of women with talcum powder. They coated ours in turn, adding flirtatious blows to our legs and shoulders with fists grasping hard peaches. The blows hurt, but I laughed, happy to be away from drab academic parties, even as my face was being painted with shoe polish.

Like my companions, I became very drunk, but, unable to navigate the mountains as well as they did, I huffed as I tried to keep up. Even after I had been in the Andes for more than a year, women carrying children on their backs, men, some without shoes or in sandals made of old truck tires and lugging heavy record players, usually had to wait as I struggled to get my breath and negotiate the stones on the path. In spite of my awkwardness in getting around and in understanding their Quechua (so different from the controlled environment of a classroom), I felt lucky to get to know so many people and to participate so riotously in their lives in the first month of my stay. "He's a good person," people began to say, "Allin runa, Buena gente," usually adding, "He eats and drinks whatever you give him."

Not all my early encounters were positive. "Stone eyes," someone might yell, or some similar gibe, done as part of Quechua joking behavior or out of suspicion that I was a communist or a spy, sent by the CIA or the Peruvian government to steal San Pedro's mythical hidden gold. Others thought I might be a *pistaco*.

"Come here," a companion called to two terrified children shaking behind some bushes as we walked in the countryside. Tall and light skinned, I looked like a *pistaco* and could not convince the children otherwise. Believed in by most rural people, *pistacos* are depicted as fearsome blue-eyed creatures that kill dark-skinned natives to sell their rendered fat for use in airplanes and other machinery. Although *pistacos* are imaginary, the belief in them evokes poignantly the relationship between rural communities and the exploitative outside, which drains their economic fat.[1] On the whole, however, such experiences were minor rifts in the general welcome.

Pablo and Claudia: Peasant Farmers

A few days into the revelry I found myself next to Pablo de la Cruz at a *cortamonte* celebration, one of the major activities during Carnival. I joined a circle dancing around the *yonsa*, a cut tree planted in the street and decorated like a Christmas tree with paper chains, fruit, bread, cigarettes, candies, and small bottles of *trago* (the local rum produced from sugarcane). I danced along with the rest, making ineffective but appreciated attempts at the difficult steps of the native *huayno*. I love to dance, but it took a good while before I was able to dance the *huayno* well. "Gringo, stamp your feet! ¡Zapatea!" amused women called out, politely covering their mouths as they laughed at my leaping instead of tapping out the beat with my feet. "The woman's

3 *Cortamonte* celebration around the *yonsa* tree

beating you!" My dance partners always won, some shamelessly knocking me off stride with their behinds as they gracefully continued to dance.

At his turn, Pablo entered the circle to take a few chops at the tree with an axe provided by the fiesta givers. "You childless, sterile thing!" a few young people taunted. "Cut down the tree and give the fiesta next year! You're rich!" Pablo was frequently heckled (I later learned) because he had never fathered any biological children. "Dammit!" Pablo shouted as he drank the maize beer offered to everyone after their turn at chopping, "I've given much more important fiestas than this piddling one. Here's my son!" he pointed to me. "I always told you my son was a gringo and lived in the United States. He's returned!" I laughed and embraced him. "Papay, my father," I called. To general enjoyment we played at father and son until one of the couples felled the tree, setting off a scramble for its favors, children jumping from the sidelines to strip the branches of goodies. The hosts toasted the couple who felled the tree and noted their names, for they had to give the fiesta in the same place next year.

I forgot the incident until a week or so later when I met Pablo drinking in a storefront cantina, a green leaf on a pole outside the door advertising that maize beer was for sale. I did not recognize him, our initial encounter embedded in the overwhelming blur of extravagant impressions of my first months in Peru, but he invited me to drink and related with relish to his wife's brother, Víctor, the story of our meeting. We laughed and I again embraced him and called him "Papay." I invited them to a round of drinks, then left after I shook their hands and excused myself with the standard, polite "With your permission, Permiso."

The next day Pablo and Víctor, carrying two sacks of fresh maize and potatoes, the "first fruits" that parents give to children from their fields, arrived at my house. Pablo told me how happy he was to know me and how grateful he was for the drinks I extended, "given just like a son." "God will repay you, Dios pagarasunki," he ended, giving the standard Quechua "thank you."

I'm glad to know you too, I said. I was nervous. How does one establish ties across great cultural and age differences? I decided to relax and "go with the flow." I served *pisco* brandy, a luxurious drink for San Pedro, and accepted his invitation to visit his home.

Busy finding my way around ("Where do I go to the toilet?"), establishing relationships, and interviewing other San Pedrinos ("How · *Pablo and Claudia* do I keep their names straight?"), I did not visit Pablo until several weeks later. Not knowing the way, I asked my friend Horacio to take me. We started out in the late afternoon, hoping to catch Pablo after he arrived home from weeding and loosening the soil around his potatoes and maize, a task then occupying most farmers. It was the rainy season. Fields were bright green. Footpaths were lined with rows of thorned, fleshy maguey leaves and pale green prickly pear cactus, brightened by yellow flowers and rosy fruit. Horacio hurled an occasional pebble from a woven sling to scare the birds attacking ripening maize. They rose squawking, only to settle on other plants a short distance away. Although the dark clouds threatening rain held off, an early afternoon downpour had saturated the ground, and we had to pick our way to avoid the mud.

We stopped at a rough-made wooden gate abutting a crude adobe house wall about twenty minutes below town. Unfaced with gesso, the adobe was pitted by rain and mottled with the tiny pieces of straw used in its construction. A terrace wall of fitted but undressed stone stood about six feet high to our rear. The house was in the intensively cultivated maize zone, and most fields were terraced and well fertilized.

"It's just me, my father, Ñuqallaymi, Taytay," I called in the high-pitched greeting voice, using the Quechua honorific, one that did not imply Pablo was actually my father. "Taytay" is a respectful way of greeting any peasant man. Peasant women are called "Mamay," my mother.

Pablo's wife, Claudia, quieted the snarling guard dog and invited us into the unpretentious farmstead. We stepped into the patio, an open space created by three unpainted and unadorned adobe rooms

14 arranged at right angles. A corral to guard barn animals at night formed the patio's fourth side, the collected manure, a valuable fertilizer, giving off a musty but not unpleasant odor. A covered veranda fronted one of the rooms, and a small, low adobe shed, the kitchen, clung to the wall of another. As I discovered many months later, after I was allowed into the interior, Pablo and Claudia slept in one of the rooms on a wooden platform covered with sheepskins and old woolen ponchos. Windowless, the room was dark and Spartan, its rough walls softened only by clothing and tools hung on pegs and a few old calendars and newspaper photos of soccer teams. A cross made of flowers, generally wilted but hung fresh each New Year to mark their identity as Roman Catholics, hung just inside the entrance. The other two rooms were used for storage. Like most

people, Pablo and Claudia did most of their work and living on the patio or the veranda, not inside.

Claudia waved away the chickens that foraged freely on the patio, then sat us on two low stools, first covering them with sheepskins. (Men never sit directly on the ground or on stools, for vapors can enter their testicles and make them sick.) Like almost everything in the household, the seats were of local manufacture, made from maguey stalks. Claudia had been grinding maize, effortlessly rocking a heavy oval stone about the size and shape of an American football over a slightly concave larger stone that sat just outside the kitchen doorway. She quickly cleaned up the debris. Pablo hurried from the adjacent field. "He's my son," he called to the neighbors hoeing his maize with him. "I'm proud of him."

The neighbors were working for Pablo in a reciprocal system known as *ayni*. Pablo was not paying his neighbors, but he owed each of them a day of labor in return. *Ayni* is always tit for tat, balanced reciprocity. The neighbors would not work for Pablo again if he ignored his obligation to return the work within a reasonable time. He also had to provide them with coca leaves. When San Pedrinos help one another without the explicit promise of future recompense (generalized reciprocity) they call it *yanapay*.

Horacio and I had come upon them during the late afternoon coca break. Coca breaks punctuate the day's rhythm, just as coffee breaks do in a New York office. Farmers take five to six coca breaks, lasting about fifteen minutes each, in a workday. They chew the leaves with a bite of the *tokra*, a mixture of water and ash from burned quinoa stalks that has been hardened into a small stone. Although unprocessed coca leaves are the source of cocaine, they have little, if any, narcotic effect. Peasants say that coca prevents them from feeling cold, hunger, and fatigue, although I have never experienced any impact other than the numbing of my lips after chewing a great many leaves. Nor have peasants ever reported to me any mental or euphoric changes caused by chewing the leaves.

Pablo offered us some leaves to chew, but I declined. Although it is unacceptable to refuse offers of alcohol or food, one can refuse coca leaves, which I usually do. They taste like dried grass cuttings to me. I had also brought coca leaves as a gift, my standard practice in San Pedro. Pablo held out his hat and Claudia her skirt to receive them. "God will repay you," Claudia thanked me. We chatted. Horacio helped with my Quechua. Serving chamomile tea made with the fresh herb she had plucked from the kitchen garden, Claudia complained that I had not visited them sooner. I explained my research. I had read about San Pedro and studied Quechua in the United *Pablo and Claudia* States, I told them, and I wanted to know more about their customs and to learn to speak the language better. They were surprised that schools teach Quechua in the United States, accustomed as they were to outsiders considering it an inferior tongue.

"Do you have a family?" Claudia asked.

Both my parents had died recently, I told her, my father of lung cancer and my mother of heart failure.

"Poor thing, *Pobrecito,* you're an orphan," Claudia commiserated.

I showed them a family photo and told them the names of my five brothers and one sister. They did not think it a large family, as people in Brooklyn, where I grew up, did. Pablo and Claudia agreed to help with my work, and as I left, Claudia gave me two eggs and some farmer's cheese.

I returned two days later in the early evening, as I had promised, with new hats for each of them. Claudia had not prepared a special meal as she had doubted that I would come. She apologized, but served me the everyday food she had prepared, a wheat soup. Pablo then asked me to become his adoptive son. Although Claudia had a daughter by another man, she also asked to adopt me. We all had fears: I worried that I might be taking on too many obligations; they worried that I would be ashamed of them and would not bring friends to visit. Deciding to take the risk, we chose the godparents for the adoption and set the date for the ceremony. (See Chapter 2 for a discussion of godparenthood.)

A few weeks later, accompanied by friends and relatives, we knelt before statues of the Virgin and San Martín de Porras. "I henceforth consider Pablo de la Cruz my father and affirm it before San Martín and the Virgin," I said in Quechua, guided by our godparents. I repeated similar words about Claudia, and she and Pablo echoed similar sentiments about me. We kissed the statues. Everybody embraced to the racket of exploding firecrackers, and we continued the celebration with rum, maize beer, and a meal that Claudia and her daughter, Yolanda, had prepared.

I never regretted the relationship. Claudia and Pablo were among the first people to show me San Pedro life, teaching me much about farming, herding, religion, and economic life. They took care of me, supplying me with food and pack animals when I wanted to travel.

"Come here! ¡Hamuy!" Claudia commanded as she pulled me from a group plying me with alcohol during the patronal fiesta. She later admonished me not to let people do that, trying to protect me from my own irresponsibility in allowing what she considered the self-interested behavior of others. Women are supposed to protect their husbands, sons, and fathers from their worst excesses.

When I left San Pedro in 1967, after nearly two years, Claudia and Pablo slaughtered a sheep for my farewell party, my *despedida,* and promised to hold the *chacra partición,* dividing their lands between me and Claudia's daughter, when I returned.

I also cared for them, contributing presents, arranging for a free cataract operation and eyeglasses for Claudia.

"Gringo! Get your father! He's drunk!" neighbors called, sending me to rescue Pablo during the bullfight in the patronal fiesta. Terrified, I entered the plaza, where bulls roamed about, pawing the ground. My father, quite drunk, was waving his poncho to attract them, but unlike the bullfighter, who steps to one side of his cape, Pablo was still wearing his poncho! I pulled him away, as a good son should, saving him from his folly. People laughed at my visible fear, but I was already beginning to reject the box of masculinity that imprisons so many men. It was only many years later, however, that I felt fully comfortable in my skin, liberated by my therapist: "Whatever you do, Bill, is what a man does."

My link to Pablo and Claudia also connected me to the entire community, both in San Pedro and Lima. Several of her grandchildren have worked as my assistants, and a nephew in Lima is my godson. In December of 2000 I received an e-mail from my godson's daughter, asking advice on how to search the Web for a university assignment. College? E-mail? The Web? In 1966, as I sat in Pablo and Claudia's humble farmstead offering them coca leaves, when there was not even a telephone in Ayacucho City, I never dreamed that a grandniece of Claudia's would be attending university, nor that I would be in contact with anyone from San Pedro except by the rare letter, which took

a month to arrive. Nor for that matter could I have imagined that
I would be sitting at a computer writing these words.

Like most of his contemporaries, Pablo spoke hardly a word of Spanish, had never attended school, and was unable to read and write. He was little more than five feet tall. His straight, black hair was peppered with gray and his jaw was covered with rough gray whiskers. Years of walking barefoot on stony footpaths had raised thick calluses on the soles of his feet, but by the time I met him he wore rubber-tire sandals. Mud and grime nonetheless still coated his sockless feet, testimony to long hours toiling on his farm. He dressed in peasant clothing: homespun woolen trousers, a blue-checked manufactured shirt, a dark brown woolen poncho redolent of lanolin sheep oil and woven so tightly that it shed rain, and a hat of vicuña skin that shielded his face and eyes from the sun. He rarely changed except to wash; he owned little additional clothing. In 1973 Pablo claimed to be ninety-six years old, but in 1974 he told me he was sixty-five, which was the better estimate. San Pedrinos who are unable to read know which stage of life they are in, but they often do not remember their birth dates and can only guess their chronological age. This contrasts sharply with their city children, who not only know their own age and birthday, but those of all their friends and family. Urban Peruvians are astonished that I need to consult my address book to tell them the exact day and month of my children's birthdays, one more sign of gringo strangeness.

Pablo and Claudia

Claudia, also a monolingual Quechua speaker without formal education, plaited her hair in the two long braids of peasant women. She wore the regional dress known as *huali* or *centro:* three ankle-length skirts, placed one over the other; a plain blouse; and a colorful shawl. She tucked a corner of the topmost green homespun skirt into a woven belt to reveal the now-faded but once-beautiful embroidered border of the skirt just below. A brown, broad-brimmed felt hat and thin, torn black-plastic shoes completed her attire. Like most peasant women she wore no underclothing and would squat in the street or field to urinate. There is no shame in urinating in public for either men or women, although genitalia must be hidden. Modesty conventions are hard to break, and I always felt uncomfortable urinating on the wall of a house or cantina.

Claudia's birth certificate told me she was born in 1907, but constant exposure to the sun and wind had wizened her face, and she looked considerably older than her fifty-nine years, a perceptual aging accentuated by my own youth. Nonetheless, even then, Claudia was truly frail and her vision clouded by cataracts, conditions that worsened as she aged. The strong ultraviolet radiation of high equatorial altitudes damages both eyes and skin.

I was much closer to Pablo than to Claudia, possibly because she already had a child. I also spent more time with him. We went together to the hot springs of Quris Baños, a week-long trip that we shared with other San Pedrinos and that bonded us closely. Although I had invited Claudia, she remained behind to protect the house and care for the animals and sent her daughter, Yolanda, in her stead. We were a family group on vacation, first sharing a rude tent we constructed of cheap plastic, then moving into an adobe shelter when it became available.

Yolanda had brought eggs and chickens to prepare, a richer diet than usual to protect us from the beneficial but dangerous hot waters. I became languid soaking in the steaming pools, the heat penetrating my body. I usually soaked too long for Pablo's comfort. "Don't get a chill, a *choque con el aire,*" he would admonish, bundling me up and rushing me from the bath. Close in meaning to what Americans call a "chill," a *choque con el aire* (literally, an air shock) is considered an important cause of disease, especially when a person is in a weakened state. Pablo used the healing mineral waters to soften the thick calluses on his feet, but risks lay in wait for him as well. "I heard a *manchachico* on the path!" he reported one evening as he returned to the camp, frightened that this mythical dead person, condemned to wander the earth, might seize him (see Chapter 5). In spite of the dangers, we were refreshed in body and spirit as we climbed the steep and very long path back to the road a week later.

We also had become closer. I became Pablo's son, his *churi,* Pablopa *churin.* I loved his warmth and well remember his smile. I liked the smell of his body: a sensuous combination of sweat, old woolen clothing, and masticated coca leaves. Although roughened by years of farmwork, his hands similarly felt warm and welcoming when they enclosed my own. I also felt the loss of my parents, the absence of my family, the separation from my home. "Churiymi, my son," he usually whispered softly, a smile crossing his face when he saw me.

The Peasant Economy

Pablo and Claudia lived alone, following the preferred pattern in which a homestead is usually inhabited by parents and children. They were unusual in that they had no children together, although Claudia's grandchildren often slept in their home. Ideally, a man brings his wife to live in his parents' house for a year of trial marriage, after which they move to their own house built on land given by the man's father. These preferences, however, can rarely be achieved, for there is usually insufficient land for even the parents. Like many others, Pablo lived far from his natal home.

Pablo had been born to poor parents in a rural hamlet dominated by several large haciendas. Until 1966, when the system was changed, these haciendas commandeered the hamlet's irrigation water six days a week. Irrigation allows farmers to cultivate maize, their most important source of protein, at higher altitudes than would be possible with rainfall alone.[2] In this hamlet, peasants could take drinking water for free on Sundays, but during the rest of the week they had to buy water to irrigate their farms from haciendas that demanded their labor in return. Partially to escape these claims on labor, Pablo's parents had migrated to the high-altitude grasslands, the *punas,* of a nearby town, where Pablo learned the trading business.

Pablo and Claudia

Pablo liked to talk about his life as an *arriero,* a muleteer. In one interview in 1973, as we sat in the sun, he looked up and sent Claudia's grandson, Miguel, into the bedroom to get a small tin box. Pablo opened it and took out receipts for coca leaf purchases made years ago. They were worn and faded, but, smiling broadly, Pablo asked me to read them to him, wanting to know if his license to sell coca leaves was still good. Spurred by my reading, he recited the names of his trade routes like a litany: Puquio in Ayacucho, the Colca Valley in Arequipa, Ica on the coast. He described the major footpaths, the *caminos reales,* that connected San Pedro to the rest of Peru. There were few automobile roads then, and even in 1999 San Pedro's hamlets were connected mainly by footpaths, and, except where deterred by political violence, people continued to transport produce along them on mules.

When he was young, Pablo usually made two trips a year. Accompanied by another muleteer, he took a string of eight mules loaded with milled wheat, freeze-dried potatoes (*chuñu*), and commercial goods to the eastern tropical forest to barter for coca leaves. Sometimes he returned directly to San Pedro or to the market in Ayacucho City, where he sold or bartered the coca leaves. At other times, he traveled with the coca leaves to Cangallo, the next province, far to the southwest. He sometimes crossed the Continental Divide to Ica and Nazca on the coast. Often gone for months, he returned to San Pedro with money, maize, horses, burros, and mules.

Pablo used his earnings to take on important religious posts, or *cargos* (see below), and to rent and buy agricultural land. After ten years or so, he had earned enough to buy irrigated maize fields near San Pedro's central town, an area where haciendas did not control the water. In the mid-1960s, he and Claudia owned about six acres (almost two hectares) of this prime land. They had several more acres in the high potato zone that Pablo had inherited from his parents. Far more prosperous than most San Pedrinos, who on average own only about three-quarters of an acre (a quarter of a hectare), and having only Claudia's one child, Pablo and Claudia were among the minority who were able to produce most of their own food.

When I met him, Pablo did most of the farming. He did not plant contiguous fields but, like most Andean peasants, had small, scattered plots. This pattern minimized risk: if the crops in one field failed, chances were another would succeed. Small plots also allowed him to cultivate a wide variety of foods. The higher the altitude, the colder the climate, so that in the Andes tropical and arctic climates are often within a day's walk. Pablo grew cold-resistant barley, peas, potatoes, and other tubers unknown outside the Andes (*maswa, olluku,* and *oca*) in a large upper field about twelve thousand feet above sea level, warmth-loving maize and beans farther down in several fields around his home, about ten thousand feet above sea level, and wheat still lower down, about nine thousand feet above sea level. Maize and potatoes, served at almost every meal, were the most important crops. The scattered plots also allowed Pablo and Claudia to schedule their work. Different crops at different altitudes did not make simultaneous demands on their time.

A kitchen garden, or *huerta,* lay just outside their homestead. It was a pleasant spot, planted with peach and medlar (*níspero*) fruit trees and flowers that were grown not only for beauty, but also as offerings for the mountain gods, saints, family graves, and for sale. Claudia also cultivated chili peppers, onions, carrots, and herbal teas and spices there. Because the garden was supplied with abundant irrigation water, Pablo was able to plant an early crop of potatoes in late July, followed by a second of maize or greens in October. Unlike most fields, kitchen gardens were well defended against stray animals by adobe walls topped with cactus and maguey.

Pablo and Claudia were well off, but they worked long, hard days. "Tell me about your work on *yarqa aspiy,* the irrigation corvée," I asked Pablo.

"Everybody has to clean those canals that they use," he answered.

We were seated on his patio, the place where I usually interviewed him. Earlier in the day he had been drinking in the cantinas in town, taking advantage of the conviviality found on most Sundays, but he was catching the warmth of the late afternoon sun as we spoke. Pablo told me that he usually spent two days cleaning the irrigation canals in August, just before the major sowing that begins in September. Pablo and the others also worked without pay in the general communal corvée, the *faena,* building and repairing footpaths, schools, the municipal hall, and the church. Rather than hire laborers, as municipalities do in the United States, San Pedro required each household to contribute one person to work for a day; they took turns until the project was completed. Common in rural agrarian societies where cash is scarce, corvées are frequently exploitive, the poor toiling on projects for the rich. In San Pedro, townspeople avoid the corvée by purchasing a replacement or by donating money, coca leaves, and cigarettes for the workers. Pablo, however, always went to the corvées himself, usually spending a week on these communal *Pablo and Claudia* projects over the course of a year.[3]

After preparing the irrigation system, Pablo and Claudia still had much to do before planting their crops. The animals that had been brought down from the high pastures in May to graze on harvest gleanings (thereby fertilizing the fields) had to be sent back. A horse or sheep loose in a sown field could destroy a year's work, and many of the disputes among neighbors were over such damage. When Pablo and Claudia had many animals, they invited family and neighbors to an elaborate branding, or *señal,*[4] before returning their stock to the *puna* grasslands, not only branding the animals, but also asking the mountain god to care for them.

As we spoke about the branding during one interview, Claudia began to sing the special songs, the *qarawi,* always sung by two women during the branding and agricultural work groups. Using the high head tones characteristic of Andean women's singing, Claudia produced a light and whispery sound, almost like a falsetto, but one that carried far distances. I loved the sounds of hidden *qarawi* singers rising from the countryside at times of heavy agricultural work.

"When the rain comes," Claudia sang in those ethereal tones, "the calf grazing on the mountain bows his head. When he reaches the heights of Rashuillca [the highest and most powerful mountain], he again lowers his head against ice and cold." Hearing the song, Pablo cried, recalling the many sheep, cattle, goats, mules, and horses that he once owned.

After the branding, Pablo and Claudia planned their sowing carefully to match the needs of plants at different altitude levels, planting the highest fields first because crops take longer to mature there in the cold. Because this sowing begins in the dry season, San

4 Terraced fields

Pedrinos irrigate these high fields first, sending the water down the mountain slope, field by field and day by day, finishing when the lowest and warmest fields are planted with the onset of the rains nearly three months later, in November and December.

After irrigating his fields, Pablo plowed, sowed, and tended them, work that lasted from September to April. In May he harvested his maize, located near his home. In June he moved to high-altitude fields and slept in a grass hut, the *hatus,* to take in ripening potatoes and to guard them against theft. "You can find your father in Choque Mesa," Claudia would tell me in those months when I went to look for him. He carried his produce home on burros and completed the harvest in July, just in time to begin the cycle again. It was exhausting labor and the results were never certain, the yield threatened by stray animals, drought, heavy rain, hail, frost, disease, insects, birds, and human theft. "Why are cattle grazing Pablo's barley fields?" I asked Claudia's grandson in July, 1974. The rain, he responded, had delayed the sowing, and frost had ruined the crop: best to use these fields as pasture and thereby fertilize them in preparation for planting maize.

Agricultural labor is hard to come by, and Pablo and Claudia depended on Claudia's daughter and her children in return for some of the yield. Neighbors also helped in reciprocal labor exchanges, but when Pablo and Claudia needed ten or more workers, as for the hoeing of maize and potatoes, they usually held a festive work party known as a *minka.* They paid their workers in cash and in kind but, most important, they also provided food, maize beer, coca leaves, cigarettes, and *qarawi* singers. At the height of the growing season, when labor was especially scarce, people would not work for a prosperous family that did not hold such a festive work party. Besides, people enjoyed hosting a *minka*. The conviviality, good food, and attendant prestige felt good.

Even so, Pablo missed having the assistance of his own children and was often behind in his farmwork. "I've a good harvest," he told me in June of 1973, "but I can't bring the crop in by myself." Yolanda's husband worked on the coast in the cotton fields of Cañete most of the year, but was unavailable to Pablo even when he came to San Pedro. "Please tell Enrique to help me," Pablo asked. "Maybe he'll listen to you. I've given him fields, but he still doesn't help. I no longer have the strength to load my burros myself."

Claudia began her day before dawn in the kitchen, which jutted like a lean-to from the main room. The kitchen was windowless, dimly lit by the cooking fire and the sunlight that struggled through *Pablo and Claudia* the narrow, low doorway and tiny chinks in the eaves. Cooking smoke hung heavy in the air, warming the small room, but irritating lungs and eyes. Dark soot, the detritus of a lifetime of cooking, clung to the roof beams. Blackened ceramic pots crowded the small raised hearth. Three stones, placed like the points of a small triangle on the hearth, made up the simple cooking area. Claudia balanced two pots against one another on the stones, then fed the fire underneath with bits of dried brush, maguey, eucalyptus leaves, cornstalks, corncobs, or cow patties. Fuel is scarce, usually requiring long trips on foot to the higher slopes.

In the morning Claudia usually prepared a hearty soup of maize, wheat, or barley to which she added potatoes, onions, and greens and herbs. She often added beef or pig fat, reserving meat for ceremonial occasions. Bowls of potatoes, boiled dried maize (hominy, or *mote*), parched maize (*kamcha*), and a condiment sauce of chili peppers and onions usually accompanied the soup. She made a similar meal in the afternoon and evening but sometimes changed its main ingredient. If she was away from home and unable to cook, she might simply reheat the morning meal. During festive work parties, Claudia always prepared maize beer and *mondongo,* an elaborate stew made of *tripas* and hominy.[5]

Pablo and Claudia ate in the kitchen, but visitors were served on the patio or, when it was raining, on the covered veranda. Claudia served the food herself, assigning portions according to a person's importance or place in her favor. Whether it was because she was partially blind or simply careless, Claudia was one of the few women in San Pedro who generally prepared unappealing food. Several times she served questionable soup. "Was the soup bad?" I asked Horacio as we returned home after one occasion. "Maybe; it certainly tasted awful," he replied. It once smelled of kerosene, probably from a rag used to plug a hole in my bowl. Nonetheless, I remember fondly the afternoon Claudia pulled dried beef, her homemade *charqui*, from above the hearth as we squatted there, and threw it into the fire to roast. She did not see the mouse that fell with the meat and then scampered away, but I did not mind: the roasted meat was delicious. "Don't tell your father that we ate *charqui*," she said. Even though men are served first at mealtime, women control food and often eat better than their husbands, but they do not wish to broadcast the fact.[6]

During the harvest, Claudia traveled to the fields to collect the crops. After my initial two-year stay in San Pedro, I generally returned during my university vacation period, from May through August, the harvest and dry season in San Pedro. I would often find Claudia and her granddaughters on the patio husking maize, setting the yellow, red, white, and purple ears on the ground to dry in the sun, flooding the patio with color. Green squash lay on the red-tile roof to ripen. Claudia sorted their potatoes by size, placing them and other tubers in the food storage room. She was responsible for this larder and had to see that the food lasted as long as possible. She took any surplus to the Sunday market on the plaza to barter for something she lacked. Traders also came to her.

5 Harvested maize drying in sun

"What're the men with llamas doing here?" I asked Pablo when
I arrived to interview him in August of 1973. They were from the
alturas, the heights above the town, he told me, and Claudia has just
traded her maize for wool blankets. "They come most years," bringing potatoes as well as cloth, looking for the maize they can't grow in
the cold high altitudes.

Before she was blinded by cataracts, Claudia tended the animals
around the farmstead. She milked the cows and made cheese to sell
to San Pedro store owners. She salted and dried meat from butchered
animals to make *charqui* for storage and sale. Most peasant women
raise guinea pigs (*cuyes*) in their kitchens, and Claudia was no ex-
ception. An important ceremonial food throughout the central Andes, they are depicted as part of Christ's meal in a famous colonial
rendition of the Last Supper that hangs in the Cuzco cathedral. San *Pablo and Claudia*
Pedrinos live close to their animals, and Claudia's guinea pigs competed with her chickens for food scraps on the kitchen floor. She
sometimes used the guinea pigs and chickens for festive meals, but
she raised them primarily for sale, using the cash to purchase food,
clothing, medicines, kerosene, and other goods.

Claudia worked even while she walked. Like most Andean women,
she carried her goods and sometimes a grandchild on her back in
a shawl, or *kipi,* leaving her hands free to spin wool into yarn on
her spindle. When I returned in 1996, however, few women were
spinning wool. Manufactured cloth was cheaper and easier than
homespun.

Good Citizens

In the 1960s San Pedro organized its public ritual through spectacular fiestas honoring saints, celebrations that were at first won-
derfully beyond my ken. During the week-long patronal fiesta in
honor of San Pedro, sponsored alternately by the two barrios of the
town, musicians led large crowds through the streets, the celebrants
connected to one another through interlinked arms, the undulating
lines swaying one way then another, driven by the powerful sounds
of saxophone, violin, tuba, and harp.

"Gringuito! Come out!" revelers called as they passed my house
early each morning. As I joined them they proffered copious amounts
of maize beer and cheap rum.

Winding our way to the Roman Catholic church, we attended
mass, the usually bare altar decorated with flowers and lit by candles,

6 The celebration of the saints

a brilliant contrast to interior stucco badly in need of repair. The congregation, more women than men, stood, shoulders touching, as young people clustered about the entrances and spilled into the plaza. The brilliant blue, green, and red shawls covering the heads of the women demonstrated both piety and taste for beautiful colors, while the candles many of them carried lit but never fully conquered the interior gloom. A portable organ, the *melodio,* and the man playing it had been placed at the rear of the church to support the singing of the congregants, their beautiful Andean sound and the entire tableau transforming an ordinary day into an extraordinary one.

After the services, scores of men lifted heavy wooden floats to their shoulders, each float carrying a saint's statue dressed in colorful robes, jewelry, and a crown. The saint stood atop a pyramid of white papier-mâché and surrounded by hundreds of flickering candles. The priest, dressed in golden vestments, led the procession around the plaza and sometimes wafted an incense burner that unleashed deep memories recalling the processions of my Roman Catholic childhood. As many as three orchestras accompanied the procession, one orchestra for each of the three saints being celebrated. Playing different music simultaneously, they competed with one another while the tolling church bell added to both the joy and the cacophony. Rushing up the outside steps to the church tower, I jostled other young men and women also struggling to get a better

view. "I'm taking photos of San Pedro," I shamelessly cried, to jus-
tify my claim to a high perch.

After the procession, I often joined the celebrants and musicians at the houses of the fiesta sponsors, where we ate, drank, and danced. Like most of the celebrants, I escaped to my home to rest when I could, only to be called once again as the crowds sallied into the streets and paused in front of my home. In the afternoon the plaza was turned into a bullring, fierce animals scattering the onlookers as they charged. Never killed or wounded, the bulls provided opportunity for men to demonstrate their bravery. In one fiesta a man was gored to death as a bull escaped the plaza and came upon him unawares. Although tragic, the death also signified that the fiesta was a good one, that "the sponsors fulfilled their obligations to bring fierce bulls." Fiestas can last more than a week, going day and night, and involve *Pablo and Claudia* the entire community, including returned migrants. I never had the stamina to remain for the entire patronal celebration and always fled to Ayacucho City, exhausted, before the end of the week.

Such celebrations were carefully organized by means of *cargo* posts, communal burdens assigned to a married couple, who became part of the town's informal but important prestige and social hierarchy. The *cargo* of *alférez*, the standard bearer, was the most expensive, and the holder was responsible for arranging for a priest to say mass and for hiring an orchestra, generally brought from Ayacucho City for at least a week. Other *cargos* were responsible for decorating the float (the *trono*, or throne), arranging the church altar (the *altar*), providing a musician to play a portable organ (*melodio*) during the mass, and furnishing animals for the bullfights (the *novenante*). The *mayordomo* supervised the fiesta, ensuring that all *cargo* posts were properly filled.

Unlike the overtly religious *cargos*, the *varayoc* were more explicitly political *cargos* charged primarily with maintaining order. Consisting of twenty or so men in each of two *varayoc* organizations, one for each barrio in the town, the *varayoc* carried whips and were a police force operating under the orders of the governor as they arrested people accused of theft, wife beating, or some other offense. "Everyone was afraid of them," people told me. The *varayoc* also buried the dead, assisted widows in planting their fields, and generally helped the religious *cargo* holders during the communal fiestas. By the time I arrived in San Pedro, the *varayoc* and their duties had mostly disappeared, but two *varayoc* officials were still distributing irrigation water in the barrio of Urin Saya.[7]

7 The *varayoc*

Peasants were expected to accept service in the religious *cargos* and *varayoc* posts, serving for a year each time. They started with the simplest and least expensive positions and gradually accepted more demanding ones, taking on expenses commensurate with their wealth. People generally accepted these obligations reluctantly.

"What *cargos* have you taken on?" I asked Claudia while we shelled maize together. It had been a long interview session, and by this time Claudia was a reluctant source, tired of my questions. She described the eight *cargos* that she and Pablo had completed, but I double-checked her account with Pablo and interviewed Claudia about the same matter on other occasions. One has to do that. People get tired and sometimes end an interview with some curt and not very accurate reply.

Pablo was more forthcoming. He enjoyed his *cargo* participation more than did Claudia. As well as providing bulls for the bullfight, Pablo told me with pride, "I brought horn players (*waqra puku*) from Chuschi," a community far to the south of San Pedro, "when I was *novenante.*"

The *cargos* entailed extensive preparation and enormous expense. "What were you doing the other day cutting firewood with all those people," I asked my assistant Lucho in 1974. It's called "*yanta waqtay*, preparing firewood for the fiesta," he responded. "I'm *novenante*," responsible for bringing bulls to the patronal fiesta. "A week ago I went to my neighbors inviting them to drink some rum, asking them to help cut firewood for the fiesta. I'm preparing the firewood at the beginning of July because it needs to dry before I use it in September. 'Bring your axe, your rope, your burro,' I told them. On the day of the wood splitting I gave them lots of *trago, chicha,* cigarettes, and coca leaves. The women prepared lunch and sang *qarawi.* Everyone got pretty looped. I need a lot of wood because I have to invite all my family, neighbors, and friends to eat during the fiesta. I'm planning to kill some pigs and cattle for the meals."

Lucho's *cargo* of *novenante* was one of the least complex and expensive, but even so, the cutting of the wood was only the beginning. For the next two months he and his wife were busy arranging for the bulls, the horn players, and the food and alcohol for their guests. They also had to provide themselves with a wardrobe commensurate with their position. To raise the money to give a fiesta, many people *Pablo and Claudia* migrated to work on the coast, but Lucho was able to fund his *cargo* through earnings from making *retablos,* wooden shadow boxes with fold-back doors that reveal ceramic figurines.

Accepting *cargos* was the obligation of a good citizen, but most people had to be convinced, usually with the help of generous servings of rum. When farming was the major source of livelihood, taking on *cargos* facilitated the quest for farmhands. People preferred to work for landowners who gave elaborate fiestas to celebrate the saints. As farming became less important (see Chapter 3), *cargos* conferred fewer benefits, and people resisted them more.

8 Initiation of new *varayoc*

"They were just wasted expenses," one man complained as he made a ceramic pot for sale. "We spent money on the *cargos* instead of making soup for our children and buying them clothing" or purchasing trade goods. People also had to care for their children, my father, Pablo, told me. How could they do that and spend money on the *cargos*? The schoolteachers, who were generally from outside the community and trained in "modern" ideas, influenced perhaps by Shining Path at the university, also disparaged *cargo* service and the *varayoc* to their students. "If someone becomes a *varayoc*," one old man told me in 1973, "young people say 'only Indians, *chutus*, do that.' They are ashamed."

In the 1950s San Pedro fielded two *varayoc* organizations and celebrated at least nineteen fiestas, but in 1999 there were no *varayoc*, and only the patronal fiesta was celebrated with any pomp.

Pablo's Alcoholism and Suicide

I often found Pablo drinking with friends in storefront cantinas. "My son, Churiymi," he would say, encircling me in a loose embrace. Then raising a shot glass of cheap cane alcohol, he continued, "Let's drink, Upiaykusun."

"Drink up, Papa! ¡Salud! Tomaykuy, Papacito," I responded.

Downing the contents of the glass in one gulp, he threw the last drops on the floor, not as an explicit offering to Mother Earth, the Pachamama, as in other Andean communities, but as a customary gesture, just like shaking hands. It also was a way to clean the dregs from the glass, for Pablo then handed me the identical glass and I drank to one of his friends in the same way. The single glass thus traveled through the group, round after round, the moist circle of spilled drops spreading and deepening as the drinking continued even after I found an excuse to escape.

Drinking is important to rural Peruvians, and I could not refuse Pablo's offer to drink without insulting him and the others. Communal drinking ties people together, but it also generates problems. It is frequently competitive, each participant trying to drink as little as possible while making others as drunk as possible. Some used it as an opportunity to test my good nature. "Drink up, *gringuito*," they commanded, even as they limited what they drank, thereby creating a friendly tussle of wills. "How many people were drunk?" friends would ask, as they assessed the success of their fiestas, the number of plastered participants a measure of their generosity. Celebrants frequently continued drinking the morning after a fiesta in *uma hampi,* the "curing of the head." Such drinking takes a toll on both pocketbook and body, and the prohibition of alcohol under any circumstances has been one of the appeals of evangelical Protestantism.

It is possible, however, to avoid excess drinking without turning into a teetotaler. I discovered these techniques slowly, little by little learning to extricate myself from drinking more than I wanted. Everybody laughed as the hostess at a fiesta in Vitarte, a community near Lima, lifted the long skirt of my wife, Barbara Jaye, to uncover the half dozen bottles of beer she had hidden to avoid the mandatory drink if she had passed them to her neighbor. She had not said no, which would have insulted the hosts, but had secreted the bottles, an acceptable strategy. Her ruse discovered, she had to pay the fine. "Drink up," the hostess said with glee, as she poured an overflowing glass of beer into Barbara's mouth. It was done good-naturedly and was (truly!) part of the fun.

Pablo and Claudia

In San Pedro, one can secretly chuck the alcohol on the floor or, as I once saw an old woman do, rub it into the scalp. Unable to step out of a cultural past that prohibited my pitching a drink behind the sofa, I usually excused myself by claiming a bad stomach and requesting "just a little." Although a culturally acceptable defense, people often ignored my request and insisted that I drink the entire glass. Guzzling it down, I dribbled as much of the alcohol as I could down my chin, invariably soiling my shirt. To bid the partygoers goodnight was usually unsuccessful, as they would try to block my departure, so the safest route was to excuse myself to urinate and not return. I usually did that after a few rounds with Pablo.

Most San Pedrinos make the drinking system a reasonable part of their lives, limiting alcohol intake while enjoying the conviviality, but as elsewhere in the world, some drink to excess and a few become quarrelsome and unpleasant. Most cases of wife beating follow heavy drinking. Drunken soldiers were responsible for some of the worst atrocities of the Shining Path war. I certainly feared coming across a drunken and armed policeman, as happened in 1983, when my assistant and I drove a San Pedrino migrant home to a poor area of Lima. We were able to placate the policeman's offensive aggressiveness, but as we drove away we shared our fears of being shot and accused of "terrorism."

I have composed these lines with some reservation, because many outsiders contemptuously dismiss highland peasants as drunken "hayseeds." I would hate to add to these prejudices, for on the whole San Pedrinos are no less sober than people in world capitals, who drink in private or whose wealth isolates them from condemnation. Violence accompanies excessive drinking outside Peru as well. For much of the year most San Pedrinos do not drink. At fiestas they do.

Unfortunately, Pablo was among those who drank to excess. While he did not drink alone or every day, he drank a great deal. He once spent a drunken night sleeping among cactus plants. Neighbors observed that he was once rich but no longer, as his animals were stolen or lost while he was drunk. Claudia cried when telling me of these losses. Pablo, however, attributed them not to drinking, but to the fact that he had not given the mountain god, *tayta urqu,* a sufficiently good offering to protect his animals. Some took advantage of these losses to bring him down a peg. "You used to ride a horse," one man spat contemptuously in 1974, "but now you have to walk just like me." They left the cantina where they had been drinking and fought in the street.

After a drinking bout in 1977, Pablo came home alone and hanged himself from a tree. I only learned of his death in 1980, when I returned to San Pedro after a six-year absence. Claudia and her family refused to speak of it. I thought they feared that I wanted my promised inheritance, although I protested to the contrary.

I never learned much about what happened and can only speculate about the underlying causes. In many respects Pablo was an outcast, insulted for never having a biological child. He also lived apart from his own natal family, surrounded only by Claudia's family. It is emotionally difficult for San Pedrinos to live so distant from birth family, and at the time of his suicide, he and Claudia had been fighting a great deal. He drank so heavily, moreover, that it is possible he had permanently damaged his brain. How else could he have borne a frigid night sleeping among cactus plants? I certainly noted a decline in acuity between 1966, when we met, and 1974, when I last saw him. It's odd that my adoptive father was plagued by problems of alcohol, for drinking also shortened the life of my biological mother and probably that of my father, matters that have left a lasting impact on me.

I have no doubt that Pablo hanged himself, although, more than twenty years later, my friend Valentina Rodríguez (Chapter 5), a San Pedrina now living in Virginia, speculated that "maybe someone else killed him. You never know," she said. "There were bad people in San Pedro then too."[8]

Claudia's Conversion to Protestantism

After Pablo's death, Claudia turned to religion, converting to Protestantism, as did many others, something I would not have believed possible in 1966. Because I was unable to visit her during the Shining Path war, and she was too sick to travel to Lima, I do not have Claudia's own account of her conversion. I last saw her in 1980. I sent her money from time to time before she died in 1995, and her nephews in Lima kept me posted on her life, but it was only on my return to San Pedro at the end of the war that I became better informed. Ethnographic research is like that: one interacts with people intensely but only sporadically.

Claudia's daughter, Yolanda, was surprised when I greeted her in 1996 on my return to San Pedro after a sixteen-year absence. I had trouble finding her, for she had moved from the town's outskirts to a store on the highway. Smiling warmly, she invited me into the living quarters at the rear of the store. Sitting me down, she prepared *chicharrones*, a special meal of fried pork rinds. I gave her the blouse *Pablo and Claudia* I had bought for her in New Jersey. Thanking me, she put it aside without opening the package. Most San Pedrinos do not "Ooh!" and "Aah!" over a gift, which would suggest that they are interested in the material rather than the personal aspects of the relationship, but even knowing this, I still find it a bit disconcerting when people whip my presents out of sight.

How are you? How are your children? we asked one another. By the 1990s my Quechua was rusty and Yolanda's children interpreted.

My children are with me, teaching English at the university in Ayacucho, I told her.

"You have to bring them to visit," she said. She remembered my oldest son, called by his Hispanicized middle name, Timoteo, because people found it difficult to pronounce "Sean."

I asked about Claudia, and she told me that her mother had converted to the Israelites of the New Covenant, a religion that was founded in Peru in the 1960s. A mixture of Seventh-day Adventism, Judaism, and Inca millenarianism, the religion has many adherents in Ayacucho.[9] They emphasize obedience to the Ten Commandments and, when possible, dress in popular representations of clothing worn at the time of Christ. "It was my mother," Yolanda told me, "who first joined the Israelites, and brought us all to the religion little by little."

Claudia joined to alleviate her failing health. She had grown more fragile and had lost most of her sight as she aged. Although I had arranged a cataract operation and eyeglasses for her in 1967, she was nearly blind when I returned in 1973. She was also doubled over with what was probably osteoporosis (I was still unaware of such things when I was in my thirties) and required a cane to move about. Pablo had consulted a diviner, a *pongo*,[10] someone who communicated with the mountain god (*tayta urqu*) to find a cure. On the

9 Israelites of the New Covenant celebrating Passover

diviner's advice, he found some ancient bones, the remains of dead ancestors known as the *aya* found around archeological remains, boiled them in fermented urine, and wafted their vapors over her body, but to no avail.

In 1991, on the advice of neighbors, Claudia began to attend meetings of the Israelites and her health improved. "My mother gained a spiritual peace," Yolanda explained. "When she couldn't go to their meetings on Saturdays, she would feel bad. The meetings lasted the entire day, beginning at seven every Saturday morning. They praised God, Jehovah, studied the Bible, prayed, and had a small lunch."

Yolanda and her husband joined the Israelites the next year, also for their health. According to Yolanda, the pastor cured her husband of frequent nose hemorrhages through the meditative passing of his hands above his body.

I visited Yolanda again in 1999, and her daughter, Udelia, freely translated her mother's remarks into Spanish as we sat eating the meal of guinea pig and potatoes Yolanda had prepared. They took me into the veranda at the rear of their house to show me a banner displaying the Ten Commandments. I read the Commandments out loud and took several photos.

"They base everything on the Ten Commandments," Udelia said. "Every Saturday they have to rest as God told them to do, just as he rested after creating the earth, the universe. They forbid alcohol and

the celebration of saints in fiestas. They can't chew coca leaves either.
My mother still chews coca leaves sometimes, but my father has stopped completely."

"Your son told me three years ago," I commented as I turned to Yolanda, "that many people believe something bad is to happen next year in the new millennium [the year 2000], when bad people are going to die."

"We continue to think that," Yolanda responded. So do Catholics and Evangelicals, but the "Israelites are praying to postpone the calamity."

Yolanda now goes to the Israelite service only when she does not feel well, but her husband goes most Saturdays. Udelia has not joined, but some of her siblings have and others are favorably disposed.

Pablo and Claudia

"People condemned us for leaving Catholicism," Yolanda told me, as she sat combing her long hair, once quite dark but now peppered, like mine, with gray. "Even now some people still detest us. 'You're crazy,' they tell us. 'You're wrong to belong to this religion!' They fault us for keeping the Sabbath and trying to dress like Jesus Christ, even though I wear my tunic only during fiestas." They criticize the men for their beards and long hair. "'You're Israelites because you're cheap,' they say, 'and don't want to spend money on the fiestas and coca leaves.' But we have already fulfilled our obligations!"

Indeed, they had. Yolanda and Enrique were the standard bearers, the most expensive *cargo* of the patronal fiesta, in 1971. I had interviewed Yolanda about their service in 1974. At first she and her husband had not wanted to take the *cargo*, she had told me; it would take too much time and money. But the *mayordomo* was desperate. Another person had initially accepted the post, but then refused, saying he was going away. Shortly after the refusal, he accidentally killed two persons with his truck, certainly a punishment sent by the saint. The *mayordomo* and the nuns then resident in San Pedro visited Yolanda and Enrique nightly, plying them with rum, pressuring them to take the *cargo*. Yolanda had a dream telling her to accept the post, and they did so, hiring a band from Ayacucho City for six days. They had certainly complied with the obligations required of prosperous farmers.

Pablo and Claudia illustrate key features of San Pedro's peasant life in the mid-twentieth century. Relying primarily on farming, they still had to seek additional resources. Pablo worked as a muleteer to obtain farmland and water free of hacienda control. He also used his trade to finance his part in the fiesta system. Fiesta service was expensive but pleasurable. It also gave them access to farm labor. People would not work for stingy farmers, an attitude that allowed the poor to leverage what they could from the rich. Pablo's muleteering trade also sustained them during droughts and other catastrophes. Claudia supplemented her farmwork with small-commodity production, selling cheese, guinea pigs, and dried beef to store owners in the central town, thus obtaining money for food, fiesta service, medicines, and other goods.

Most of their peasant contemporaries lived like Pablo and Claudia, although few were as prosperous. Some worked cyclically on the commercial cotton and sugar plantations on the coast, migrating there for a few months and returning with cash to supplement the meager production from their small farms. Others remained on the coast, as Yolanda's husband did, sending cash home, and finally returning with money to buy additional farmland. Still others produced guitars, hats, or ceramics, bartering their craftwork for the food that they lacked. Nearly everyone, like the llama traders who came to Pablo and Claudia's house, exchanged agricultural produce they had in abundance for food they lacked.

In spite of their need for nonfarm income, Pablo, Claudia, and other San Pedrinos remained peasant producers. Dominated by landlords and government officials, they strove for greater access to land and water to increase their production, but they farmed primarily to produce food they consumed themselves. Their goal was very different from that of one of my New Jersey students, who had never tasted the crops raised on her family farm for sale to ethnic food markets in New York City. Nonetheless, San Pedro's productive system and that of San José were already being transformed when I arrived in 1966. Rural families were getting larger at the same time that crop income was declining. Peasants were increasingly unable to sustain themselves by farming.

TWO

Horacio and Benjamina

GENDER, RACE, ETHNICITY, AND CLASS

"Teach me how to say 'shit' in English!"

Always a joker, Horacio Gutiérrez and his wife, Benjamina Enríquez (women retain their maiden names after marriage), were among the first people I met in San Pedro, and their warm welcome on my first day is still vivid. Their lives illuminate many of the gender, racial, and class hierarchies that structure San Pedrinos' relationships with one another and with other Peruvians. They also were major figures in the development of San Pedro's artisan commerce, a matter discussed in Chapter 3.

On arriving in Ayacucho, I had heard that two Peace Corps volunteers had been thrown out of San Pedro, accused of being *pistacos* and responsible for killing several people who had fallen into ravines. I later learned that the unhappy volunteers had isolated themselves, rarely accepting food and drink, refusing to dance at fiestas. But I had not known this and was unnerved by the story that they had been pelted with prickly pear fruit, as ferocious as "prickly" suggests.

Horacio and Benjamina quickly put me at ease, pleased that I had rented a room in the compound that housed them while they were building their home across the street. They invited me to lunch. We joked and laughed, and the invitation extended to other meals and gradually became standard practice. I reciprocated by buying fruit and vegetables at the Sunday market. After dinner they often climbed the outside stairs to my second-floor room to chat about the day. We were all young: she was twenty, he was twenty-four, and I was twenty-eight. They had a six-month-old son whom I nicknamed "Smiley."

Our two-story house in the central town was elegant in conception, but unfinished, neglected by its migrant owners. Built around a patio, the house was adorned with window frames, a rare amenity, but it lacked glass or shutters. I sheathed the openings with opaque plastic and, in the coldest months, covered them with wool blankets at night. My furniture was rudimentary: wooden crates nailed to the walls, a Primus stove on a rickety homemade wooden table, a bed that sagged like a hammock, and an inverted wooden carton for a night table. The corral in the rear served as our toilet, giggling young women occasionally climbing the five-foot adobe walls to peek. Until the town installed electricity and piped water, a year into my stay, I read by the light of two or three candles (an extravagant expense) and drew water from the irrigation ditch at the head of town. "It's not dirty there," I was told.

Small in stature and thin in build, Horacio had an open, pleasant face graced by a playful grin that was accentuated by an unruly cowlick jutting from jet-black hair. He dressed in store-bought boots, trousers, a buttoned shirt, and often a pale yellow cotton cardigan for warmth. He put style above comfort: he rarely donned a poncho for warmth, a hat for protection against the sun, or home-spun trousers or jacket. Such clothing would mark him as Indian.

Benjamina's "really crude, *chusca*," her brother cautioned me about her temperament. She had reason to be angry with Horacio, but she rarely smiled and usually met everyone, even her infant son, with a scowl. She dressed in long skirts similar to Claudia's, but cleaner and more elaborate. Two dark plaits hung down her back, reaching the colorful red, blue, and green shawl holding her son. Like Horacio, she wore manufactured shoes, but unlike him, she covered her head with a broad-brimmed brown felt hat.

Born to Quechua-speaking families, Horacio spoke poor Spanish and Benjamina hardly any. They were from rural hamlets located about one hour on foot below town.

With everyone other than his wife, Horacio was a joker, always testing the limits of civil behavior by his antics and outrageous, often sexual, remarks. Some people thought he took too many liberties with me. "Señorita," he said, as he tried to kiss me, "you don't have a penis but a vagina." He called me *waqra*, a Quechua word meaning "horn," but used to mean "adulterer," and teased me about my presumed relationships with Peace Corps volunteers. I laughed, but the joking sometimes wore thin. He once infuriated me by smearing potatoes into my hair, but my anger diminished when I discovered that young men and women often played this game at the potato harvest.

He passed the bounds of my tolerance when he flicked a spoonful of soup at me. I had been in the field for more than a year and was tired of being the center of attention, observed night and day, tired of speaking Quechua and Spanish, tired of the teasing and joking. I exploded, dumping the bowl of soup (it was cool) over Horacio's head and storming to my room, upset at my actions but still livid, venting my anger into my diary.

Horacio also was very generous to me. He would search for me if I was out at night, afraid that I might fall on the unfamiliar and uneven footpaths. He brought me to fiestas, presented me to his family and friends, instructed me about farming as he worked on his parents' fields. More hindrance than help, I pitched in to do what I could, as Horacio taught me how to behave like a San Pedrino.

"Be careful how you keep your apartment," he told me as he walked into my bedroom one evening. I was lying in bed reading an English novel, a favorite escape. "Gossips are saying you parade around town with your hair well combed," he continued, "but that you live like a pig, just like Indians, *chutus,* in the countryside." Clearing his throat, Horacio spat on my bedroom floor several times as he spoke, rubbing the spittle into the rough floorboards with his foot. He meant no disrespect, and I was quietly amused. Horacio and I had contrasting notions of cleanliness, illustrating mutual ethnocentrisms. I tossed dirty laundry into the corner of my room and left unwashed dishes standing in a plastic bucket, but I would call my room untidy rather than a pigsty. Similarly, Horacio's spitting was an acceptable behavior in rural San Pedro, even if not to most educated San Pedrinos.

Horacio and Benjamina: Gender, Race, Ethnicity

"Sometimes we're angry with one another," Benjamina remarked about the three of us, "but we also make one another happy and laugh." She was right. I was Horacio's friend, companion, and confidant, less so that of Benjamina. Horacio had taught himself to read the hour hand on his watch and was grateful when I showed him how to read the minute hand as well. I made sure, "just the way a brother would," that his chickens did not escape into the street. I once padlocked the couple in their bedroom every night for a week. Peruvian soldiers had descended on the town, entering the church during the Easter service to impress young peasant men into military service. It was the *leva,* a periodic military levy. The soldiers combed the streets in the day and swept into homes at night, locking their captives in San Pedro's jail and continuing their hunt until they met their quota.[1] Horacio escaped into the fields during the day but sneaked home to sleep behind the padlocked door, which fooled the soldiers into thinking that nobody was at home.

A year into my stay, Horacio and Benjamina, who was carrying their eighteen-month-old son in her shawl, came to my room.

40 Benjamina was still nursing the baby. Women nurse children until they are two and even older, and Smiley sometimes toddled across the floor to suckle at his mother's breast. Horacio was carrying a bottle of cane alcohol. "Drink up," he offered. "You've helped take care of Smiley, buying him medicines. We're planning to hold Smiley's first hair cutting, his *corte a pelo*. Would you be the godfather, his *padrino?*"

"I'd be honored."

San Pedrinos rarely ask a favor directly, but cushion it by first offering cane alcohol or a meal. The context is affectionate (you must ask with *cariño*), but at the same time, it is coercive (I find it difficult to say no). In this case, I was a willing participant. A few weeks later, aided by the godmother, the *madrina*, a mutual friend, I steadied Smiley on top of a roughhewn wooden bench. "You cut first," people told me. Smiley was in tears as I removed a lock of his thin hair and placed it into a plate with the equivalent of about U.S.$10 in Peruvian soles. How much to give? Nobody can give more than the *padrino*, I had been told, but the amount "depends on you, your *voluntad*." Well, what's the usual amount? People would not say, but I knew my $10 was very generous by local standards. The *madrina* followed, then all the guests, each giving less and less. The money was set aside for Smiley's education.

Smiley was my first Peruvian godchild. As his *padrino*, I was expected to give him little presents (*propinas*) from time to time and to help him develop morally and economically. When he got older, he was expected to help me by doing little tasks, and if I had continued to live in San Pedro, by working in my fields.

San Pedrinos use godparenthood (*padrinazgo*) to establish ties beyond the family. In addition to the first hair cutting, they seek godparents for baptism, confirmation, marriage, and even the building of a new house or any other important event in a person's life. The ties between the godparents and the child (*padrinazgo*) tighten the relationship between the godparents and the parents (*compadrazgo*), thereby creating a web of mutual support, a network of people who, like kinspeople, can be called on for help. Parents often look for upper-status godparents, but at the same time are wary that the relationships do not become exploitive, with godparents demanding free labor but giving little in return. We are now *compadres*, Horacio and Benjamina told me, co-parents, expected to help one another.

As my *compadre*, Horacio became more respectful, although he never completely stopped his practical jokes. I was incorporated more closely into his social network and expected to *acompañar*, or accompany, him during celebrations and family obligations. I brought a case of beer to his birthday party in 1967, carrying it around the room on my shoulders, as I should, advertising my generosity. "Help yourself, Sírvete," I said as I went from person to person with a jug of maize beer, helping Horacio attend to his friends and relatives. "Attention, San Pedro," the radio blasted as we danced into the early morning, "congratulations on your birthday from your *compadre* Bill Mitchell, with the song 'Huayno Serenade.'" Five other relatives and *compadres* paid for similar announcements. Many others brought beer and helped prepare the food, some doing it as balanced reciprocity (*ayni*) and others as generalized help (*yanapay*), for which they expected no specific return.

Horacio and I often spoke while he shaped his clay into a church, an *ukumari* (a mythical half-bear and half-human sexual predator), a *toro* (a bull-shaped receptacle for serving maize beer), or some other figure. He usually sat on a sheepskin on the ground, one leg close to his body and the other straight out, fashioning his clay in the triangle between his legs. I sat on a small bench across from him while he worked. I was lucky to have a person I could interview who spent so much time seated, happy for my company, even though he sometimes became irritated by my incessant questions.

At first I was uncertain how to proceed. What questions should I ask? How should I phrase them? I gradually learned to ask open, rather than closed, questions, to ask, for example, "How did you get married?" rather than "Did you first live in trial marriage?" I also learned that the more specific the question, the better the answer: to ask how Horacio got married rather than how people in general got married. I had no tape recorder on my first trip (portable recorders were not yet readily available), so my notes in a stenographer's notebook are filled with answers to questions posed to clarify information rather than long narratives. We also spoke as we walked in the countryside to work in his parents' fields, located on a thin, flat peninsula jutting sharply into Tutapa Gorge, its precipitous sides falling rapidly to the river below. We sometimes sat on low stools covered with sheepskins in the shade of eucalyptus trees growing at the side of an irrigation canal by his father's house, providing welcome protection from the noonday sun.

Horacio led my initial excursions into San Pedro beliefs and knowledge. I used his commentary to formulate questions for other informants, to check and cross-check the information, and to discover new insights as I learned my trade. He spoke to me about ceramic production, about his family and love life, about religious processions and other ceremonies. He told me about the *varayoc*,

Horacio and Benjamina: Gender, Race, Ethnicity

10 Festive work group to hoe maize

the rural political organization that his father and grandfather had served in. He related stories of the *amaru,* the golden ducks, pigs, and cows that live under the earth and cause landslides; of the *uma,* the detached heads of witches flying through the air; of the *aya,* the ancient pre-Columbian people whose bones were dangerous. He educated me about how San Pedrinos conceived their lives. When I told him that some men had turned angry when I took their photograph while they were eating, he explained that San Pedrinos did not like to eat in front of people, that they were afraid of being criticized for slurping their food. "When my father was the mayor of the *varayoc,*" he elaborated, "he always gave the food he was served to someone else to avoid such embarrassment."

Gender

When I met Horacio and Benjamina, they had been married in the Catholic Church, but had postponed a civil wedding until they could build a "house and raise money for a grand fiesta." Instead of a single wedding, marriage in San Pedro is solemnized by sequential activities, some taking place years apart: courtship, trial marriage, a civil wedding, and a separate religious one. A few San Pedro townspeople try to arrange the marriages of their children, but most young people initiate courtship on their own.

Like most couples, Horacio and Benjamina avoided parental disapproval by meeting secretly. Horacio told me that he courted Benjamina by saying, "I want to get to know you, sweet mother, *mama
linda*. I want to marry you, buy you food and clothes." He seized her
embroidered apron as a *prenda,* an intimate token designed to lure
Benjamina to retrieve it and thereby yoke her to him. Like most
women, Benjamina protested, telling Horacio that her parents would
be angry.

Although parental opposition to a child's prospective marriage
partner is common (see the account of Valentina Rodríguez in
Chapter 5), Horacio had a different experience. He visited Benjamina's parents, and her father remained at home, signaling that he approved of their courtship. Benjamina's mother later asked Horacio's
father: "What're we going to do with your son and my daughter?"

"Do you want to marry Benjamina?" Horacio's father queried.
"You have to work if you marry or you can't buy clothes," he cautioned. Horacio agreed that he would "work and serve her," that he
would fulfill the mutual obligations of their relationship. The two
families held the fiesta called "taking the woman, *warmi qurquy,*"
and Benjamina went to live with Horacio's birth family in trial marriage (*uywanakuy*).[2] After a few months they held a Roman Catholic wedding, and shortly later left for their own rented house in the
countryside.

I do not know what impelled Horacio and Benjamina to have a
Roman Catholic wedding before a civil one. By the 1960s women
had begun to push for the civil weddings that made child support
more likely from husbands in the event of a breakup, an increasingly
common phenomenon as men migrated for work (see Chapter 4).
Schools, moreover, required children to produce the civil marriage
papers of their parents, further encouraging the practice. A Catholic
marriage also entailed an elaborate fiesta, so most people made it the
last step in their marriage plans.

This was not Horacio's first relationship. In 1966 he already had a
four-year-old son by another woman, a child born out of wedlock,
an *hijo natural* (literally, a "natural child"). Horacio told me that he
didn't marry the child's mother because he was ashamed that they
shared last names. San Pedrinos receive two last names, a common
pattern in Spanish America: the first and most important comes
through the father, the patronym, and the last from the mother, the
matronym. Horacio's patronym was the same as the woman's
matronym.

Shared patronyms would certainly have placed them in the same
ayllu, or kin group, but their case was ambiguous. Because the

*Horacio and
Benjamina:
Gender, Race,
Ethnicity*

woman was from another hamlet, Horacio claimed she was not related to him. Benjamina, however, charged that the common names made her his cousin. "Qarqacha," she yelled insultingly during one of their many fights, calling him by the name for a creature part llama and part mule that roams at night as a punishment for incest. Most San Pedrinos would agree with Horacio, but the shared names were tinged nonetheless with implications of incest.

In 1966 the woman filed a complaint with the police and demanded child support. Benjamina and Horacio did not want to comply. "I don't want to pay," he told me, "but if I'm forced to, I want my son to live with me so that I can see he's educated." After a night in jail, Horacio began to send the support. His initial refusal was not unusual; men often avoided financial and emotional responsibility for children born out of wedlock.

In 1968 Horacio told me the names of eight women with whom he had sex after his marriage. Benjamina often fought with him about these assignations. "We're married," she told me, and "if he goes with another woman, I can send him to jail." Nonetheless, she once helped Horacio escape the wrath of an unmarried girl's father who, on finding Horacio with his daughter, tied their hands to the rafters, allowing their feet barely to touch ground. Informed of the punishment, Benjamina plied the man with alcohol until he was drunk, thereby allowing Horacio to escape. Did Benjamina have affairs? I do not know, and I neglected to ask her and other women about such matters, a lapse I regret today, although I doubt that they would have confided in me as they might have in a woman researcher.

Horacio sometimes beat Benjamina, and I once restrained him as he went after her with a log. Men refer to such violence as "highland love, *el amor serrano*," a phrase sometimes employed with a knowing grin. "A woman isn't satisfied with her husband if he doesn't give her a beating every now and then," Horacio said to me and Benjamina, "but with the occasional beating, a woman becomes tranquil and contented."

"I doubt women like to be beaten," I responded. "What do you think, Benjamina?"

"I don't understand," she answered with a smile. We were chatting in my room after our evening meal and had been using Spanish, rather than Quechua. I am convinced that she had understood, but did not want to start a fight.

At other times she argued with Horacio, insisting that all men do not beat their wives. "Do they?" she asked.

"They don't," I said. "I think it's cowardly."

"Men are pigs, *cochinos*," Benjamina complained another time, privately. "They abuse us" and try to force us to have sex when they find us alone in the countryside.

Most San Pedrinos believe that men dominate women and beat their wives as a result of their intrinsic natures.[3] Nonetheless, not all San Pedro men beat their wives, or harass women sexually, but it is difficult to estimate how many do so. I am more likely to hear accusations of wife beating than reports of gentleness, usually through secondhand gossip about some egregious offense.

Even so, I was surprised when Valentina Rodríguez (Chapter 5), told me, "Ah, Bill, my chest hurts. That's where Roberto [her husband] beat me. He was jealous, but he never had reason to be."

Valentina and Roberto were my friends, people I had known for more than twenty years before I heard these allegations. I never would have suspected that Roberto beat his wife.

These are not the only cases of wife beating or discussions of *el amor serrano* that I have encountered in San Pedro and San José, nor are these matters unknown elsewhere in the Andes.[4] The issue puzzles me, running around my head like some keeper melody, in this case, a dissonant one, perhaps because I find wife beating so alien to my own sense of self—even though I know as an anthropologist that humans often do peculiar things to one another. "Why," I wonder, "do so many assume wife beating to be natural?" I believe answers lie at least partly in how conceptions of gender in San Pedro intersect with poverty and extreme social inequality, creating a combustible mix often ignited by alcohol.[5]

"It's difficult to imagine a time when anthropologists didn't have the concept of gender," Ruth Behar reflects.[6] "But it really wasn't all that long ago that we traveled around the world, seeing gender everywhere but not really seeing it because we didn't have a name for what we saw." In the 1960s and the early 1970s, gender was for at least some of us omnipresent but unnoted as such, except for reporting on what we called "the sexual division of labor." I did not investigate wife beating then as I would today, but nonetheless my early research offers some clues.

Although overt physical affection between men and women is infrequent, they often speak endearingly to one another. "Mamacita Linda," a man might address a woman, or "Niñacha" in Quechua, during courtship or when requesting a favor, while the woman responds in a similarly sweet voice, calling him "Sweet Father, Papay," or "Niñucha."

Horacio and Benjamina: Gender, Race, Ethnicity

Signs of tension are also common.[7] "The woman's winning!" by-standers might shout to a man and woman dancing the *huayno*, competing to outdo one another in the cleverness of their footwork. Such exhibitions are a great deal of fun, and I have enjoyed them with the rest, but they are competitive. Being hit by a woman with a hard peach during Carnival is far less pleasant, but it is nonetheless part of flirting. Indeed, the phenomenon of marriage by capture, as happened to Valentina Rodríguez (see Chapter 5), or the seizing of a token, or *prenda*, from a girlfriend, as happened with Horacio and Benjamina, expresses this tension between men and women, in part a tension between responsibilities to one's birth family and new bonds created by marriage.

Women in San Pedro and San José have considerable economic power and independence. They do most of the marketing and trading and continue to own the lands that they inherited from their parents.[8] During the Shining Path war, women developed autonomous mothers' clubs to grow and prepare food together, clubs found in San Pedro and San José.[9] Wives frequently manage household money, a source of conflict when they refuse their husbands' requests for money to pay for drinking or personal expenses the women consider wasteful, although they usually accede to the men's demands.

Women also are in charge of the larder and the distribution of food, which they use as a way to express approval and disapproval. Everyone waits to be served by the woman responsible for the cooking; she decides how much will be given. Horacio once asked me to buy food for him on the plaza because Benjamina refused to cook for him and he could not cook for himself because the kitchen was her domain. He was too embarrassed to admit his predicament to the food sellers.

One might expect women's economic power to permeate other areas of life, but their independence is part of a "patriarchal bargain," one of the strategies they use to survive in an overarching system of male dominance.[10] In southern Peru, men are "valued for showing strength, authority, and autonomy, women for diligence, motherhood and nurturing," in the words of Penelope Harvey, descriptions also true for San Pedro and San José, if we allow for the fact that individuals differ in their adherence to these values.[11] Men are also expected to be dominant, to be the head of the household, while women exert power through the important but informal mobilization of opinion. Both men and women call a man believed to be controlled by his wife a *saco largo*, a "long coat," a terrible insult impugning his masculinity.

In spite of their household power, and their considerable economic independence outside the household, women depend economically on their spouses and frequently have to struggle to make fathers responsible for children. As men leave rural communities to look for work, women have an even harder time, as they take on the work of the men and struggle to keep their families fed and their husbands attached. Ever on the economic edge, many women are faced with the alternative of resisting wife beating, and possibly rupturing economic support, or accepting and rationalizing the situation as an aspect of the nature of things.[12]

Women also are bedeviled by notions of shame and, when they complain, seldom receive much help from their families or from the police.[13] "Why did you allow Roberto to beat you?" I asked Valentina Rodríguez as we were relaxing together in my home in the United States on Christmas Day in 2003. I was reviewing my notes with her.

"Bill, we believe that the husband is the second Saint Joseph and to fight with him is to fight with Saint Joseph. But I really don't believe that, only *ignorantes*, ignorant people, do. I was afraid of a scandal. My sister even told me to call the police after he destroyed my store [in a drunken rage], but I didn't want to. They would take him to the station and create a scandal. That's how women thought then, but it's changing, especially after women got the right to vote [in 1979] and began to realize they had rights."

"Would you let him beat you now, if he were still alive?" I asked.

"No! Even when we were living in Lima, I began to tell him 'You hit me and I'll punch you back.'"

Valentina had developed psychological strength through a lifetime dealing not only with her husband but also with her children and the many challenges of her complex life. She also began to resist her husband's violence when her children were grown and she was no longer as dependent on him. In Lima, moreover, she discovered that such violence was not inevitable.

I witnessed the growth of such personal empowerment in Comas, a poor area of Lima, as five women discussed wife beating while they sat around a rectangular table in the darkened dining area of a communal kitchen, a *comedor popular*, that they had helped organize (see Chapter 9). Resting after the lunch crowd had left, the women were tired but animated.

"Does your husband have the right to beat you?" Camelia, the leader of the group, asked.

At first, they each said "Yes," then gradually they modified their answers in response to Camelia's probing "Why?" and her use of me as a foil. "Do you beat your wife?" she asked.

Horacio and Benjamina: Gender, Race, Ethnicity

In the course of an hour and a half, they concluded that wife beating was unacceptable. I was impressed. Beginning in the 1960s such experiences became more common. Women gained strength as they organized in response, at least partially, to the international women's movement, and continued during the Shining Path war when women united to defend their homes and to search for missing husbands and sons.[14]

Clearly, women's lives are difficult in Peru, but so too are those of men. In San Pedro men are supposed to be brave, using physical force if necessary to defend themselves and their families against rustlers, occasional brigands, and other thieves. They also must protect community lands and water against ever-present threats from outsiders, duties exacerbated during the Shining Path war. Although women also take on such tasks, the primary responsibility rests with men; many more men than women were killed during the war.

Men brave such matters "a lo macho," pushing through difficulties regardless of physical or emotional danger. They also act out these real-life risks in bullfights and in ritual battles as two men whip one another on the legs or hurl hard peaches at one another from a sling or fight in massed groups in competitions held during Carnival that often draw blood. Such bravery cannot be easy for them. When bulls roamed the plaza during the bullfights celebrating saints' fiestas, I, fearing injury, climbed to the top of the fountain in the plaza center, much to the laughter of the crowd, as other men risked their lives in macho displays.

11 Masculine strength: mutual whipping of legs during Carnival

Horacio and Benjamina: Gender, Race, Ethnicity

11A Masculine strength: firing a peach at opponent during Carnival

At the same time that they must prove their bravery, men must be subservient to the rich and powerful, women as well as men, humbling themselves to catch economic crumbs. They tip their hats and speak with deference and humility, only altering their behavior in occasional communal defiance of egregious offenses. The long legacy of repression and inequality also is important to our understanding, for powerful outsiders (soldiers, priests, hacienda landowners, government officials, townspeople) have exploited the rural poor, often sexually dominating women and thereby creating models of behavior.

The psychological tensions of being simultaneously brave and humble in a context of extreme social and gender inequality lead

50   some men to act on what they have learned as acceptable behavior, *el amor serrano,* and to exult in their power to hurt women, usually in a drunken rage. This explanation requires investigation, and the situation may be changing as women take more control over their married lives, but the explanation is supported by research in other areas and helps explain why some men—but not all—beat their wives.[15] As we will see, Horacio fits the model. He suffered considerably as he rose in the social hierarchy. Labeled an Indian as he struggled to assert himself, he took heavily to alcohol as he grew older. In the mid-1960s, when I lived with them, Horacio beat his wife when he was drunk.

Race, Ethnicity, and Class

Horacio grew up speaking Quechua and wearing rubber-tire sandals and homespun clothing. "When I first put on shoes," he told me, "I felt like I had rocks on my feet and I could barely walk." He had never attended school because his "father wanted [him] to work." Like most rural people, his Spanish was poor, learned on the fly as he interacted with people from the town. Nonetheless, he was widely regarded as one of the great ceramicists and was made a teacher at the new school for artisans in 1965, at which point he and Benjamina moved to the central town.

In spite of Horacio's skill with ceramics, the appointment shocked many townspeople. "How can he be a teacher," complained a store owner, "when he can't read or write?" Some disparaged him as a "*chutu,*" or "Indian." Others belittled him more subtly. "Hi, there, wearer of boots!" the owner of the store fronting our house sometimes addressed him, the sweet words underlying his contempt. Horacio hated the salutation, muttering to me about it, for by calling attention to his new boots, it reminded the world of his lowly background. He had worn shoes for the first time only recently.

Most San Pedrinos have nicknames, and Horacio had inherited his, Chutu al Aire, from his father and paternal grandfather. Roughly meaning "Ethereal Indian," the name is simultaneously derogatory and complimentary. On the tongues of some, "al aire" had an agreeable flavor, alluding to the family's beautiful ceramics, but others ungraciously said it referred to the pottery's fragility. In Horacio's case, "al aire" also commented on his somewhat unpredictable behavior.

Quechua insults are far milder than their Spanish or English counterparts. To call someone a "dog" in Quechua (*allqo*) is hardly an insult, but the same word in Spanish (*perro*) is offensive. We bring our cultural baggage into the field, and even though I was aware of these differences in meaning, Quechua insults often distressed me as much as did English or Spanish ones. Horacio, however, did not mind being called "al aire," even with its ambivalent connotations, but he resented the "chutu" in his nickname or in any other context. "It's the powerful people, *apu runa*, who call ceramicists *chutus*," he told me in 1967. "They have money and don't respect anyone and think they can buy San Pedro."

It is difficult to write about San Pedro's class and ethnic/racial divisions, because the terms used to describe them change meaning, depending on context. I came to Peru with the scant anthropological literature on the Andes in my mind and thinking that San Pedro had two hierarchical groups: mixed-bloods (*mestizos*) and Indians (*indios* or *chutus*). My perception was reinforced by an anthropology student at the university in Ayacucho City who had lived in San Pedro for six months and who told me early in my stay that the community was divided into *indios* and *mistis* (*mestizos*). (I later discovered that San Pedrinos rarely used the term *mestizo* or *misti*.) San Pedro, moreover, was an officially recognized indigenous community, a *comunidad indígena*, a designation that helped fix the notion of Indian in my mind.

San Pedrinos similarly divided the world into two seemingly fixed groups. Some spoke of *chutus* ("Indians") or *campesinos* ("peasants"), on the one side, and *llahta runa* ("townspeople"), *apu runa* ("powerful people"), or *gente decente* ("decent people"), on the other.

I brought to these divisions a white sensibility that I had learned in the racially homogeneous neighborhood of my Brooklyn childhood in the 1950s, a view describing races as distinct biological groupings.[16] After a short time, I realized that matters were more complex. I was puzzled that some people I thought of as *mestizo* were the children of what appeared to be Indian parents. I noted that one educated and powerful town official spoke excellent Spanish, wore manufactured clothing, and did not chew coca leaves. His father, however, lived in rural San Pedro, had been born a peon on an hacienda, and, although a wealthy peasant, spoke only Quechua, chewed coca leaves, wore homespun clothing, and walked in truck-tire sandals. His mother similarly was a monolingual Quechua speaker who dressed in braids and long skirts similar to Claudia's.

Horacio and Benjamina: Gender, Race, Ethnicity

12 Lunch during festive work group

How could this be if the divisions were as rigidly drawn as the literature and my preliminary thinking suggested? And what does one make of *cholo,* an amorphous category sometimes used to describe people like Horacio and Benjamina who fell in the middle? I asked my adoptive father, Pablo (among others), what *chutu* meant, and he replied, "That's what they call the people who live in the *puna,* the high-altitude grasslands. Because they don't have any schools, they call them *chutus.*" Don't they ever call the people here in San Pedro *chutus?* "No, there are none here, although some petty officials, *tenientes,* and hacienda owners called people *chutus* as an insult."

Pablo was telling me that *chutus* are those who live higher up, above the maize zone. But altitude is relative, and residents of the high grazing zones say *chutus* live even higher up, in some other community, over there but not here. Others say that *chutus* are from the *bajíos,* the lower, rural areas of the community. Claudia, on the other hand, emphasized education and clothing, telling me that "*chutu* is what they call low people, *gente baja,* who do not have any education and who wear ponchos, rubber-tire sandals, and hats." She started to laugh, amused by the irony. "Maybe some people call me *chutu!*"

The meaning of *chutu* depended on context. Are there *chutus* in San Pedro? I asked Horacio. "No," he replied, "they're only found in the *puna,*" but another time he used *chutu* to refer to any rural San Pedrino. "Don't go to the fiesta," he told me about a fiesta being held in a hamlet well below the *puna.* Why? "Because they'll be drinking *molle* beer, *chicha de molle,* and it will hurt your stomach." Why do the people drink it, if it's bad? "*Chutus* drink it." Who are *chutus?* "They're Indians."

The lexical history of Peru's ethnic terms has added even more complexity. Until the 1970s *indio* and *indígena* were commonly used to refer to Quechua and other non–Spanish speakers, but in the 1970s the Velasco military regime (1968–1975) successfully replaced the words with "peasant" (*campesino*), even changing the name of "indigenous communities" like San Pedro and San José to "peasant communities."[17] *Campesino,* however, still carries much of the pejorative freight attached to *indio* and *chutu.*[18] In polite speech, upper-status San Pedrinos generally distinguish between *campesinos* and *gente decente* (decent people), but they employ "*gente decente*" to refer to townspeople who are both cultured and born to the position, a practice that is eerily similar to that of characters in nineteenth-century English novels speaking of "gentlemen."

Horacio and Benjamina: Gender, Race, Ethnicity

It became clear that in San Pedro (and Peru) terms that initially appeared racial to me (*indio, chutu, misti,* and *mestizo*) were not rigid biological categories but flexible ones that employed biological and social and cultural characteristics to create an ethnic hierarchy. Education and competence in Spanish were (and are) the most important determinants of social position, spurring people to educate their children, often at great sacrifice. Because of this desire to educate both girls and boys, Peru's literacy rate is high (90.2 percent in 2001), helping to raise Peru to eighty-second out of 175 countries in the 2001 United Nations Human Development Index.[19]

Location and clothing are also important in defining the social hierarchy. People in the central town were known as "*vecinos del pueblo*" and were "more respectable, *decente,*" as one former hacienda owner told me in 1983. The farther from the town, the less respectable. Homespun clothing and a poncho marked men as *campesinos,* as did coca chewing, although the long dresses, broad-brimmed hats, and shawls of the women did not necessarily mark them as *campesinas.*

Wealth also was important, even though San Pedrinos have a strong ideology that downplays such differences. "Manuel," I asked my thirty-year-old research assistant while we were discussing the concept of rich and poor in 1974, "what do you call yourself?" We were walking in the countryside, talking about wealth differences, as Manuel was taking me to interview his relatives about farming different altitude zones. The midday sun was hot. I had already removed the sweatshirt that protected me from the morning chill, but I stopped to take off my jacket, draping it over my field bag. Taking the bag to carry, a sign of respect, Manuel answered my question. "I'm a poor person, *wakcha.*" I decided to provoke him to elicit a detailed response. Our relationship was comfortable enough for me to do so. "What? You're not poor!" I exclaimed. "You walk about in nice clothing!"

He looked up at me. "I'm poor!" he laughed.

"No, you're not!" I shot back. "You may say that, but you really aren't! You have your fields, your animals!"

He laughed again, this time more exasperatedly, and said, "William! We don't have any animals!" I ignored the remark.

"Listen, there are people who have nothing, no? They hardly have enough to buy coca leaves. Someone like that is poor. And you aren't." I named some people poorer than he and others who were richer. He finally acknowledged the differences.

"I'm in the middle, mediano, tumpa wakcha," he said.

Can you tell people that you are medium poor? "No," he responded, "I can't say that I am a little poor or a little rich. I have to say that I'm poor."

Just as most North Americans say they are "middle class," most San Pedrinos must claim to be "poor." Nevertheless, they vary in wealth, and that wealth helps position them in the social hierarchy.

Skin color is another important marker, and whiteness had — and still has — power. Parents will sometimes treat a light-skinned child, affectionately called *gringuito* or *misticha* ("little white one"), more favorably than other children. These values are constantly affirmed by popular culture. Most of the saints and certainly God and Jesus are depicted as white, often with blue eyes.

Skin color, however, is not as important as language and formal education in determining social position. Although San Pedrinos sometimes conceptualize social groups as varying in skin color ("A *cholo* is brown skinned, but a *mestizo* is light skinned," Triga's father told me [see Chapter 6]), they do not use color to form racialized ethnic groups, as people often have done in the United States.[20] People of differing skin hues are found in the same group, even though color tends to lighten as one ascends the hierarchy. Nonetheless, if you speak Quechua and are unschooled, you are a peasant, regardless of skin color. My adoptive father, Pablo, was bearded and fairly light skinned, but most would call him *campesino* and some used the term "*chutu.*"

Because people can be characterized in a variety of ways, allowing for many permutations, they occupy a shifting place in the hierarchy, depending on who is evaluating whom.[21] Even as some townspeople insulted him as a *chutu* or, if they were being polite, a *campesino* or a peasant, Horacio was a rich townsperson to his rural family. "They made me drink," Horacio complained on returning from visiting his birth hamlet. "They told me that I'll only drink champagne and won't drink with poor people because I'm rich. I couldn't say no."

To a Limeño or Ayacuchano, on the other hand, everyone in San Pedro might be an *indio* or a peasant. In the 1960s many school-teachers called nearly everyone in San Pedro "*ignorante*," almost a synonym for "peasant."

Just as gays have embraced "queer" in the United States, however, some people have made the negative terms their own. "We are *indios*," they may say with pride, "*cholos*, the original inhabitants of this country." The meaning becomes clear in context: said with a deprecatory tone, the words are offensive, but with an affirmative one, they are statements of self-esteem. Alejandro Toledo capitalized on these sentiments in his successful campaign to be president of Peru in 2000, touting the slogan "Cholo sí, chino no," referring negatively to the Japanese-descended Pres. Alberto Fujimori.[22]

In spite of its conceptual fluidity (and social mobility for some), San Pedro's hierarchy was clearly visible. During public fiestas, important townspeople occupied the municipal balcony and other places of honor. In a household fiesta, they were seated at a table and served first, while poor rural people sat in the courtyard without a table. The separation was quite distinct; an educated townsperson might seat his uneducated parents in the courtyard with the *campesinos*.

The hierarchy also had (and has) real consequences for wealth and power. Townspeople are the small shopkeepers, selling coca leaves, kerosene, candles, alcohol, and other goods to rural folk. They control the police and the legal system and garner the best government jobs. One of the first teachers in the government's artisan school was a townsman who knew nothing of *retablo* manufacture but who was mayor when the school was established. (To his credit, he taught himself the craft.)

The powerful also take irrigation water at will, allowing themselves two crops instead of one. Townspeople rarely work in the labor corvée, but by paying a small fine, they rely on rural people to clean the plaza and streets of the central town, repair the footpaths, and maintain the irrigation system. During the war townspeople paid peasants to take their place in the peasant militia. Until the 1950s two peasant *varayoc* officials rotated each week to serve as

Horacio and Benjamina: Gender, Race, Ethnicity

personal servants to the priest and the governor. Although the practice had ended shortly before I came to Peru, the priest had the right to harvest about a row of each peasant family's crop, a right known as the *primicia*. He sold these rights to townspeople who rushed to harvest the crop, although they often encountered opposition as they did so.

Townspeople also receive most of the free outside aid and other resources. "Here, take two cans of powdered eggs," the mayor told me in 1967. Donated by the U.S. Alliance for Progress, the eggs had been sent for the workers constructing the new dam, not for me or for the many other townspeople given precedence in their distribution. "How do you cook them?" Benjamina asked as I gave them to her. "Are they poisoned?" The eggs not only lacked instructions on use, but their label was in English!

We have strayed far from Horacio and Benjamina, but this system of hierarchy is important in understanding their lives and the lives of other San Pedrinos, and even for comprehending the brutality of the Shining Path war. Pablo and Claudia were clearly *campesinos*, although they would resent anyone's insulting them as "*chutus*." Horacio and Benjamina occupied a more ambiguous position. Horacio was not only illiterate and called Chutu al Aire, he was a ceramicist, an occupation that most San Pedrinos scorned in the 1960s. Pablo (and others) insulted potters as Indians and *chutus* and referred to them as "makers of cooking pots, *olleros*" and "eaters of the earth, *allpa micuy*." Horacio preferred to be called "*alfarero*" rather than "*ceramista*," although both mean "ceramicist," because "*alfarero*" carried more dignity.

Even so, Horacio's rural past followed him through at least his early adulthood. Horacio's an Indian, a *chutu* who wears rubber-tire sandals and chews coca leaves, Valentina Rodríguez told me in 1966, during a conversation about San Pedro's class system.

"No," I disagreed. "He rarely chews coca leaves, and he wears regular shoes and even has boots."

"Well, he wore rubber-tire sandals until recently," she responded disparagingly.

As a teacher, and a rich townsman, Horacio could never be seated with the rural peasants at a fiesta but he could be spoken of contemptuously and be mistreated with slights both small and large. "If I were able to read," Horacio told me, "the director and other teachers in the artisan school would treat me better," a sentiment he voiced again and again. Some patronized him. Horacio has "grown too big for his britches," a townswoman from a family of once-powerful *hacendados* complained in 1983. "When I travel to San Pedro from my home in Lima," she continued, "I speak to him with the same affection as before, but he sometimes doesn't respond and simply looks at me. When people get too much money, they take on airs." But I knew Horacio when he spoke only Quechua and walked in truck-tire sandals, she concluded haughtily. "People are like that, they don't recognize you anymore once they rise in the world." In spite of the popular conception of all *hacendados* as fabulously wealthy, she was not rich, but might be described as a lower-middle-class Limeña.

Horacio and Benjamina were careful to act in ways that would avoid their being called *chutu* or *campesino*. They never chewed coca leaves in the presence of people who might criticize them. Horacio spoke his poor Spanish to townspeople (Benjamina less so) and tried to dress well, but at home he preferred to speak Quechua. In the *Horacio and* countryside, Horacio and Benjamina might remove their shoes to *Benjamina:* protect them from being scuffed on the dirt footpaths, but they al- *Gender, Race,* ways put them on when returning to town. The condition of one's *Ethnicity* shoes is a major mark of social position. Prodded by friends, I have kept my shoes cleaner in Peru than in any other place I have lived.

Horacio and Benjamina used wealth to inch up the status hierarchy. "What good is a *cargo?*" Horacio speculated in 1966. At that time he thought that it was all right to make a fiesta for a birthday or a baptism but not for the celebration of some saint in the town. As a ceramicist, with no agricultural land of his own, he had no need to participate in the communal celebrations that brought expense and little return. He also was rejecting the many *cargos* associated with rural people, like the *varayoc*. In 1970, however, just a few years after this remark, Horacio accepted the costly *cargo* of *alférez* in the fiesta for the patron saint. In 1973, he told me with pride that he had spent U.S.$2,000 to hire the orchestra and provide the food and drink for the fiesta, an extravagant sum for a teacher earning US$117 a month. He had recorded the music and still played the tapes as often as he could three years later. The *cargo* had been meaningful and it was pleasant to be admired, but most important, that admiration elevated him to a social rank more commensurate with his position as professor and townsman than with his birth status of rural peasant.

Horacio and Benjamina also decked their house with material goods. In 1966 they owned three radios, two record players, a sewing machine, and a bicycle—a phenomenal number of luxury items. Rented out from time to time, these items provided income, but they also "make a person feel superior" Horacio claimed. Wealth could not erase Horacio's and Benjamina's poor Spanish, lack of formal education, and rural background, but by employing it well they tried to mitigate the negatives.

Horacio contested the hierarchy with humor and outrageous behavior. "Merde alors!" he yelled at me and others to demonstrate our ignorance of French and his knowledge of at least this one phrase, which he had learned from someone who had studied in France. "How do you say 'small balls?'" he asked, wanting to add new phrases to his foreign repertoire.

"We don't say 'small balls' in English."

"How do you insult people, then?"

"Fuck you!" and "Shit!" I responded.

"Teach me to say them," he asked, rehearsing them over and over
to pronounce the words well.

He used these epithets to great effect against the police in 1966 (at least, as he told the story). Uncertain if a radio he had bought from a stranger might have been stolen, he took it to the police in Ayacucho City to inquire, but instead of helping, they placed him in jail as a reminder not to buy stolen property. They added to the indignity by insisting that he make them adobe bricks. Angry, Horacio let loose with his foreign vulgarities, telling the police, when they inquired, that the phrases meant, "I'd like to do that right away for you, sir."

Benjamina and Horacio sometimes joined rural people in mobilizing against egregious abuses. In 1967 a particularly offensive townsman collected signatures on a petition to request a high school for San Pedro. He neglected to tell the many illiterate farmers who signed with an X that they were agreeing to be taxed, an explosive matter to people living a marginal existence and retaining memories of tribute demands like the *primicia*. By offending so many people on such an important issue as taxes, the man had gone too far. "He's a communist," Benjamina said. "He wants to charge people for using the land." They were not leaders in the movement against the man, but they participated in the public assembly that gave him twenty-four hours to leave town and that appointed an executioner should he remain. Nobody dared intervene and he left, escaping to Ayacucho City, although several months later, when tempers had cooled, he started to sneak back from time to time to visit his family.

But Horacio and Benjamina usually reacted to prejudice against them with quiet resignation. Some months before the school fracas, this same townsman had taken stones Horacio had collected to build the foundation of his house. The townsman claimed he had a document proving that they were his. "Where's your bill of sale?" the man demanded. Horacio was angry and fumed about the injustice but did nothing. He knew he would lose in a direct confrontation with an upper-status person, man or woman.

Horacio suffered emotionally because of his ambiguous position (Benjamina less so). He loved being with me in part because I was North American, a gringo, and the positive valence attached to me, an educated foreigner, helped compensate for his marginal status. In me, he also had a friend who admired his knowledge and skills rather than disparaged them. Horacio was thrilled in 1973, when the daughter of a powerful family of *hacendados* attended the special earth-oven feast, the *pachamanca,* that he made to celebrate my return to San Pedro. "This is the first time you have visited my house," he told her repeatedly. "Please teach me how to behave. You know how and I don't." I squirm for him even as I write this.

In spite of his own ambiguous class position, or perhaps because of it, Horacio sometimes treated rural people with prejudice. He was quite amused that I had been adopted by Pablo de la Cruz and called me "Indian de la Cruz, *chutu* de la Cruz." He was sometimes cruel. "What language is that?" he asked two monolingual Quechua speakers who had come to San Pedro to participate in the patronal fiesta. "Oh, it's *chutu!*" he continued disdainfully in Spanish. "It's *chutu!*"

Similar dynamics were most likely involved in his beating of Benjamina. In later life, Horacio turned increasingly to alcohol. I do not know if the pain of his marginal status was a cause of that alcoholism, as it might have been for Pablo, but it certainly did not help.

Horacio and Benjamina: Gender, Race, Ethnicity

THREE

Horacio and Benjamina

CONFRONTING VILLAGE POVERTY

In San Pedro ceramic figurines perch on roof peaks, like the chimney pots of English towns. Weathered by intense wind, rain, and sun, many of these small ceramic replicas of churches, deer, bulls, and tropical forest indigenes (*chunchus*) appear old, but San Pedrinos say they are recent, as are the tourist shops that sell them.

When he was young, nobody had such ceramics, my adoptive father, Pablo, told me. Horacio Gutiérrez agreed, asserting that decorative ceramics were unknown before the mountain god, *tayta urqu*, taught the craft to a man named Mauricio in the 1920s.

"He was a *pongo*," Horacio added.

"What's a *pongo*?"

"He's a diviner, someone who converses with the mountain god," Horacio answered, annoyed. Like a young child, I constantly asked questions and was often repetitious, sometimes irritating friends.

"Mauricio asked the mountain god to teach him to make ceramics," Horacio continued. "The god sent him to bathe at a waterfall in Tutapa Gorge at midnight, then a few nights later, sent him to Lake Yuraqucha in the *puna*, again at midnight. Mauricio entered the lake, which "almost ate him," but he was rescued by "a *señora*, a Virgin, all dressed in black."

I was interviewing Horacio in his workroom. The bare cement room was cold in the early morning. I excused myself to get a sweater. Handling frigid clay, Horacio was cold too and asked to borrow a jacket. I owned an old army jacket that he liked to wear.

"Which Virgin?" I asked when I returned.

"She's known as Mamacha," Horacio responded. "Mauricio grabbed her belt, and she pulled him out of the water. But by the time he got to land, she had disappeared, and he couldn't find her." On returning home, Mauricio made ceramics for the first time.

Whenever he returned to the lake and waterfall, and he did so often, "the mountain god taught him how to make ceramics."

"Did he see Mamacha again?"

"She only came to the lake once, because that was the only time he had been drowning."

In this widely shared story, Horacio and other San Pedrinos, employing European and pre-Columbian beliefs in a blend characteristic of Andean religion, give the craft a sacred origin. *Tayta urqu,* the mountain god, is central to San Pedro belief.[1] Each mountain has a god, the higher the mountain, the more powerful the god. These gods care for animals, appear in dreams, and can be dangerous as well as helpful, sometimes demanding human life. The god from Rashuillca, the mountain that stands higher than any other, a frequent subject of myth and the mountain that Claudia sang about in Chapter 1, once grabbed an airplane, many have told me, gobbling its passengers into itself and refusing to set them free.

The Virgin is also significant in Horacio's account. Before the advent of Protestantism, she was the Christian symbol most prayed to and looked to for support. A different manifestation of the Virgin was said to have appeared beside another spring and commanded the people to build a church and found San Pedro there. Lake Yuraqucha is similarly enchanted, associated with many stories of drowning and hidden gold. It is also the water source for one of the irrigation systems.

According to Horacio, Mauricio taught the new craft only to Horacio's grandfather, Maurelio, and one other person. Maurelio taught his children, including Horacio's father, Guillermo, who in turn taught it to his children and ten other men. This, of course, is Horacio's history and he certainly neglected to tally and include ceramicists in other hamlets. It is also likely that San Pedro's ceramic tradition is older than this genealogy or the origin myth would indicate.[2] Nonetheless, the total number of ceramicists in the 1940s could not have been more than a few dozen. A census by the artisan school in 1966 counted fewer than fifty. Today there are hundreds of ceramicists, perhaps more than a thousand, in both San Pedro and Lima, and at least two have worked in the United States.

Until the 1940s ceramicists scheduled their work around the agricultural cycle, working part time in exchange for food, especially maize and coca leaves. In addition to utilitarian pitchers, plates, and large storage vessels, they occasionally made roof adornments, ceramic musicians (given to festival performers), and ceremonial drinking cups.[3] During the irrigation festival, *yarqa aspiy,* women served maize beer in small cups shaped like vicuñas, covering the cups with flowers to make them even more beautiful. Other decorative cups held offerings to the mountain god.[4]

Unglazed and fragile, these decorative pots carry a folk-art charm. During the 1940s San Pedro ceramicists began to market them outside the community. They moved in this direction at the same time that many other rural Peruvians took to commerce and other cash activities to supplement farming. Why would this be so? Horacio's genealogy provides significant clues. I recorded the genealogy in 1966–1967 because, like taking household censuses, it is a basic task of ethnography. It tells us who is related, how they are related, what they call one another, and where they were born and live. We use the kinship ties divulged by genealogies to help us understand how people create families and secure shelter, labor, and other help. Horacio's genealogy also reveals the demographic and economic pressures underlying his family's decision to manufacture commercial pottery. I was unaware of this significance when I first collected the data. While not random, research results are often fortuitous.

Maurelio, Horacio's paternal grandfather (Table 1, row A) is credited with starting the family ceramic tradition. He had one sibling, a half brother who left San Pedro for the nearby province of Huanta, where he reared four daughters. I have no further information about them. Maurelio, however, lived with his wife in one of San Pedro's rural hamlets. His wife bore 11 children, but only 3 (one of them Horacio's father) lived to adulthood. Maurelio also had a daughter by another woman, or a total of 4 children out of 12 who survived past age five. By 1967, when I recorded the genealogy, these 4 had 27 surviving children (Table 1, rows B and C), an average family size of 6.75, a huge increase over their father's 4 children. When I recorded the genealogy, moreover, not all of Horacio's relatives had finished their reproductive lives.

The families of Horacio's father, aunts, and uncle did not become larger because they were having more children. On the contrary; their families increased in size because fewer of their children were dying. Table 1 illustrates this change better than words. Only 33 percent of Horacio's paternal grandfather's children survived past five years of age, but 60 percent of Horacio's father's children did so, and 83 percent of Horacio's.

In spite of this decline in infant mortality, funerals of little children are still too common. "A child's death is a happy one," I was told over and over, because "children go directly to heaven, bypassing this miserable life to be with the angels." This belief was certainly a potent salve for the pain of frequent loss. People mourned an adult death

TABLE 1. GROWTH OF HORACIO GUTIÉRREZ'S FAMILY   63

	Horacio's Relatives	Relationship to Horacio	Total No. of Children	Children Surviving Past Age 5	Percentage of Surviving Children
A	Maurelio	Paternal Grandfather (Fa's Fa)	12	4	33%
B	Guillermo	Father	10	6	60%
C	Clara	Fa's Sister			
	Elisabeta	Fa's Sister	N.d.	21*	N.d.
	Mardonio	Fa's Brother			
D	Horatio	Self	6	5	83%

Horacio and Benjamina: Village Poverty

Source: Rows B–D from genealogy collected from Horacio in 1966/1967;
Row A given by Horacio in 1999.
N.d. = No Information
*Total children of paternal aunts and uncle

but drank and danced at a child's funeral. Even so, parents wept as they danced, especially when their child had died not at birth but, as many did, when only one or two, or even four or five years old.

The experience of Horacio's family is typical. Peru and much of the developing world experienced similar declines in infant mortality in the mid-twentieth century, paralleling similar declines in Western Europe in the eighteenth and nineteenth centuries that also had led to increased numbers of people.[5] Scholars are uncertain of the cause of this reduced mortality, although economic development and public-health measures improving nutrition, sanitation, and health care (especially infant vaccinations) may have been significant components of the modern decline.[6] Nonetheless, the causes are complex and may have varied from place to place. The single best predictor of infant mortality is the mother's educational level.[7]

Several San Pedrinos concerned about their many children repeatedly asked how couples in the United States manage to have so few children. "How can I abort my fetus?" a pregnant woman asked me in the 1960s. I didn't know and told her so, but I let her and others know about the birth control pill, the diaphragm, and IUDs. "Can you get them in Ayacucho?" I was asked. "How much do they cost?" One man tried to buy birth control pills in 1966 but was told that such things did not exist, even though I knew that the pharmacy

13 Weaving woman's shawl

stocked them. The couple had another child, one the father tried to abort by severely beating his wife in the abdomen. Whatever their method, this couple did limit their children to three. "Little by little, young people are learning about birth control and trying to use it, but when I was young I knew nothing of that," a San Pedro migrant to Lima told me in 1983. He had five children, the oldest of whom was sixteen years old.

Even as each woman has given birth to fewer children, the decline in infant mortality has created the exponential growth illustrated by Horacio's genealogy. As families increased in size, parents were faced with the prospect of providing for more children. The likely response of farmers would be to increase the size or productivity of their farms. In Peru, however, farmers found that the value of many of their agricultural products, especially wheat, a major cash crop, was declining in national markets, forcing them to sell more sacks of wheat than previously just to stay even in purchasing power for medicines, kerosene, matches, noodles, clothing, school supplies, and other goods they needed. Life is harder, people invariably tell me whenever I return to San Pedro. It's harder and harder to make do, "to defend ourselves," they say.

How could all twenty-seven of Maurelio's grandchildren have survived as farmers in San Pedro? They could not, and when young adults most abandoned the town to seek work on the coast.

"Why did your Aunt Clara go to Lima?" I asked Horacio about his father's sister. "Where is she going to find work here?" he responded incredulously. "Why should she live here when she has her own house and work on an hacienda in Lima?" [8]

In each generation, only one or two children have remained in San Pedro. To do so they turned more and more to commerce. At first, Horacio's parents remained in San Pedro, but they had to barter utilitarian and decorative pots to make ends meet. In 1952 they were running out of food. As the oldest son, Horacio told his father that he would take some pots to barter for maize. He was only seven years old but, accompanied by a neighbor, he loaded utilitarian pottery onto a mule and returned five days later. Traveling on foot, he chewed coca leaves for the first time to combat the cold, hunger, and exhaustion. He and his companion slept in caves, cajoling the mountain gods with offerings not to turn their animals into wild *locos*. But the journey was worth it. In San Pedro, Horacio could exchange a vessel for the amount of maize that fit inside it, but on this trip to another peasant village far from San Pedro and any automobile road, he obtained twice that amount. He continued to make similar excursions to other areas.

It was through the sale of decorative pottery, however, that his family obtained its best returns. Horacio's grandfather began the business in the 1940s, making his the first family to sell ornate ware to a shop in Ayacucho City. "She was a really good person, *muy buena gente*," Horacio said of the shop owner. "We brought the pottery to her on burros, and she gave us food and a place to sleep when we arrived."

I interviewed the woman in her dingy cement store, where she also sold straw-filled mattresses, in 1967. She lived in the rear. I am uncertain of her age, but she appeared ancient to me when I was twenty-nine. "I was the major buyer," the woman told me, "but I'm no longer able to manage because of poor health." At first she sold the pots in her store, but in 1947 she began to take them to Lima, thereby encouraging increased demand and production. Horacio's father responded by turning his home into a small workshop, where he taught apprentices the craft in return for their labor. He bought the land where they mined clay to solve problems of supply. Neighbors had objected to the theft of clay from their lands.

In the 1950s a second Ayacucho businesswoman started coming to San Pedro in a truck to buy pottery. No longer needing to haul their goods to Ayacucho City, Horacio's family began to deal with her. At first they bartered ceramics for coca leaves, bread, cigarettes, cane

Horacio and Benjamina: Village Poverty

alcohol, and rice. Later they demanded cash, but the woman often advanced money when they were hard-pressed, thereby leveraging cheaper prices. To prevent shortchanging, Horacio taught himself to write numbers and to add. He calculated the sums in anticipation of the woman's arrival, advising his father what amount they should receive. In 1966 Horacio still made arithmetic errors because he did not align the numbers in straight columns. I taught him to do so.

In spite of her tough business practices, this second woman expanded the market by exhibiting the pottery at Lima artisan fairs. A North American expatriate also began to sell the pottery at his tourist shop in Lima and suggested new designs to the potters. The Peruvian government encouraged the craft by sponsoring artisan fairs in Lima and establishing the San Pedro artisan school, which employed Horacio in 1965. This was the decade of the Kennedy administration's Alliance for Progress and the Belaúnde administration's Popular Action programs. "Economic development" was in the air.

Because they manufactured pottery almost entirely for the Lima market, Horacio's parents moved there with four of their children in the early 1960s, thereby eliminating third parties, shipping costs, and breakage. In the dry climate of Lima, moreover, they were able to work year round. In San Pedro, the rainy season halted production for almost half the year.

At first, Horacio's parents used clay and paints shipped from San Pedro, but they later found local sources. His father left Horacio in charge of the farm but returned for the harvest and took most of the food back with him to Lima. Horacio missed his father a great deal. "Without your father, you're without your *patrón,* the person who will always defend you," he told me in 1967. "I've been left alone, and it's almost as if my father has died, almost as if my family doesn't exist. I can't talk to anyone about getting his fields planted, and I don't feel like eating. My father would give me anything."

In the mid-1960s Horacio had no fields of his own other than one his father lent him. Benjamina also had a small field from her parents, but their combined yields did not provide enough food. Benjamina supplemented their larder through rural trade. I accompanied her on one of her trips in May, 1966, the height of the harvest. She loaded coca leaves, sugar, rice, and bread on three burros and set off at daybreak for the potato-producing upper reaches of the district. The world lay below us, swathes of green fields, their verdant color accentuated by the many eroded gullies and desiccated lands unconnected to irrigation. Entering a field, Benjamina squatted to help the farmers sort their harvest of tubers, as did I.

*Horacio and
Benjamina:
Village Poverty*

14 The harvest

The harvest is hard work, but also a happy time, and farmers almost always roast potatoes in an earth oven. "Serve yourself," a
woman dressed in homespun told me as she handed me a plate filled
with potatoes. "Gracias, dios pagarasunki," I responded, accepting
the plate from a hand roughened by years of work. Dipped in chili
sauce, the potatoes were delicious. No lowland potato can compare
to Andean ones grown at more than ten thousand feet above sea
level, the plant's native habitat. After about an hour of chatting and
helping, Benjamina exchanged her goods for some of the crop. By
the end of the day, she had bartered five soles' worth of trade goods
for twenty-five soles' worth of potatoes and other tubers (*olluku, oca,*
and *maswa*), a healthy return of 500 percent.

In spite of these farm resources, Horacio and Benjamina lived
mostly from Horacio's teaching salary and their combined income
from ceramic sales. They produced ceramics whenever they could,
although in the rainy season they were too busy on their farms to
make pottery, and the wet, cloudy days also prevented them from
drying any pots or firing them at a high temperature. Matters were
different in the six-month dry season, however. Then the patio was
filled with decorative pots in various stages of production, and
Horacio and Benjamina had to employ others to help paint and decorate them. They sold their goods at artisan fairs in Lima and little by
little introduced new designs to maintain market share. "I have some
big expenses coming up," Horacio would tell me, "and have to make

15 Tourist crafts (incised gourd, *retablo,* and ceramic piece)

some pots." They had come full circle. In the 1950s Horacio and his family had used ceramic production to subsidize their farming, but by the end of the 1960s, pottery manufacture brought in more than the fields. As the decades progressed, moreover, craft sales became ever more important to Horacio's household, especially after he left teaching.

The tables have turned. Rather than being the prime source of livelihood, farming has been reduced to a secondary position, and, from a certain perspective, his farming (and that of others) now can be viewed as helping to support commerce.

My departure from San Pedro in 1967 at the end of my initial field-work was emotionally difficult. I found myself immobilized, para-lyzed by the thought of leaving so much unfinished work and arriv-ing home to much uncertainty about my life. Do I even want to be an anthropologist? I thought. Horacio helped considerably, giving me a hand to pack my things, helping me focus on completing my work. We corresponded for a while, then stopped. I was establishing my life at home; he was getting on with his in San Pedro, and it was surely difficult to get someone to read my letters and write his, a task that I had performed for him. Nor did we resume our intimacy on subsequent trips.

Janet Malcolm has underscored that journalists behave like con-fidence men who ultimately betray the people they cover, that the reporter has goals that are in inevitable conflict with those of the subject.[9] A similar problem, even if unintended, exists in anthropology. As much as I love the people I work with, I am focused on my research. On subsequent trips to San Pedro, I could remain only for short periods, and I assigned greater priority to my work than to my friendship with Horacio. I was traveling about the countryside investigating ecological adaptations instead of sitting and listening to stories of mythology and customs while Horacio worked. Horacio wanted to play and I wanted to work. He had also taken to frequent drinking. I had had my own problems with alcohol in the 1960s, and I did not want to be drawn in. I felt sad and guilty that I no longer visited him regularly, but my interests had changed, as had his. He had also replaced me in his affections with another gringo, another "great guy, *muy buena gente,*" an archeologist whom he had met. "Do you know him?" he asked.

Horacio and Benjamina: Village Poverty

Nonetheless, I still inquired about the ceramicists, and on my return in the summers of 1973 and 1974, I found that changes had accelerated. Potters were no longer insulted. "People have come to understand what ceramic making is all about," Benjamina's brother Lucio explained. Working as my assistant in 1974 to help measure altitudes throughout the countryside, Lucio spoke as we rested in the shade of an adobe wall. "Before, we were ashamed of being potters, but not now. Everybody's a potter today." Many of these artisans were former townspeople who had once despised ceramicists as "*chutus,* earning money from the earth," but the trade had brought San Pedro not only money but also fame, attracting tourists who came to buy and to see the artisans in their shops. A once-despised occupation was now one of the best.

The success that ceramic production would become had not been apparent at the beginning. In 1965 the three artisan teachers had to scour the countryside to convince reluctant farmers to send their children to the school. Thirty students finally registered, but few attended regularly. I accompanied Horacio the following year as he canvassed for students. He was able to register six, but many more parents refused, preferring to send their children to the academic school. After the first years of the artisan school, however, when most rural economic activities had become increasingly precarious, the teachers rarely had to search for pupils. By the end of the twentieth century, most ceramic shops were filled with young apprentices trying to learn a craft that has brought economic success to many.

Children have also flocked to other schools. In the 1940s few people attended the one-room school covering kindergarten and first grade, but by 1987 ten primary schools, one high school, two

16 Parade of schoolboys and schoolgirls

nursery schools, and two artisan schools were teaching 2,171 pupils. "Everybody sends their children to school," Benjamina told me in the 1960s. "You can't get any work without education." She and Horacio planned to educate their children at the central school rather than the artisan school. Nonetheless, they feared the school's corrupting influence. "Kids who go to the central school," Horacio told me, "become thieves, stealing eggs to buy candy." They do not tip their hats in greeting the way rural children do, he told me.

I do not know how successful Horacio and Benjamina were in realizing their educational plans. Some of their children had only a poor command of Spanish in 1999. Their oldest son, Smiley, however, like great numbers of his contemporaries, did go to high school.

After 1980 the Shining Path war kept me away from San Pedro for the rest of the decade. I did not see Horacio again until 1999, but in 1983 I ran into Benjamina at an artisan fair in Lima. I had not seen her since 1974 (she had not been in San Pedro in 1980), and I was startled by her changed appearance. She had aged considerably, probably hastened by hard work and the damaging rays of mountain sun. What did she think of the changes to my face? I thought. She told me that she carried ceramics to this fair every year and that Horacio went to another. Gold fillings glittering in her mouth testified to her prosperity, but she still wore the long dress of peasant women. "I wouldn't want to cut my braids," Benjamina told me. "I'd look ugly and like a man." Many years before, she had laughed when she saw my wife in dungarees, telling us, "I couldn't wear them because I'm uneducated." Although it was certainly an emotional matter for Benjamina to dress like a peasant woman, it also could have been a business strategy. At a craft fair people are more likely to buy "authentic" ceramics from a woman in "indigenous" dress than from someone in dungarees, a strategy that has been noted for market women in Mexico and Bolivia.[10]

In the early 1980s she and Horacio had bought four hectares in the tropical rain forest (the *montaña*), Benjamina told me, and, using farm laborers brought from San Pedro, were cultivating cacao, coca leaves, and fruit. "We have to pay for everything," she said, "their transport, food, everything." They had no trouble obtaining the peons. It had been a terrible agricultural year, a result of a severe El Niño weather disturbance, and poor farmers were anxious for the work. Smiley (she still called her son by my nickname for him) was traveling between San Pedro and the tropical forest to supervise their work, but he had to return to school, and she was planning to go in his stead.

Horacio and Benjamina: Village Poverty

The following year, in 1984, just as we sat down to dinner I opened a letter sent to my home in New Jersey. I slumped into my chair. The military had entered San Pedro and had killed Smiley and thirteen other young people. Just as they had during the *leva,* the soldiers had entered homes and seized the young, but this time they tortured and machine-gunned them on the heights above the town. I sobbed as I told the news to my children. The deaths did not have much impact on them. They were young and had not known Smiley or the others, but they responded to my emotion. The letter was from Roberto Quispe, Valentina Rodríguez's husband, who wrote of his own fear. He had visited his parents in the *bajíos* of San Pedro that same day and had narrowly missed encountering the soldiers himself. Headlines about the Shining Path war and its brutality were suddenly transformed into flesh and blood, the mutilated corpses of people I knew.

Smiley was nineteen when he was killed. Or should I say "murdered"? Word choice is important here. I had not known Smiley as an adult, but as I look at the scribbles he made in my field notebook, I think of the human being behind a war statistic, of the two-year-old toddling around my room, demanding "Upa, upa" when he wanted me to lift him onto my lap. At the end of my first trip, Horacio had asked to buy my typewriter, not only as a symbol of high status (the only one in town other than that in the municipality), but also so that Smiley could use it in school. I gave it to him as a parting gift.

Was Smiley a guerrilla? Perhaps. And perhaps not. This question has no easy answer. Many San Pedrinos say he was involved with Shining Path, but what that means is unclear. As we will see in

Chapter 6, many Ayacuchanos collaborated with both the guerrillas and the military, less out of conviction than fear.[11] What is certain, however, is that Smiley and the others were murdered by masked men, presumably the military, without a trial and without any independent verification of guilt or innocence.

After the killing, Horacio and his family fled to hardscrabble Santa Anita on the eastern outskirts of Lima. I visited them in 1999, stopping before their house and calling, "It's just me, Ñuqallaymi," as in the sierra. They lived on a brown, dusty street a short distance from the noise and fumes of the Central Highway, a torrent of trucks, buses, and cars. Benjamina, now dressed in slacks, invited me inside. She and her children were making ceramics. Their combined house and workshop was a ramshackle affair constructed of reed mats and earthen floors. As when I had first met them in the sierra, they were in temporary quarters, waiting to build a more permanent structure.

Horacio was visiting San Pedro, Benjamina said, but he'd be at their *cortamonte* celebration the next week (see Chapter 1). "Come to it," she invited as she handed me a printed invitation.

Officially, the celebration was to begin at noon and last until the "final consequences," the final inebriation and pleasure, but when I arrived with my wife, Barbara Jaye, and a Peruvian colleague at 5:00 PM, few people had gathered and preparations were still under way. Horacio had returned from San Pedro and was spreading water on the ground to tamp down the dust. Benjamina was marinating beef hearts, which were to be barbequed and sold to the guests. She served us maize beer, and I bought a few commercial beers. This fiesta was very different from those in the sierra, where everything was served rather than sold. "It's a business," my friend Valentina Rodríguez said to me when I told her about the charges. "It's a business." I danced a few *huaynos* with my wife and one of their daughters, but the real party did not begin until around midnight, well after we left.

Busy with his preparations, Horacio did not have much time to talk. He was visibly older and seemed less playful, perhaps shy, or even angry, after years of separation. Like him, I too was reticent, reluctant to engage him in intimate conversation. I felt uncomfortable in my relative wealth and safety and did not want to pry, so I did not ask about what had happened to Smiley (what could I possibly say?).

Fleeing to Lima had removed Horacio and his family from the war. It was safer there; people were less subject to arbitrary brutality and murder, even though such repression occurred in Lima as well. But like many refugees, they remained in Santa Anita long after the danger had passed. Horacio was repeating the history of his father: by

moving to Lima he could now produce pots year round and was
closer to national and international buyers. As in previous generations, only one son remained in San Pedro. Most of his children,
moreover, preferred gritty Lima to beautiful San Pedro. It had more
of everything: people, goods, and entertainment.

From Farming to Commerce

Among the many changes in San Pedro since 1966 (paved streets,
electricity, and piped water in the central town), the ubiquity of ceramic and artisan shops stands out. There were only a few shops
with meager displays back then, but when I returned in 1996, nearly
every street was filled with craft shops. Several had elaborate displays *Horacio and*
of not only pottery but also incised gourds (*mates*) and woven fab- *Benjamina:*
rics, some still made with natural dyes but most glowing with im- *Village Poverty*
ported aniline colors. Shopkeepers also carried a variety of the
wooden shadow boxes known as *retablos*. Once carried by muleteers
as portable altars, the *retablos* in the stores now depicted secular as
well as religious scenes. They also sold peasant baskets identical to
those that raised raucous laughter when I used them in the 1960s. By
carrying goods in an "Indian" basket, I had violated rules of appropriate use, much as a boy in the United States would be laughed at
for riding a girl's bicycle.

Retablo, gourd, and ceramic manufacture have not been the only
commercial route taken by San Pedrinos. They work at almost everything: highway repair, carpentry, tailoring, hat making, guitar manufacture, weaving. Some have harvested and sold cochineal, an in-
sect used to make a red dye that lives on the underside of the prickly
pear cactus. A few San Pedrinos own small jitneys to carry passengers to and from Ayacucho City, while others have trucks to haul
goods throughout the country. "I was born poor," one man said to
me. He was fashioning a *retablo* and paused as he continued. "But I
have bettered myself by working. I have worked in farming, weaving,
pottery, and muleteering."

Many opened up fields in the tropical rain forest, a day's journey,
to produce coffee, cacao, and fruit for national and international sale.

A few entered the cocaine trade, although it is difficult to estimate
how many. "I learned how to extract cocaine from coca leaf," a research assistant told me in 1973, inserting his remark into the last of
four interviews we had conducted with others inquiring how a poor
person could become rich. "Why don't we become partners? I'll

17 Wall hangings for sale to tourists in Ayacucho market

make the cocaine and you can take it to the United States. It's the only way a poor person can become rich," become a millionaire.

"I'm a professor," I demurred, "and don't know anything about business. I do research and teaching."

Did he become a cocaine dealer? I do not know, but his request illustrates his line of thinking. Nor was his interest sparked by dire poverty. He was better off than most of the people we were interviewing. Although he had no land himself, he was well educated, spoke excellent Spanish, and had a thriving business taking ceramics to Lima once a month. Poverty had created the conditions for the cocaine trade and for the Shining Path war, but not in a simple, linear causality.[12] My research assistant, like Horacio and so many others, was searching for a way to support himself and his family at a time of serious demographic growth and economic pressures on peasant farming, conditions that encouraged everyone, rich and poor, to seek alternative sources of livelihood.

Artisan manufacture and migration have been the most common routes San Pedrinos have taken to deal with their economic pressures. At the end of the twentieth century, hundreds of artisans and several cooperatives in San Pedro and Lima had created many new shapes and had experimented with novel media. They sold their pottery, *retablos,* gourds, and colorful textiles to the United States, Europe, and Japan. In Lima some of them marketed their production over the Web.

Although the changes in San Pedro have produced economic suc- cess stories, as this chapter describes, I do not want to leave the false impression that all San Pedrinos have been able to pull themselves up by their bootstraps. Large numbers continue to work as impoverished peons.

In 1999 I returned to San Pedro during Holy Week. National and international tourists, including many returned San Pedrino migrants, crowded the town. Horacio and Benjamina were there as well. They had brought with them ceramic churches, crosses, and other ceramic figures that they had made in Lima but that they peddled as "authentic" and "traditional" San Pedro pottery. They sold their entire stock. Nobody barters ceramics anymore, and few make the utilitarian jugs and storage jars that once were the raison d'être of the enterprise.

Horacio and
Benjamina:
Village Poverty

FOUR

Martín

CONFRONTING MIGRANT POVERTY

"When we speak of San Pedro we have to think of people in lots of different places, in Santa Anita, the tropical forest, the *montaña*, Lima, Punta Madera, and the cotton haciendas on the Coast," a San Pedro university student told me in 1983. "Although we don't have a single territory, we are a nation of San Pedrinos. We're like the Jews when they didn't have a territory, but they were a nation, just the same."

Martín Velarde

"Do you know any San Pedrinos who live along the coast?" I asked Valentina Rodríguez, a San Pedrina then living in Lima (see Chapter 5). "In Santa Anita and Punta Madera," she said. "The Velarde family is in Punta Madera. My son Julio can take you."

I had just arrived in Lima in 1983; the Shining Path war was ravaging the sierra. Unable to travel to Ayacucho, even though I had been invited to teach at its university, I decided to work with San Pedro and San José coastal migrants. Because my wife and two children had remained in New Jersey, I limited my stay to just three months.

I climbed onto the number nine, a rickety white bus, with Julio. He was twenty-one, studying business at one of the many new private universities educating migrant children struggling to get ahead. He was pleased with the diversion and the chance to work as my assistant.

"I've got a friend in Punta Madera," he said.

We climbed into an even older bus at the central highway, diesel fumes and ear-piercing noise spewing from its broken muffler. Miles of squatter settlements abutted the highway, rising into distant sandhills, dense with adobe houses that furnished scant contrast to the earth from which they were formed. Great crowds packed in and off the bus ("Be careful of pickpockets," Julio warned), then thinned as we crossed farms and cotton fields to arrive at Punta Madera an hour and a half later. Buses travel frequently to the remotest parts of metropolitan Lima, making it easier to get around without a car than in most U.S. cities.

Julio had only a vague idea of the location of his friend. "Do you know the Sánchez family?" he asked at the market.

"Why do you want to know?"

"We're paisanos," he responded, "I'm a friend from San Pedro."

Directed to one of the barrios, then climbing a street cut from the driest dust I had ever seen, we found a cousin of Julio's friend. Retracing our steps, we scrambled up another narrow lane crowded with poor cement housing to locate his friend. He introduced us to *Martín* other San Pedro migrants and they to others, including several branches of the Velarde family, related to me through my adoptive mother, Claudia Velarde. In this way I constructed a sample of 102 migrants in Punta Madera, Callao, Pisco, and many other coastal areas, as well as Santa Anita and Vitarte along the central highway.

Once a rural center north of Lima, Punta Madera was gradually being incorporated into Lima's cosmopolitan sprawl, although it still had a rural feel in 1983. I occupied an unfurnished and Spartan room on the top floor of a cement house in the town center. Crowds passed the house throughout the day, rushing to homes, buses, and the market. I slept on a mattress on the floor, awakened about

18 Recently erected squatter settlement

two o'clock every morning by the challenges of fighting cocks in the next room, the bare cement walls amplifying their clamor.

A few months before my arrival, some people whose homes had been destroyed by an earthquake had quickly thrown up reed houses along the street in front of the house, creating a *pueblo joven*, or "young town," as such squatter settlements are called.[1] Such invasions are a common strategy of Peru's landless poor, who fight off police and raise Peruvian flags throughout the complex to secure their claim. Because they initially lack water and sanitation (as well as electricity), these densely settled squatter settlements are deplored by many Peruvians, but I found the reed houses and flags a pleasant sight, a symbol of human resourcefulness used to carve a foothold somewhere, somehow. Unlike many, however, the Punta Madera invasion was unsuccessful. Blocking the center of a major street, the settlement was too prominent and was destroyed by the police shortly after I returned to the United States.

Outside Punta Madera's bustling center, dirt roads led to former cotton plantations on the west, now organized as cooperatives, their irrigated fields, one flat row after another, extending seemingly forever. Small settlements, many created through land invasions like the one on my street, clung to the sides of bare sandstone hills that rose to the east, one house edging another, spread like vines along mountains of dust. Ancient buses, one lacking a roof and most of one side, hauled people and goods between the towns, while trucks carried water to household cisterns for purchase. The hills loomed large, but the view was deceptive, and a friend and I climbed what appeared to a huge hill in only half an hour.

Situated amid these sandy hills, dirt roads, and small towns, Punta Madera seemed far from Lima, but this distance was as deceptive as the height of the hills. Punta Madera was physically near Lima, and the value of its cotton and the consequent availability of work were greatly affected by decisions made there, as well as in Washington and other world centers, about trade, farm subsidies, and support for one government over another.

In the process of finding people to interview, I stumbled across an assistant who had worked for me in San Pedro in the 1970s. He introduced me to his older brother, Martín Velarde, Claudia Velarde's nephew. Martín received me warmly. *I've heard about you,* he said. I interviewed Martín several times in 1983, but I do not know him as well as I know most of the people in this book. Interviewing a large sample of respondents, I sacrificed depth of knowledge for breadth, so I saw Martín only occasionally during my two months in Punta

Martín

19 Temporary shelter in new squatter settlement

Madera. Martín lacks the ability of most of the people profiled in this book to put together a coherent, compelling account of his life. I include him because his life illustrates a common migratory pattern and because it embodies a too-common tale of the debilitating poverty that has constrained people's lives and limited their choices.

With few skills, little education, and seven children, Martín has had a hard time managing his poverty. The course of his life reminds me of Jude Fawley's in Thomas Hardy's *Jude, the Obscure* (1895), a poor man driven by desire and belief but forced by circumstance to make the "least bad" decision among terrible alternatives.

In 1983, when I conducted most of my interviews, Martín lived with his wife and children in a rented, dark house with dirt floors.

Peruvians would characterize his demeanor as *humilde,* a poor person who knows his place and speaks softly when addressing the educated and wealthy. He calls me, in a warm, respectful voice, "señor Guillermo."

"I'm interviewing people about their lives, especially how they came to live on the coast and what has happened to them," I told Martín, as I did everyone I was interviewing. "I want to know how they've managed to get by, how they've defended themselves. When were you born?" I asked as I began to record the interview. I paid Martín for his time, but he would have cooperated without pay. Like most of my respondents, he had little opportunity to hear his voice on tape, so I also played back a portion of the interview for him.

I was born in San Pedro in 1939. My father's name was Víctor. He left for the coast because he only had a small field, and the economic situation in San Pedro was pretty bad.[2] My grandparents still owned all the lands; our house was falling down and was too small for us. We had a large family with lots of small children. My father left to look for a better life and to save money to build a new house and buy another field. When he returned, he was able to buy enough land to give us about two yugadas *[a quarter of a hectare]. After my grandfather died and my grandmother distributed the lands, we got a little more.*

Like most migrants, Martín's father had been recruited by a labor contractor, a *contratista* or *enganchador.* Generally a townsman from the same locality as their recruits, these contractors established regional migration patterns by sending migrants to certain areas instead of to others. *Enganchadores* offered people an advance, the *enganche,* or hook, that committed recruits to the work. One San Pedro townsman started contracting around 1920, working with his godson, another San Pedrino employed on a Punta Madera cotton plantation. "It wasn't a difficult task," his daughter told me. "He announced that work was available during the Sunday market, advanced part of their salary, and wrote down the names of those who said they would go, then set off with about forty to fifty people on several buses to Punta Madera."

Some *enganchadores* were honest; others cheated the workers, offsetting promised salaries with inflated expenses for travel, food, and housing. "The contractor told us that 'expenses' ate up our salaries and we weren't going to be paid," one migrant from San José complained bitterly in 1983. Recruited to harvest coffee in the tropical forest for three months in 1971, he and the other workers were given "nothing to eat, nothing, no vegetables, no meat, only plain rice that didn't even contain spices." They complained in vain to the

Martín

20 Migrant coastal farmworker

plantation owner. He had paid the contractor in advance, he told them, and it was no longer his concern. The crew abandoned the work, slipping away at night "without any money."

Martín's father, however, had a positive experience. *When my father returned home, he told us that things were better on the coast: that there was lots of excitement and lots of work. He told all this to my mother. And we saw that nearly everyone who went to the coast returned well dressed, carrying radios, shoes, and other new things. People were coming back with money to build houses and buy farmland.*

We got fired up like everybody else and left for the coast too, more or less around 1945. I was around six. There were no buses, so we rode in the back of a truck, costing 45 soles for the fare from Ayacucho to Lima. The truck was crowded with passengers, everyone with luggage. We got to Lima after three days on the road. Lima was much smaller then, located mostly around the government palace. Everything was farmland and haciendas. There were few cars. Mules, burros, and wagons carried green vegetables and bread into the city.

When we got to Punta Madera, my father went to work in the cotton fields, the chacra. In those days men earned 2.2 to 1.8 soles daily.[3] Women got 1.5 soles to do the weeding and raking. I was only six years old, but I helped my mother rake and weed. It was easy to get work in the 1940s. They only planted cotton then, but they said that the hacienda once grew sugarcane. The hacienda had everything, a bakery, a movie theater, a restaurant for single people. Married people had their own living quarters and kitchen. We were given a place in the married people's housing. The hacienda had a school, so young children could attend and older ones could work. Those between fourteen and sixteen worked with the women, but at sixteen boys began to work with the men.

"Why did you go to Punta Madera instead of some other place?"

The first paisanos came to Lima on foot. When they returned they told us about the work in Punta Madera. It wasn't possible to go to a place where you didn't have a contact, where you didn't know anyone. People always came with a person who had already been to the coast, someone who was able to find some paisano who would put you up for a few days and ask the field boss, the mayordomo, *to give you work and housing.*

Like Martín's family, most San Pedro migrants were first drawn to the cotton plantations around Lima, a route taken by 55 percent of my migrant sample (56 of 102 people). A few San Pedrinos have been attracted to Lima primarily by its excitement. "San José is ugly, filled with mountains and ravines, but Lima is flat and beautiful," a friend confided in 1967, presenting a concept of beauty the opposite of mine. "In San Pedro everyone remains at home, except during fiestas, but in Lima they're in the streets," he continued.

Most migrants, however, like Martín's father, were pushed out of home communities by economic necessity and drawn to Lima and its environs by available work.

In their first year on the coast, Martín's mother fell ill and they had to return to San Pedro. *"You need a change of climate," the doctor said to her, "or you'll die."* I have no idea what sickened Martín's mother, nor do I have data on work-related illness on Peruvian cotton plantations, but in later years Martín's father cared for the plow oxen and the horses and mules used to fumigate cotton with *arcenato,* probably calcium arsenate or lead arsenate. I neglected to ask what type of work Martín's father did in their first year, but I wonder if he and his wife also had worked in insecticide administration then, possibly causing Martín's mother to fall ill. Once used on cotton and food crops in the United States, calcium arsenate and lead arsenate were banned by the Environmental Protection Agency in 1988 because of "cancer risk to workers and acute toxicity to the general public."[4] In Mexico migrant laborers on produce farms have died from improper use of insecticides.[5] It is also possible that Martín's mother had caught malaria, endemic on the coast in those years and a frequent reason migrants returned to the sierra.

Martín was eight when the family returned to San Pedro. He attended kindergarten but left school after a year, to set off once again

for the coast with a paisano. His parents, brothers, and sisters remained in San Pedro but joined him on the coast a short time later.
Unlike most of his siblings, Martín has little education, even though
he is the oldest child. Instead of attending school, he worked with his
parents on a cotton hacienda for the next four years and entered first
grade only when he was thirteen, after they moved to an hacienda
with a one-room schoolhouse. On that hacienda, Martín worked in
the fields until 1:00 PM, ate lunch, then attended class. He finished
second grade, the final year offered on the hacienda, but went no
further. To continue would have required bus fare to Punta Madera
center, about five kilometers away.

In those days education wasn't given as much importance as it is
today. My parents were interested in work, not education; my mother
didn't take any interest and didn't push me to study. I also began to Martín
work with the men when I was sixteen, and my salary rose to six soles
a day.

In 1959, when he was twenty, Martín returned to San Pedro to
marry. He lived in San Pedro with his wife, Isabela, and her parents
but, in need of money, he left for the coast after six months. Isabela
remained in San Pedro, beginning the intermittent separation that
characterized their marriage, during which they sometimes lived together but often did not. They both loved the sierra more than the
coast but they were caught between the harsh reality of uncertain
food production in the sierra and insufficient income on the coast.

Here on the coast in Punta Madera I have nothing, no farm, only my
job. Everything is money here. I like it better in San Pedro and I want to
be with my family. In San Pedro I can plant food and raise animals but
I can't survive without some kind of business to supplement the farm.
We have enough lands but no oxen to plow them, and if there is either
too much rain or too little and we lost our crop, what would we do?

Martín's dilemma was a real one. Rural farmers have no system of
crop insurance or help for crop loss. I spent one of the saddest days
of my life the day after a catastrophic hailstorm in March, 1996, devastated Rumipata, a hamlet in the lower reaches of San Pedro (see
Chapter 7). More than twenty-four hours after the storm, pebble-
sized hailstones still clustered in the shade. Birds killed by the force
of the storm remained impaled on cactus plants. *Molle* trees lay bat-
tered on the ground, surrounded by half the maize, peas, and wheat
plants, cut down as if by a scythe.

"How will we eat?" an old woman blinded by cataracts asked.
"How are we going to live?" her companion wanted to know, his face
wrinkled by years of work and sun. "How can we pay back the loan of
seeds we received from the *caja rural,* the rural bank?" a younger man

asked. The young man could migrate to look for work, but the old people had to hope for remittances from family working elsewhere.

Martín and Isabela's difficulties on the coast were also common. "What do we eat in Lima, doctor?" a woman complained in 1996. She had returned to San José with a group of former neighbors to rebuild their hamlet, abandoned for economic reasons in the 1970s, a ghost town of crumbling chapel, road, bridge, and houses. In Lima "we earn only a minimal wage, not enough to feed us," the woman explained. "We earn just 8 soles a day [U.S.$3.20], doctor. Not enough to buy bread or milk. Many, many are suffering . . . some can't even afford a ticket to return . . . but there is no work in Lima. At least in San José we have our fields, our animals. That's what they say, doctor."

Martín and Isabela solved their economic problems by living apart and sharing resources, Martín on the coast and Isabela and the children in the sierra, a common pattern. I often am astonished at the number of Peruvian couples who live apart. "How do they remain a couple?" I ask myself. Everyone profiled in this book has experienced some significant separation from parents, children, lover, or spouse, painful experiences memorialized in the department's haunting music. "Ayacucho Little Orphan Bird," the department's popular hymn, laments that people are forced by the "claws" of poverty to live in "strange lands."

After his marriage, Martín toiled as a field hand, a *peón agrícola*, on coastal plantations, sometimes treated well and sometimes not.

"Velarde, how are you doing? Where are you working?" a friend of my aunt who was a field boss, a mayordomo, asked. I was about thirty.

"I'm working in Mala" [an agricultural region to the south of Lima].

"Well, how much are you earning? We need a good, responsible tractor driver on my hacienda. Other drivers don't know how to care for the machine and they break it. I know that I can rely on you, and we'll pay a little more than you're earning now."

He promised me the job and a house. I was bored with the job I was on and had relatives near the new place, so I accepted. But when I arrived, there was no machine, no house, nothing. I was angry and argued with the field boss. "Why did you cheat me?" I demanded. "Why did you make me quit my job for nothing?" He shouldn't have done that, but he ignored my complaints and told me to rent a house and come to work. My brother Sergio lived nearby and I went to see if I could stay with him.

Confused by Martín's reference to Sergio as his brother I interrupted, "What brother?"

Sergio.
"Oh," I responded, "your *primo hermano,* your cousin-brother."
"Cousin-brother" describes the kin relationship known as "first
cousins" in my background, a family tie that is very close in Peru.[6]

*I told my brother my story and he gave me a place to stay. I traveled
to work from my brother's house, but after a week the boss told me that
I had to work at night because someone else was going to drive the
tractor in the daytime. I told the Japanese guy running the plantation
that I couldn't work at night. I lived too far and couldn't get home
after finishing at two in the morning. I quit.*

*I let my brother know what had happened that night. I told him that
I knew of a company that had just received a contract to build side-
walks in Ventanilla. "Maybe we could get jobs there," I said to him. We
went to the company and were hired as masons.* *Martín*

Ventanilla is a huge residential area just north of Lima and near
Punta Madera. When Martín began to work there in 1969, Ventanilla and the rest of metropolitan Lima were growing exponentially, flooded by highland migrants experiencing economic pressures similar to those of Martín and the others in this book. As a
mason, he earned four times as much as a field hand, seventy-five
soles a day instead of eighteen.

*Everybody left the hacienda for construction, and so I left farming
forever, going from one masonry job to another. Isabela and I thought
I could use the savings from my masonry work to return to the sierra to
live permanently. She had been living on the coast, but went back to the
sierra with our four children to build our house. She arranged for the
manufacture of adobe bricks, and I sent her saws and money to buy eucalyptus wood for the beams. When the walls were half done, I left my
job to finish the house in San Pedro. We were building it along the path
leading to the central schools, a perfect place for selling school supplies.
We planned to put a stationery store in the front. My daughters and
wife could run the store while I worked in the fields. I also bought
another small field to farm.*

Martín and Isabela miscalculated. They thought that Martín's final
pay, the *liquidación* from his masonry job, would be enough, but they
ran out of money before finishing the house and store. Martín once
again returned to Punta Madera to look for work while Isabela and
their five children (two others had died in infancy and two more were
yet to be born) remained in San Pedro. It was 1969. Martín was
thirty-one years old. Reared during relatively prosperous times, he
was filled with hope and viewed his absence from the sierra and his
family as temporary. *I wanted to finish the house and open the store.*

21 Coastal street peddler

I even bought land in San Pedro, not knowing that I'd be stuck on the coast until today.

Martín's plan to earn money on the coast and then return to the sierra was not unreasonable. Other San Pedrinos, including his father, had used a similar strategy successfully. It is easy to plan, but plans easily go awry when you earn a marginal income. In contrast to his previous experience, bad luck and Peru's deteriorating economy in the 1970s stalked Martín. Unable to find suitable work, he became a peddler, an *ambulante,* selling fruit, vegetables, candy, clothing, and whatever else was available from a pushcart for most of the ensuing year. Because peddlers earn little and are subject to police harassment, San Pedrinos peddle only when they have no alternative, and they speak of these experiences unhappily. Even so, Martín sometimes endured weeks without even this work.

And there in the sierra were my wife and children, Martín told me regretfully. *I sent money when I could, but I often had none to send. My wife was angry. Because I sent so little, she thought I might have another woman. She couldn't understand why I didn't return to the sierra if I couldn't find work on the coast. But if I worked only the farm, we wouldn't have money for clothing and food. There is no income in San Pedro, only expenses. I told my wife that we had to finish the house in San Pedro and open a business.*

Isabela's suspicion that Martín might be philandering was not without reason. I do not believe that Martín had another family, and

his brother Homer tells me he did not, but many other men have es-
tablished multiple families under similar circumstances, some even abandoning their families in the sierra. Martín's cousin-brother Sergio, for example, bragged to my assistant of his many families. Even allowing for male braggadocio, dual families were not uncommon. How does one live apart for so long?

Martín was recommended by a friend (a woman) and finally was employed as janitor of a night school. The pay was so low, however, that he still had to grab *cachuelos,* odd jobs, during the day, a common practice of migrants who, like adjunct faculty in American universities, can provide for themselves only by piecing together various jobs. Martín was quickly promoted to janitor of the day shift at a better salary and was responsible for general handiwork and cleaning the school.

Martín

It was a temporary position, but the director knew me. He was fond of me because I did whatever he asked. He would call me for the smallest thing, and he sometimes slipped me something extra, a propina. "You're intelligent," he told me, "unlike the person you're replacing."

Martín's relationship with the director illustrates his *humildad,* the ingratiating behavior he often expressed toward upper-status people. Such humility, establishing relationships that hopefully will be repaid with assistance, is one way poor Peruvians seek the favor of the better-off.

The director recommended Martín for the permanent position, but the Ministry of Education appointed a woman in his stead, putting Martín out of work once again after only three months. His cousin-brother got him odd jobs loading sacks of fish meal, but after a few agonizing weeks, Martín's luck changed. The woman who had replaced him had joined a teachers' strike and never returned.

The job was too difficult for her and I returned to the school, but it took the Ministry of Education eight months to process my first pay. I suffered a lot. I borrowed money from here and there to eat. I sometimes got odd jobs and I sent that money to San Pedro to take care of my family. In 1972 I was officially named to the post and received my back pay.

Martín's experience with pay is not uncommon. In the 1960s San Pedro schoolteachers often waited weeks before receiving their salaries. "Can you lend me some money?" Horacio Gutiérrez (Chapter 2) asked me. "I haven't received my pay and I need to get ready for my birthday fiesta."

After paying my debts, I sent a letter and money to my wife, telling her that I had a steady job and that she and the children should join me. We moved into a temporary house, but my salary was too low to support the whole family [six of his seven children had been born]. *My wife wanted to stay, but I spoke to her trying to make her understand. "How are we going to manage?" I asked her. "We have a house in the sierra and it is empty for no reason. Now that I have steady work, I can send you money every month and you can plant the fields and, if anything is left over, finish the construction of the house." She returned to San Pedro and I stayed on the coast.*

I do not know what Isabela thought about this and other matters. I never interviewed her and know her primarily through Martín's eyes. I had not planned to use my interviews with Martín in other than a statistical and summary way, or I would have obtained an account from Isabela as well.

Martín miscalculated again. Hardly earning enough to pay for his food in Punta Madera, he could not save anything and was rarely able to send money to his wife for food or for the payments for the fields they had bought. Afraid that even the small amounts he sent to San Pedro would be stolen in the mail, Martín entrusted the money to traveling friends and relatives. When nobody was traveling, Martín sent money through a commercial agency, an additional expense for the money order and for Isabela's travel to pick it up.

To be separated like that wasn't good, Martín regretted. *She was in San Pedro for two years and I only went there on vacation and for my birthday. Isabela would complain, crying, telling me about her hard life, running our farm and rearing the children on her own. She couldn't get farmhands, so she did most of the work herself. She had to search for cooking fuel, a terrible problem. We didn't own any trees to provide fuel and had no money to buy firewood, so Isabela had to travel up the mountain [to the wild underbrush zone], renting four or five burros to bring back enough kindling for two weeks. I never should have built my house in San Pedro, nor should I have bought the land. They were useless expenses. I thought I was doing well in building my house. I wanted all of us to go to San Pedro to live.*

Away from his family, Martín was lonely. Being alone and being lonely are not the same, but this is a distinction that many San Pedrinos rarely make. "I'll sleep at Barbara's to accompany her," my friend Valentina Rodríguez said to me as my wife was clearing out her house, getting ready to move. Why does she need someone to accompany her? So that she is not alone, so that she does not have to deal with everything by herself. *Acompañar*—to accompany—someone carries a special meaning. It refers not only to being with somebody, but also to taking care of him or her, helping out, serving food. It is

often a hierarchical relationship: younger people accompany older
folk, and the less powerful accompany the wealthy and more powerful. One is not supposed to be alone, and I was often asked if I wanted
somebody to accompany me on some trip or other activity.

San Pedrinos rarely live alone. If they do not reside with a spouse
and children, they try to live with parents, siblings, aunts, uncles,
cousins, or godparents. In part this is economic; by living together
they share expenses. But the preference is also emotional; to be alone
is to be lonely.

Martín was lonely and he spent his Sundays drinking with men in
one of the San Pedro migrant associations, where he was a leader and
often spent much of the money he had earned. Highland migrants
often form associations of people from the same town.[7] When asked
what the clubs are for, members respond with mission statements, *Martín*
generalities that represent aspirations rather than accomplishments.
They frequently speak of creating industry back home to provide employment, but most migrants place first priority on helping their
families financially, then, secondarily, the town. From time to time
they purchase some gift for the town—a church bell, clothing for the
saints, books for the school library. The Historical Society, a San Pedro club located in Santa Anita, bought the land on which the central
school in San Pedro was built. The Association of Progressive San
Pedrinos, the club Martín was active in, has devoted itself to helping
San Pedro pave its streets and provide lighting along the paths leading to the school.

These are significant accomplishments, but the clubs are mainly
places where San Pedrinos obtain help in getting jobs and housing
and where they can enjoy themselves in the company of people they
have known since childhood. Like many expatriates, they want to associate with people who have familiar assumptions, shared values,
and common experiences. They get together informally, as Martín
did each Sunday, and more formally during Carnival, saint's day celebrations, barbeques (*parrilladas*), and soccer games. These activities not only ameliorate feelings of isolation, they also sustain the social networks necessary to find work. Social networks are important
to all of us, but they are vital to the poor. My social network provides
happiness (my family and friends) and professional success (my colleagues). Martín's network not only provided happiness and success,
but it has sustained him during his most difficult times. Yet maintaining such a network had a negative side: Martín spent money on
standing rounds of beer at club events that he could have used to
build his planned-for store in San Pedro. When he was older and

reunited with his family, he came to regret money spent on alcohol, even though he had used it to form relationships that had helped him survive.

Isabela finally came to live with me on the coast in 1980, Martín told me. *We left the children in San Pedro in the care of my oldest daughter to let them finish school. It was very sad when we were all separated, and I sent for the children to join us at the end of the school year. In 1983 we live together as a family but we are still in economic crisis. Every year gets worse. There is even less work than before because the cotton plantations are gone, turned into cooperatives. The cooperatives have no money and can't plant most of their fields, so my wife can get only minimal work as a farmhand. But that farmwork helps at least to buy meat and vegetables.*

The agrarian reform in the late 1960s and the early 1970s transformed the former cotton and sugar plantations into cooperatives organized around former plantation workers. These cooperatives were sometimes successful, but they often were not. Many of the cooperatives had been undermined even before they began. Aware that land reform was imminent, many plantation owners were unwilling to invest in property that they thought would be taken from them. Some stripped their farm's assets, sometimes deliberately sabotaging the property, and left the cooperatives without adequate equipment. After President Velasco, who had initiated the land reform, was removed in 1975, moreover, the Peruvian government shifted away from fomenting social transformation and provided even less help to the cooperatives. The cooperatives were further undermined by reduced international demand for cotton, now replaced by synthetic fibers. Developed-world subsidies to their own cotton producers added to the economic pressures by undermining prices.[8]

In 1983, when I conducted these interviews with Martín, many cotton cooperatives lacked the capital to purchase seed, insecticide, and fertilizers. They teetered near bankruptcy, their tractors rusting in the fields and the earth, their source of future sustenance being sold to be made into bricks for Lima housing. They had no money to hire workers, so the migration of *serranos* to the cotton fields had all but disappeared, as had the occasional fieldwork that Martín and Isabela had often relied on. In 1983, moreover, a disastrous El Niño had warmed the sea and altered rain patterns, devastating Peru's fishing industry and farming, creating even more unemployment. It was a terrible year throughout Peru and, worse yet, Isabela was sick with the flu, unable to work for the two weeks before the interview.

Martín

22 Shoe repair shop of coastal migrant

I'm paid monthly, but it isn't enough, and we have to pay for food on account. Last month we spent 70 or 80 thousand soles [U.S.$62 to $71] *of my salary to pay for food that we had already eaten, leaving 20 thousand soles* [U.S.$18] *for the coming month. Isabela's the only one who helps me, and we don't have enough even for bread. They're operating on my son next week, and I had to buy medicines. My children don't eat as they should and they rarely drink milk. We sometimes buy milk on Sundays, but even that milk is diluted with water and isn't healthful. In Punta Madera we're going to die of hunger.*

Keep in mind as you read this: Martín had a full-time job! And although he related all this straightforwardly and without anger, he was desperate. I was paying Martín to assist me. It is possible that he exaggerated his poverty to receive a higher salary, but his siblings confirm his account. So did the general poverty around him. Many Peruvians complain, as Martín did, that "right now we are worse off than ever." They are right. Life is more difficult every year for many (and perhaps most) Peruvians. As population has grown and as Peru has had to compete in the ever-more-cutthroat global economy, the poor have fallen further behind.

In spite of their hunger, Martín and Isabela had not sown their sierra fields in 1983. Even though San Pedro potatoes and maize taste better than store-bought produce, the high costs of fertilizer, seed, insecticide, labor, and transport made the food too expensive in comparison with provisions bought in the market. Martín and Isabela were unaware of the government policies (see Chapter 9) that made store-bought food relatively inexpensive, and food was still costly, but they knew it would not pay to travel to San Pedro to grow their own. Usually only wealthy migrants in Lima planted their lands in San Pedro, as they could easily arrange for field hands and retrieve their harvest while in the town to visit family, check on property, and hunt for household servants and other workers for coastal enterprises. (As we will see in Chapters 6 and 8, Triga and Anastasio Huamán were recruited for work on the coast in just this way.)

Too poor to travel regularly to San Pedro, Martín and Isabela left their fields and home in the care of a relative. *We want the fields sown continuously, to prevent grama grass from growing and making it impossible to plow.*

"Do you charge any rent?"

No, but if he wants, he can send us some of the produce.

Like most Peruvians, they hesitated to rent their home and land because they feared losing possession. Many San Pedrinos believe that if they contribute to the value of something through residence or unpaid labor, they obtain rights of ownership, a conception often in conflict with rights conveyed by formal deed. "My house in San Pedro is empty," Valentina Rodríguez (Chapter 5) told me in 1983. "I'm afraid if I rent it, the person will say, 'It belongs to me because I've lived there.' I'd rather see the house tumble down than for that to happen."

In the early 1970s these different conceptions of property led to a furious public dispute in San Pedro. Advocates of the agrarian reform, especially university students and representatives of the government agency known as SINAMOS (Sistema Nacional de Apoyo a la Movilización Social, National System to Promote Social Mobilization), sought to make landownership dependent on active cultivation, urging San Pedrinos to work their lands as a cooperative. They claimed that because San Pedro is a registered peasant community, a *comunidad campesina*, private ownership does not exist; only those who work land can claim title to it; and lands left idle for two years must revert to the community for redistribution. "To my way of thinking, these changes are a good thing," my assistant Miguel told me in 1974. "Private ownership of land was imposed by the Spanish. Under the agrarian reform, there won't be any inequality in land. Whoever wants to work will have enough farmland to do so."

Large landowners and migrants opposed these changes and led the fight for private property. We've been a *comunidad campesina* only in the higher altitudes, they argued, and have always bought and sold lands in the maize zone. "People here want to become communists," one opponent of the changes told me. "They don't want anyone to be property owners and they want everything to be owned by the state. We won't even be able to rest or drink maize beer." Still another commented, "We don't live on the lands of the community but on our own lands, which we bought with our own money and through our own efforts." A few were noncommittal. "Do you want to be a member of the *comunidad,* of a cooperative?" I asked in 1973. "It doesn't matter very much," my friend responded. "I don't have much land. If I did, I'd want to be a *propietario,* a private property owner."

San Pedrinos held meeting after meeting to resolve the issue, heightening existing animosities and alliances. "I don't want to go to town," my assistant Lucho told me in 1974. "There's a lot of arguing and I was even beaten up." A mini-riot broke out during Independence Day festivities in 1974, when Ayacucho university students presented a Quechua theater production in the market that urged "the community to work together peacefully." The reference to "community" was heard as a tacit call for agrarian reform, infuriating some bystanders. Only the intervention of the priest prevented a fight. When I naïvely used the word "community" to refer to the town, friends quickly let me know that "community" signified the "peasant community," not the whole town, as I had presumed, another example of the dangers of bringing assumptions into a foreign context. One confrontation in 1975 grew so hot that the district governor fled to the safety of the police post, and police reinforcements had to be called to restore order.

Many migrants returned to San Pedro to defend their property rights. Too poor to travel, Martín left the matter in his parents' hands. In the end, the advocates of private property prevailed, convincing the majority that, even if they had little land, they were better off as *propietarios* than as *comuneros.* Underlying this decision, I believe, was the reality of near-universal migration. So many families depended on migrant remittances that they rejected the dichotomy of self-sufficient *comuneros* versus absentee landlords. Almost every family had a spouse or child who in some sense was an absentee landlord.

After 1983 I had only occasional contact with Martín and his family. I visited them on the rare occasions I was in Punta Madera, but did not stay for long or interview them extensively. I last visited in 1999. Martín still behaved with the courtly grace of the man in my notes and memories. No longer dreaming of returning to San Pedro, he and Isabela were constructing a new cement house in Punta Madera. They had finally accepted that their home was on the coast,

Martín

not the sierra. Martín's parents and a brother were sowing their fields in San Pedro.

I think of my parents, Martín told me. *They're old and sick and need my help. We want to bring them to the coast to live, but they're used to San Pedro and don't want to come. When they visit, they return to San Pedro within a week.* "*Like any good rooster,*" *my father tells us,* "*I want to die in my own corral.*"

Martín's home, larger than his previous home and with cement floors, marked a significant improvement in his economic condition. He had retired from his janitorial job, but still worked at odd jobs. He stored fifteen three-wheeled pedicabs on the first floor and earned a total of about 7 soles a day with them (about U.S.$2.00). Unable to afford the $100 a month to rent a permanent stall in the market, Isabela sometimes worked as peddler. Their children were grown, but Isabela and Martín continued to help them economically. Like most poor migrants, they had brought several generations and families into their household and were rearing the eight-year-old child of a daughter killed in an automobile accident and helping another daughter with five children whose husband was in prison. While large families often increase interpersonal tension, San Pedrinos nonetheless try to accommodate as many of their relatives, god-children, and *compadres* as they can and rarely live in a household comprising only husband, wife, and children.

Martín and Isabela invited me to lunch, as I knew they would, even though they were aware that I was to eat lunch at the house of Martín's sister. Food ritualizes and represents social relationships and cannot be refused without rejecting the relationship. As I ate the soup and lentils that had been quickly prepared in my honor, neighbors stopped by to deliver barbecued beef hearts, a Peruvian delicacy known as *anticuchos*. They were selling the food to raise money to purchase medicine for a sick relative. Martín bought some to help out. He has needed similar help himself.

Martín told me that he had left Roman Catholicism some years before to become a Jehovah's Witness. He now found solace in Bible study, reading the Bible with the help of coreligionists, like many poorly educated Peruvians. His new religion, which prohibits the consumption of alcohol, provided Martín with needed moral support to stop drinking. To avoid temptation, he has distanced himself from the migrant association, a relationship that he also no longer needs for networking, as he did in the past.

In spite of their poverty, Martín and Isabela did not eat at the communal kitchen, the *comedor popular,* directly across from their

home. *The food doesn't taste good,* Martín complained, *and they add*
lard to the soups to extend the meat.

Begun in the late 1970s and now found throughout Peru, communal kitchens do not provide complete nutrition, but they are essential to many of the poor.[9] Women members cook the food by turns, using ingredients (wheat, lentils, rice, noodles) obtained from the government, the church, and nongovernmental organizations (NGOs), as well as food they have purchased. Inscribed members of a communal kitchen in Comas, a poor district of Lima, paid about U.S.$0.35 (one sol) for a big lunch in 1999, which they ate in the kitchen or took home to their families, and nonmembers paid about U.S.$0.52 (1½ soles). The kitchens are also a center of socialization, where members exchange information and advice about child care, cholera, infant diarrhea, women's rights, and other political and so-   *Martín*
cial issues.

Martín is poor, but not the poorest of the people I have interviewed. One family in my sample lived in a reed hut without electricity and running water and bought water from a water truck. Everyone worked to earn money, no matter how little, the children going door to door selling packages of peeled garlic cloves prepared by their mother. Martín and Isabela were better off, occupying, as they did, a cement home with water. They nonetheless were poor, struggling from crisis to crisis.

Martín, moreover, is among the poorest of his siblings. His brother Homer is far more prosperous, living in a house with flooring, a telephone, and fancy, stuffed couches. Homer had the good fortune to finish secondary school and to receive technical training as an electrician. The return to San Pedro when he was young, Homer told me, was a disaster, "ruining our schooling and reverting us to poverty." He had to struggle to study, but he did so successfully. That training has provided him with a secure income in the fish meal industry, even though in the current neoliberal climate, he lives from uncertainty to uncertainty as his contract must be renewed every six months. "My contract's up next month [or in two months or in three] and I'm not sure I'll be renewed," he has said to me often. "There's no work security in Peru anymore."

Nonetheless, Homer's stable income has provided capital to open a store in the front of his house, where his wife, Alicia, sells rice, noodles, cigarettes, sugar, toilet paper, and other incidentals. They also have rented out rooms in their house, and in 1999 they purchased another house, providing additional rents. On his days off Homer uses his automobile as a taxi. Alicia and Homer's relatively large income has allowed them to educate their children. One child completed his university education and in 2001 opened a dental practice, setting up a work area in their living room, even as he faced tough competition from other recent graduates. Another child was still at the university, while the youngest was in primary school.

Unlike Martín, who had seven children, Homer and Alicia have limited their children to three. "You can't have more than a few children if you want to succeed." He and Martín are also different temperamentally. While Martín decides something and then changes his mind, Homer carefully chooses a course of action and sticks to it. During the high-inflation years of the 1980s, when the price of an orange might double in the course of a day, he immediately transformed his pay into hard goods. Throughout the decade, one wall of his living room was lined with bags of sugar and boxes of toilet paper to be sold in their store. He also has avoided familial and other obligations that might detract from his success. He moved from Punta Madera to distance himself from these demands and to focus on his own achievements. He also avoids migrant associations except for major celebrations.

Homer's experience, however, is exceptional. Many migrants, and perhaps the majority, have experiences similar to those of Martín, and many are even poorer. Their youngest brother, Carlos, for example is bitter about his poverty. Born on the coast, he was reared and attended school in San Pedro and Ayacucho City. He set out for Lima as a young adult to earn his way and to enter a university but quickly discovered that a university education was impossible economically. He did make it to Japan, however, claiming Japanese ancestry to work at menial jobs, but reverted to serious poverty on his return to Peru.

"To be on your own, to live on your own, to be separated from your parents, is very sad," he told me in 1983. "Sometimes you don't eat anything. Sometimes relatives invite you. That's what happens when you live alone. The truth is that the first time you're separated from your parents, you suffer just like a little bird on its first flight, all beak and stomach, searching for food."

FIVE

Valentina

FROM BRIDE BY CAPTURE TO
INTERNATIONAL MIGRANT

"Comadre, you're going to be in my book too. And so's [your husband]."

"Don't make me laugh!"

"What would you like me to call you?"

"Valentina! Yes, Valentina. I don't know why but the name just came to me. I like it. And you'll change the name of my husband? Let's call him Roberto."

I first met Valentina Rodríguez in San Pedro in 1966, but she has lived in the United States on and off since 1991. When we first met, Valentina and I were friendly but not close. Mistakenly believing that there was some "authentic" Andean culture, I wanted to work with monolingual Quechua speakers, not an upper-status townswoman who spoke reasonably good rural Spanish.

In San Pedro Valentina dressed very differently from most of her neighbors. In 1966 San Pedro had a stricter dress code for women than for men. An uneducated peasant woman had to wear *huali,* the characteristic blouse and long skirt similar to that worn by Claudia Velarde and Benjamina Enríquez. Educated townswomen and returned migrants, however, could dress in *traje*—a knee-length skirt, heavy stockings, a blouse, often covered with a light sweater—and could wear their hair short, without braids. Valentina could have walked unnoticed on the streets of New York.

Valentina lived in San Pedro only occasionally in 1966, and I referred to her in my initial notes as "the woman across the street, *la vecina.*" I am not good at remembering names and often used descriptive tags attached to a key to refer to people at the beginning of my acquaintance. When she began living in San Pedro, she borrowed my kitchen implements and offered me food. In the evenings, she and Roberto sometimes visited my room, and she would sing

23 Ayacucho market woman

Ayacucho songs in a sweet, high voice. In 1983 I lived near her in Lima, and now she lives in northern Virginia, which has allowed us to come to know one another well.

Valentina was born comparatively rich, but she has had a difficult life and today relies on gifts from her children and odd house-cleaning jobs in Virginia. Nonetheless, by any economic measure, Valentina is considerably better off than is Martín Velarde (Chapter 4).

Valentina's Story

I was a natural child, born out of wedlock, an hija natural. *I couldn't believe it when I looked at my birth certificate. My grandmother hated my father, Néstor, because he was from the rural area below the central town, the* bajíos. *She thought he was an Indian, a* cholo. *She was from a higher level, a family of social importance,* de la sociedad. *Because my grandmother didn't want them to marry, my mother and father escaped to Chancay on the coast, where I was born in 1939. They were married by the town mayor after I was born, but never had a church wedding because of my grandmother's opposition.*

In Chancay, my father was boss, a mayordomo, *of a work crew, and my mother cooked meals and washed clothing for the workers. My*

mother got tired of living so poorly, and when I was around two, we
returned to San Pedro. After two or three years in San Pedro, my fa-
ther died.

"What did he die of?"

I don't know. Either typhus or typhoid, something contagious that
hit San Pedro and killed my father and many others. There were no
doctors, no medicine.

My grandparents were very rich and my grandfather was very pow-
erful. He was governor of San Pedro and also justice of the peace. They
were hacendados *and owned an hacienda and two large farms with*
about fifteen families of peons. Other campesinos also worked for my
grandparents, but they lived on their own fields.

Whenever Valentina speaks of her grandparents, she always refers
to her mother's parents, probably because they were richer and more   *Valentina*
powerful than her paternal ones. Knowing that haciendas monopo-
lized land and water to capture the labor of peons who lacked one or
both resources, I asked, "Did the peons on the estate have to work on
your grandparents' fields in order to receive the land they lived on?"

No. My grandparents paid them for their work like everybody else.

"Why would your grandparents give peons land if they weren't
getting people to work in return?"

That way they had people near their fields who would always work
for them. But they had to pay them like any other worker.

Like many of us, blinded by a belief in the inherent fairness of our
families, Valentina was unable to see the coercion in her grandparents' relationship to their peons.[1] In San Pedro small *hacendados* and
townspeople often established godparent and other affective ties with
peons, partially obscuring the servile nature of the relationships. It
was only after I questioned her carefully that Valentina revealed that
each week members of one of the families on the hacienda walked
several hours to town to serve as unpaid resident cooks, maids, and
general servants in her grandparents' home. It is also probable that
they had to work in her grandparents' fields or in caring for their animals, a fairly typical relationship. In addition, Valentina said that the
peons who lived off the estate had to pay for drinking and irrigation
water by working in her grandparents' fields, much like the obligations that had constrained farming for the parents of Pablo de la Cruz
(Chapter 1).

Lands in San Pedro are inherited more or less equally by legitimate children, regardless of gender, a system of partible inheritance
that reduces the size of landholdings over time. After the death of
Valentina's grandparents, the hacienda was divided among four children, but the portions were large enough that Valentina's mother,

Elisabeta, remained rich and powerful. Like her parents, she dominated local society, utilizing income from several large farms (or
fondos), a small store where she sold cane alcohol (which she was
fond of herself), and a business in which she hired women to weave
cloth at home that she sold in the market in Ayacucho City.

After her death in 1960, the majority of Elisabeta's lands were divided equally among her five daughters, creating parcels too small to
support any of them.[2] Valentina and her husband wanted to buy her
sisters' shares on credit, paying them with projected farm earnings,
but they refused, insisting that the land be sold and the proceeds divided among them. *If we hadn't been poor, they would've sold us the
land,* Valentina says, lamenting that she has no farmland.

"You and your sisters inherited your mother's lands equally," I
said. "What would've happened if you had brothers too? Would
everyone still have inherited equally?"

*The lands would've been divided equally among all of us, brothers
and sisters.*

Responding to further enquiries, Valentina elaborated that lands
specifically assigned to a child in the *chacra partición,* the division of
the fields, are *interés.*

"What's *interés?*"

*Lands inherited from parents that you didn't pay for. Unlike lands
you buy, these lands have to stay in the family. But things are changing
today and people sell everything.*

"Well, then," I asked, "if you can't sell inherited lands, how come
you and your sisters sold your mother's lands?"

They weren't interés! *My mother died from a cerebral stroke before
she had told us, "This field belongs to you, that one to your sister." If
I had been given my field, I never would have let my sisters sell it. My
mother had already given the maize field near San Pedro center to my
oldest sister. She only stopped planting that field recently, when she
grew too old. The field was* interés *from my mother.*

"Did you get any lands from your father?"

We built my house on his lot. He died young and hadn't held the
chacra partición, *but my mother told me and my sister* [the three
other sisters had different fathers] *which parcels he had wanted us to
have. She respected what he wanted and told us the parcels were ours,
not hers.*

"What happened to the plot and house when you married? Did
they belong to you or to you and Roberto?"

You know that Roberto was real machista, *thinking he could order
me around because he was a man, and he cheated me out of the title,*

putting only his name on it, not mine. But usually a couple owns their property together, not separately.

This last observation illustrates the contested way in which cultural rules are implemented. In this case, gender trumped inheritance.

Because of this system of partible inheritance, Valentina and her sisters are poor in comparison to their ancestors. *Billcito,* Valentina has told me in a variety of ways, *it pains me, [me duele], because I have nothing of my mother, nothing. People in Ayacucho City are surprised I have nothing. My mother and grandparents were very rich.*

These diminished circumstances inspired several young men to dig for buried treasure in the former home of Valentina's mother several years after her death. I heard of their plans while interviewing Horacio Gutiérrez and three of his teacher colleagues in the artisan school in 1966. A young boy in tattered trousers, a student at the school, was stomping a mound of clay with his bare feet, mixing and softening the clay with water while we spoke.

Valentina

"Valentina's mother's a *manchachico,* a *condenado,*" Horacio told me. "She was rich, but her children aren't. She must have buried her money and never told them about it. We're gonna dig for it tonight."

"What's a *manchachico?*" I asked, not for the first time.

"People who die without telling their family about buried money," Horacio answered, grabbing a piece of the clay being worked by the boy to test its consistency. "They're condemned by God to become *manchachicos,*" the wandering dead, worms wriggling in their mouths, preying on unwary travelers to take their places.[3] Horacio and his friends uncovered rocks that night, but nothing more.

They were wrong, my mother wasn't a manchachico, Valentina complained incredulously when I told her the story many years later, omitting who had told me. *But my grandfather hid money and told no one. The man who bought one of his houses found real sterling, making him rich. But he saved my grandfather, letting him return to his grave. If the money had remained buried, my grandfather would've wandered forever as a* manchachico.

Many *hacendados* lost their power about the same time as did Valentina. Not only had farming become less profitable, but peons strapped for land were seizing farms. The anticipated agrarian reform unsettled matters still more. Nonetheless, prepared culturally and educationally for urban life, most *hacendados* were able to establish relatively well-off lives elsewhere.[4] Even though she was fluent in Quechua, Valentina spoke Spanish as her first language at home. She also was one of the few San Pedrinos (and even fewer women) to attend school in the 1940s and the 1950s.

When she was ten or eleven, Valentina completed first grade in the one-room San Pedro schoolhouse and transferred to a school in Ayacucho City, as did other San Pedrinos able to continue their education. Her memory of this first trip to Ayacucho City is harrowing.

My mother placed me on top of a truckload of fuel, asking the driver to take care of me, telling him that my sister Luisa would be waiting for me in Ayacucho City.

"Did your mother know the driver?"

We didn't know him. He had just come through San Pedro. When I got to Ayacucho City, my sister wasn't there! "Who will you go with?" the driver asked. "Do you know your house?" I was in Ayacucho City for the first time and I knew nobody.

"Wait here," the driver told me. "Your sister will surely come along." Then he left.

I didn't move, but my sister still didn't come, so I began to look for her. Crying, I walked around Ayacucho City until I bumped into a San Pedrino who recognized me. He took me to our rented room and told me to wait for my sister, who had gone to school. My mother had forgotten to tell her that I was coming.

Valentina attended school with her twelve-year-old sister. Sometimes a neighbor was paid to feed them, but they often cooked for themselves. Although she lived with her sister, Valentina missed her mother.

On the very first Saturday, we returned to San Pedro on foot, going by way of the highway, holding one another's hand and bringing bread from Ayacucho City. It took about six hours, walking uphill, but we hurried, afraid of thieves.

"Why did you come?" my mother asked.

"We were lonely," we told her, "and wanted to be with you." My mother began to cry.

We returned to San Pedro every weekend, but sometimes I escaped before that, setting off on Thursday or Wednesday, leaving my sister behind. I was really tied to my mother and I missed her a lot. That's why I never really studied, or finished primary school. My sister told my mother that I cried all the time and that she had to come live with us. My mother hit me then, admonishing me to stay in Ayacucho to study, saying she would come see me once a week or once every month. That just made me worse. I didn't want to leave San Pedro, and my mother finally said, "Well, if you really don't want to study, you can stay in San Pedro with me." I finished only third grade, nothing more.

In 1952 my brother-in-law Nemesio arrived from Lima. He lived with my oldest sister, Lourdes, and had come to San Pedro to check on their house and fields.

"Mamá," he said to my mother, "I'm going to take Valentina to live with us in Lima to accompany her sister, Lourdes. Valentina isn't going to school and is just wasting her time. Perhaps she'll go to school in Lima."

I was thirteen and my mother didn't want me to leave. "Valentina will be even worse in Lima," she told Nemesio. "She went crazy, crying all the time, just going to Ayacucho City."

"Lima is pretty," Nemesio said, trying to convince me to go with him. "You won't cry with your sister. If you want to go, I'll take you."

I was excited at the thought and told my mother that I wanted to go with him.

"But you won't cry?" she asked. "You won't miss me?"

"No, Mamá," I told her, and she agreed to let me go.

Intrigued by the twists and turns in her life, I interrupted Valentina to comment that she began living in different places at a very young age. I was seated at her round kitchen table in Lima in 1987, recording her story, one of several that I have collected. She was preparing the family's luncheon of potatoes, rice, carrots, and chicken and was peeling potatoes as she spoke, deftly removing the potato skin so that it fell in a single spiral, a skill sharpened by years of practice. Potatoes are eaten at almost every meal. Prompted by my interruption, she set the knife to one side, straightened her short, permed, hair, somewhat disheveled from the morning's work, then agreed with my remark as she sat across from me.

After just a week in Lima, my sister and her husband placed me in a house as a maid. I was thunderstruck! I cried and cried. I no longer lived with my sister, but slept and ate in the house where I worked. Even though my cousin worked in the house as a cook, I was not used to cleaning and the other household work. My sister came to get me on Sundays, and if she didn't come, the woman of the house wouldn't let me leave.

The woman was mean. "Why do you cry, serrana?" she heckled when I cried. "You serranas are just a bunch of filthy pigs, cochinas covered with lice."

She insulted me like that and I cried all the more. When my sister came one Sunday, I said, "Lourdes, the owner of the house insults me telling me that I'm a serrana, a pig, and covered with lice. I'm going to leave, I can't work here."

"Señora, why do you treat her badly?" Lourdes confronted the woman. "You don't know us. We're not just anybody that you should treat my sister like that. Yes, I have brought her to this job because I'm not yet ready to take care of her. My husband is a carpenter and I'm busy taking care of him and don't have anyone to help me care for my sister, but I didn't bring her here so that you should treat her as you are. My sister's not going to work for you anymore."

The woman pleaded; she wanted me to stay. "I won't speak to her like that again," she promised, but Lourdes didn't want me to stay. And I didn't want to either.

Lourdes took me to her house and began to fight with her husband. "Why did you bring my sister here?" she demanded. "She isn't used to work. She never worked as a maid and now she's crying because they treated her badly at that job. My mother's going to find out and I don't know what she'll say because she didn't know that Valentina was working."

"Well, we have to send her back to San Pedro," he said.

"How are we going to send her back by herself? She's a girl who knows nothing. We have to wait until my mother comes."

Without letting my sister know, I already had written my mother, telling her that I was suffering and asking her to take me back. My mother went crazy when she got the letter. She came for me, but almost died on the journey. She was too fat, just like my sister Fátima. She couldn't breathe crossing the mountain passes, and they had to give her oxygen.

"My daughter shouldn't suffer," she told me when she finally got to Lima. "If I sent her away it was so that she could be with her sister and nothing else. I'm going to take her back with me."

I stayed with my mother in San Pedro until I got married in 1957, when I was sixteen going on seventeen. At first I didn't want to marry Roberto, but he persisted, visited us often, and my mother finally accepted him. She told me I had to marry him, even though I told her that I hated him.

Later, when I wanted to marry him, my mother changed her mind. "Why are you going to marry that cholo?*" she demanded, hating him because he wasn't from the central town, the* llahta, *but was from the* bajíos, *the lower regions of San Pedro. "He's a* cholo!*" my mother complained. "How are you going to marry someone like that? You're going to suffer." It was just like what happened with my father. She talked like that until I became disillusioned and didn't want to marry him.*

The marriage of a child is a potential source of friction in all societies, but is especially so in San Pedro and San José. Time and again people have told me of the opposition of parents, especially mothers, to their choice of spouse. Even though she is aware of the hardship that her mother's attitudes brought her, Valentina has absorbed many of them and has fought with nearly all of her children about spouses, even opposing her own daughter's marriage to an Ayacuchano because he was a *cholo*.

Roberto Quispe, Valentina's husband, came from far less elite status than Valentina but had risen high. He had been a monolingual speaker of Quechua until he attended school at age eleven, when he learned Spanish and set aside his rubber-tire sandals for shoes. His father had decided that his children were not going to be untutored *ignorantes* and struggled to send Roberto and his siblings to school. "It's okay for me to be unable to read or write," Roberto's father told them, "but not my children."

Roberto first attended the San Pedro school, but had to continue his studies in Ayacucho City. He obtained a scholarship and finished his education in Huanta (a nearby provincial capital), where he learned tailoring and carpentry. Despite this schooling, he was never able to erase all signs of his rural origins. Later in life, after he had reached some prominence in San Pedro and Ayacucho, Roberto revealed to me that he sometimes felt embarrassed that he did not speak the fine Spanish of his associates.

In spite of her own uncertainty and her mother's opposition, Valentina ultimately married Roberto. *He kept trying to see me, calling me little princess, princesita. One night he climbed over the wall on a ladder and entered the bedroom I shared with my mother and sisters and forced me to have sex. I was too ashamed and afraid to say anything. I got pregnant. I've never told this story to anyone before, not to my mother, sisters, or children. I was too ashamed. If I had told my mother, she would have sent Roberto to jail because I was a minor.*

I have other accounts of men sneaking into the family sleeping quarters, usually a single room, to have sex with girlfriends. I do not know the extent of women's agency in these experiences. It probably varies, but Valentina felt coerced, and in a separate account she used this experience as an example of men raping educated as well as uneducated women. I'm surprised that nobody woke up when Roberto entered the bedroom, or while they were having sex, but under conditions of crowding people learn to exclude certain noises, much as the person living on a busy street expunges the sounds of traffic, only to be driven awake by the chorus of tree frogs in the countryside. The loud radio that frazzled me one night in Lima bothered nobody else. "What radio?" my hosts responded in the morning. In Valentina's case, moreover, her mother usually drank every day and was probably further deafened by alcohol. She also employed a watchman, thereby providing a false sense of security, unaware that he was susceptible to Roberto's bribe.

I told Roberto that I was pregnant, and he treated me with respect, but I still didn't like him, and he also began to take advantage of me, saying he was my owner, my dueño.

Valentina has ambivalent feelings about having had a *dueño*, a man who protects and claims ownership over her. She resented Roberto's claim when he was courting her. But in the 1990s, some ten years after Roberto's death, as we listened to a popular Hispanic song in which a woman lamented that she no longer had a *dueño*, I questioned Valentina about what a *dueño* meant to her. She was visiting my summer cottage in the Catskills. The day had been full. We had hiked one

of my favorite Catskill trails, had eaten a communal meal with friends, and, joined by my wife, were relaxing before retiring for the night.

"Do you want a *dueño?*" I asked.

Yes, I miss Roberto. He always took care of me, never let people abuse me.

During her courtship and marriage, however, Valentina rebelled.

I decided to run away to Lima, to escape Roberto, but I planned first to hide at my mother's farm until the search for me died down. I sneaked out at night with Jorge, my sister Fátima's son. Although Jorge was my nephew, he lived with my mother as her apra, her adopted child. In those days a grandmother would take her daughter's "natural child," her "hijo natural" [child born out of wedlock], *doing so with force if she had to, making the child her apra.*[5] *My mother raised Jorge as if he were her own son. He lived with us, and I took care of him, carrying him on my back in a shawl and giving him his bottle. He called me "Mamá" because he didn't know his mother. I reared him, and he slept with me.*

Although men and women are not ashamed of having had a natural child, as Valentina and others have told me on many occasions, people often resent resources given to their spouses' natural children, which sometimes transforms those children into Cinderellas, treated badly by both parents and stepparents. Many natural children lament childhoods in which they were household servants deprived of the education and other resources given to legitimate children, the *hijos políticos*. Valentina loved Jorge, but she has little love for Roberto's two natural children, barely acknowledging their existence. I saw one of them only once, when she came to clean Valentina's home in Lima. When I asked him how many children he had, Horacio Gutiérrez included only his children with Benjamina, ignoring his natural child. Roberto did the same.

The institution of *apra*, in which the grandmother cares for the natural child, mitigates some of this discrimination and provides a child to accompany and attend the woman as she grows old—often after the death of her husband. San Pedrinos also enjoy young children. *"What use is a house without a child?"* Roberto told Valentina when her early pregnancies ended in miscarriages. *"Maybe we should adopt one."*

Jorge, my mother's apra, was about five years old when I carried him to my mother's farm, far from town. I also took my mother's maid, her muchacha. She was my age, about fourteen or fifteen, and spoke only Quechua. My mother always had a muchacha. I asked the muchacha if she would accompany me until the next morning. Then she could return home. She agreed and the three of us set off.

When we were walking, walking at night, traveling on the footpath below the town, we heard noises. At first we thought they might be manchachicos and started to hide, but as the sounds became clearer, we knew that they were people and we waited.

I had told the maid, "If someone comes, we're gonna hide."

"No, Mamá," she said, "we'll go with them, because it's very dark and I'm afraid."

"Well, I guess so," I replied.

When the people got near, they recognized me. It was just a strange coincidence, but they turned out to be Roberto's parents. It was destiny. If I had reached Lima, my life would've been very different. By now they knew that I wasn't going to marry their son. I think my mother had told people that I had run away and that they should send me home if they found me.

"Señorita," my mother-in-law said.

"Who is it?" I replied, because it was still dark out.

"Señorita Valentina," she said to me.

"Who are you?" I asked.

"I'm Roberto's mother."

"Where are you going?" I asked in Quechua.

"To the hacienda to buy maize. And you, where are you going?"

"I'm going below to my mother's farm."

"No, señorita," she said, "that's suspicious. Why would you be going to the farm so late at night? Where are you really going?"

"No, señora, my mother sent me to the farm."

"No, señorita," she replied. "My son will go crazy! You aren't leaving!"

My mother-in-law at first didn't want Roberto to marry me. She wanted him to marry a woman from the campo, the rural countryside, a woman dressed like a peasant in huali, *but he told them no! He was going to marry someone from a different race* [raza], *not someone from the countryside.*

When my mother-in-law found me on the path, she grabbed me like a cop, with my father-in-law helping. "We don't want you to leave," they told me. "You're coming with us."

They took us to their home, the first time that I'd been there, then locked us in a room with a padlock. Jorge cried. "Let us out," I pleaded, "my nephew's crying." She didn't want to do that; she first had to let her son know that I was there.

Meanwhile, my mother was crying and looking for me all over. She lodged a complaint, and two policemen went to Roberto's house in town, waking him up, telling him I was a minor and he had better return me to my mother.

Roberto was really surprised. He knew nothing about my plans. He went to see my mother. "You stole my daughter," she told him, "and you're going to bring her back to me. If you don't, I'll send you to jail. Do you think you're going to marry my daughter? She's your patrona, *your boss, you no-good Indian!"*

"Señora," Roberto told her, "I know nothing about what happened. I haven't even seen your daughter." My mother scared him and he began to search for me everywhere. He went to the maid's house, thinking that we might have gone there. When he got there, the girl's mother began to cry, demanding, "Where's my daughter?"

Roberto came back and told my mother, "Señora, your daughter isn't at the maid's house and the maid's gone too. Why do you blame me? I haven't seen your daughter."

The corporal from the police post came to Roberto's parents' house. I was listening from inside the room and heard him.

"Señora, is señorita Valentina here?"

"No, señor, she isn't."

"Yes, she is," he said. "Her mother's going crazy looking for her. She's a minor, and if you don't produce her, your son's going to jail. He's already in detention."

That's what he told them. I was listening to everything.

I had left my bag on the patio of the house. The corporal recognized it and said, "The señorita's things are over there. Why did you hide her?"

"We haven't, señor."

"Okay," the corporal said. "I'm going to take her things, and if you don't produce the girl by this afternoon, I'm going to send your son to jail in Ayacucho City."

"Why didn't you call out to the policeman?" I asked some years later, when I was checking details of the narrative with Valentina.

I must have been tired and afraid of the police, she responded, clearly puzzled herself.

My mother-in-law was frightened, and when the corporal left she opened my door. "Señorita," she told me, "we're going to your mother and I'll speak to her."

They sent a young boy to tell Roberto that it was urgent he return, in that way letting him know I was with his parents. He had no idea that I had been in his parents' house. He was very upset.

"What're you doing here, my little princess?" Roberto asked. I told him to set me free, that I wanted to continue my journey, but he refused, saying that nobody would believe that he had nothing to do with my disappearance. He told me that I had to go to my mother and tell her the truth. Valentina

They kept me in their house while Roberto and his mother went to ask my mother for my hand. My mother chased them away, but on the second visit asked them to bring me to her, that it would depend on what I wanted. She asked me why I wanted to run away, and I lied, telling her I just wanted to be on the hacienda. *I didn't tell her I was pregnant.*

"How long were you in Roberto's parents' house?"

About a week. I sent the muchacha, *the maid, back to my mother, but told her not to tell my mother where I was.*

"It was like *warmi suway,* bride capture, then. Why didn't you want your mother to know where you were?"

Warmi suway, *yes. I was afraid they might put Roberto in jail for rape. I was a minor.*

Valentina's experience of being taken by force was fairly common in the 1960s. Known as marriage by capture (*matrimonio por robar* or *warmi suway*),[6] the custom was another manifestation of tense gender relationships, as well as a reflection of the frequent conflict between birth and marriage ties.

Some years later, as I was reviewing my notes with Valentina, I asked her to explain the woman's feelings about *warmi suway.* She was visiting my home, escaping her then-tense relationship with one of her daughters. "Does the woman want to go when the man takes her?" I asked.

I didn't want to get married and was running away, but the girl usually wants to be with her lover, Valentina responded, providing an account similar to those obtained from others in San Pedro. *She is afraid to tell her parents,* Valentina continued, *so the boy steals her, taking her to his home. His family then would send emissaries, people that the girl's parents respected, but her parents always rejected them, sometimes hitting them over the head with poles. But after five or four visits, her parents usually agreed to talk and set a time for the two families to meet to make marriage arrangements.*

In my case, I didn't want to marry Roberto, but he kept after me, telling me I should marry him, that I should think of the child. "I won't leave you alone until you accept!"

I finally told him yes, because I was afraid I might have a miscarriage. I had been working hard, harvesting my mother's primicia, *the priest's portion of a peasant's crop that my mother had purchased, and I had begun to bleed. The mayor married us shortly afterward, at the beginning of May, 1957, and the priest did so in the church at the end of the month. I was so sick during the Catholic ceremony that I hardly danced at the fiesta and went to bed. I lost the baby, but the miscarriage prevented the suffering I would have had if people had learned of the pregnancy.*

While there is no shame in having a child out of wedlock in San Pedro, the matter is not uncomplicated. As in other areas of Ayacucho, San Pedrinos condemn adolescent sexual activity, even as they are aware that it is fairly common.[7] Valentina, moreover, was *gente decente,* from the upper class, and was expected to adhere to higher standards than other San Pedrinos. Her pregnancy also represented adulthood, no matter how it came about, something that Valentina was not yet ready to acknowledge, let alone assert. She was only sixteen years old.

In this way we got married. My mother was so angry she didn't go to my wedding, and only one of my sisters went. If I hadn't met his parents on the path, I wouldn't have married Roberto. Our marriage was quite strange. Roberto used to tell me, "If it hadn't been for my parents, we wouldn't have married because who knows where you would've gone." Maybe if I had married somebody else, Valentina has told me often, *I wouldn't have suffered so much.*

The marriage was not easy for Valentina. Roberto, a charmer and skilled carpenter, was a poor provider. "I can't make money no matter what!" he once told me, complaining bitterly about political authorities who placed obstacles in the path of people like him who he believed were working for progress. Roberto sometimes risked other people's money in business schemes that often failed, and at times he narrowly escaped jail. He was not consciously dishonest. He lost his own funds and always intended to repay his loans and other money, but events often prevented him from doing so. Like most of us, Roberto was a bundle of contradictory behaviors. Capable of great love, he often brought joy to the homes in which he lived and visited.

Valentina still speaks of him affectionately, even though he beat her. I was very fond of him. He called me "my dear William, mi querido Guillermo" and was very generous with his time, knowledge, and love of San Pedro, but I also knew that it would be best not to lend him money (it would have had to have been a gift) or to have any other financial ties to him.

Valentina moved a great deal, usually in response to changes in Roberto's employment.[8] Roberto had no land of his own, only the house in the central town that he built on Valentina's lot. His parents were still active farmers and had not divided their fields among their children. In spite of a lack of land, or perhaps because of it, Roberto had great aspirations.[9] He opened San Pedro's first well-stocked store in 1952.

He had the first radio in San Pedro. It was a Telefunken, run by au-   *Valentina*
tomobile batteries. Everyone came to the plaza to hear it. Because I was
educated, people asked me where the sound came from. I didn't know.
"Were there people inside?" I wondered.

After their marriage, Valentina and Roberto moved to the nearby town of Rumi Sonqo to open another store. Business was good, but they had to transport cane alcohol and other goods with a team of ten or twelve burros, sometimes spending a night under a tree when the burros tired.

I was lonely and didn't like Rumi Sonqo. We returned to San Pedro to take over our store that we had left in the hands of others. Roberto became mayor in 1953, and remained mayor until 1956. We continued running the store in San Pedro, but Roberto's family kept taking things without paying. He was like that, always giving everything to his brothers and sisters, causing his own children to suffer. He was unable to pay his financial partner, and she pulled out of the business. We couldn't continue without her capital.

Many years later, one of Roberto's brothers claimed in a lawsuit over another brother's property that his parents had provided the capital for the store and that Valentina had pushed them out of the business after she married Roberto. This claim, made nearly fifty years after the events described, reflects the frequent and contested claims made by birth (natal) and marriage (conjugal) families over resources and loyalty that often lead to hurt feelings and anger. Other San Pedrinos give a different account, saying that political opponents accused Roberto of stealing communal funds, which is why he and Valentina had to leave San Pedro. Because similar accusations, often motivated by envy and political opportunism, are made frequently against officials in San Pedro, the veracity of any particular claim is difficult to judge.

Whatever the truth behind the allegations, Valentina and Roberto settled in Ayacucho City, where Roberto opened a carpentry shop with two brothers. After an argument with one of the brothers, Roberto sold his share, and he and Valentina returned to San Pedro, dedicating themselves to the commercial production of potatoes, financed through a large bank loan. But the rains failed and they lost the crop. It was so dry that, even after irrigating at night, the sun burned away the water the next day. Their debt from the failed potato crop plagued them for years.

After the potato crop disaster, Valentina and Roberto went to Santa Anita, near Lima, where they opened a workshop to manufacture clay ceramics with three artisans brought from San Pedro. Typical of such workshops, the employees were incorporated into the household, even if in an inferior fashion; they all lived in a rude hut and Valentina cooked for the artisans as well as for her family.

My oldest sister gave me a table but was upset. "How can you live like this?" she said. "What will be your future? Roberto's just an Indian, a chutu!*"*

Roberto brought the ceramic pieces to Lima shops and they sold like hot bread! This initial success, however, was quickly undermined by cheaper prices offered by San Pedro artisans who started to bring their merchandise directly to Lima. There may have been other problems. Horacio Gutiérrez claimed that he never received full payment from Roberto and Valentina for goods that he sent them.

After a year, Roberto and Valentina abandoned ceramic commerce and returned to the sierra. Valentina moved to San Pedro to start a *pensión,* providing board for the schoolteachers, and Roberto went to Ayacucho City to open a carpentry shop. This is when I met them. Like many Andean couples, they lived apart in order to get by economically. Unhappy with the separation, however, Valentina gave up her business after a year and relocated to Ayacucho.

Valentina's home in San Pedro was one of the finest in town: two stories of whitewashed stucco, containing eight cement rooms surrounding a large patio. She left this grand home to live in humble rooms with earthen floors in Ayacucho City, adjoining Roberto's carpentry shop.

Like most Andean women, Valentina has always tried to be economically independent, hustling in the best sense of the word. She was often the major provider, making sure, for example, that there was enough money for her children's schooling. In Ayacucho City, she rented an empty shop from her brother-in-law. Located on the

Valentina

24 Family storefront

highway leading from town, the store secured good income from sales of food and alcohol to travelers. Working there all day, Valentina missed her children. She left home in the morning before they awoke and returned after they were asleep. They were cared for by her twelve-year-old daughter. Roberto worked in the adjacent carpentry shop, but he was a gadabout, and because both he and Valentina considered child-rearing a woman's or young person's job, he was often elsewhere.

In 1980 Valentina was rewarded with a government post for her active participation in the successful presidential campaign of Fernando Belaúnde, an election that also sparked the Shining Path rebellion. When the fighting intensified in 1982, Valentina sent her children to the safety of Lima, then a short time later renounced her government post to be with them. In one sense they were war refugees, but they have never defined themselves that way. Instead, they saw Lima as a place to struggle for success. "No," her son, Manuel, has said to me, "We were never refugees. We always planned to go to Lima to study."

In Lima Roberto opened a carpentry shop in space made available by an unmarried brother. Valentina, Roberto, and children moved into the partially constructed home of the brother and helped him finish it. Migrants to Lima usually live in a new home as they build it. Lacking capital, people accumulate construction materials gradually, so that half-finished walls and piles of cement and brick sometimes dot new barrios, making them look almost like cities destroyed in war. During years of high inflation, moreover, people invested in building materials (when they could) instead of saving cash. When completed, after about ten years, Valentina's home was far more elegant than anything she had lived in previously, with parquet floors, tiled kitchen, and a modern refrigerator.

As beautiful as the house was, however, Valentina lost much of her independence, trapped as a servant, cleaning and cooking for everyone and taking care of her eldest daughter's children. Even so, she still conducted whatever business she could. In 1987 she dispatched cases of beer to another brother-in-law in San Pedro, doing so at a slightly favorable price to him, but earning money for herself.

Being jealous, Roberto did not like Valentina's work outside the home. He was dependent on her income but resented her independence and feared her potential sexual freedom, although Valentina has said that he never had to worry. He also needed to be in charge. Early in the marriage, when they had only two children, Roberto attacked her Ayacucho City shop in a drunken rage.

He was crazy. I don't know where he was drinking, but he was drunk when he got to my store, my tienda. *Roberto usually didn't drink like that; it must have been some* compromiso, *some obligation that started his drinking.*

"Close the tienda," *he ordered me, "come on home."*

I didn't want to. I still had customers. "No!" I told him.

It was just like a telenovela, *a soap opera. He went into a rage and smashed all the glass jars filled with merchandise, throwing them to the floor. Trach! The jars shattered, scattering the candies, chewing gum, and crackers, the things I wanted my customers to see. He did the same to the bottles of beer and rum, destroying them.*

I escaped into the street, ashamed that he did this in front of my customers, so many people. I fled to my sister's store, it was nearby, leaving my store unlocked. After Roberto left, still drunk, my sister went over to lock up. I was too afraid to go myself.

I stayed with my sister that night. "Don't put up with him," she told me. "Leave him. You have only two children. Why should you stay with him? He doesn't even support you and gives you nothing. Why should you stay?"

The next day, when he was sober, I became really brave, muy valiente. *I didn't return home but went with my two children to the old people's home run by the nuns. I had often given the nuns gifts of sawdust and wood shavings from the carpentry shop, which they used to make mattresses. I had never charged them, even though other people did. I told the nuns what Roberto had done, told them that he beat me and that he was too jealous. I stayed two nights with them.*

Roberto came to the home, speaking to the nuns, begging them to make me return. I didn't want to go back. I wanted a divorce, but the nuns didn't believe in divorce. "Return home for the sake of the children," they told me. They made Roberto promise to stop abusing me. "How could you destroy her negocio, *her business," they told him, "when that's what sustains your children?"*

I decided to go with him on the nuns' promise that I could come back if he mistreated me again. But even though he still sometimes beat me, I never returned. I was too ashamed. What would they think? Roberto also threatened that he would take my children if I ever left again. I didn't leave but would just cry, grabbing my children when he beat me.

I left only one other time, going with my children to an aunt who lived in Ayacucho City but far from my house. "He's not even going to know where I am," I told myself. "I'll stay with my aunt and then take my children to Lima."

"Tía, I need to stay with you," I asked her. She was a distant relative on my mother's side, but she was always fond of us. She took me and the children in, but the next day asked me to carry some merchandise to her post in the market. She had a very good business, sewing beautiful clothing. I was afraid to go into the street, but she told me that nothing would happen. I rushed through the streets carrying the goods, but someone saw me and told Roberto. He came searching for me that very afternoon. My aunt was still in the market, and only my uncle and his children were at home. I hid in my room but heard everything.

"How do you know Valentina's here?" my uncle asked him.

"I know, tío," he answered. "Someone told me."

"Why do you think she came? What did you do to cause her to leave?"

"I just want to talk to Valentina and beg her forgiveness."

"She isn't here now, but when she returns, I'll see if she'll talk to you."

I later told my uncle how Roberto mistreated me, how he destroyed my store. "I don't want to go back to him," I said.

"Give him another chance," my tío tried to convince me, but I answered, "Please understand, tío, but my aunt isn't here and I can't speak about it without her."

I stayed three or four days with my aunt. She remonstrated with Roberto, telling him that I was her relative. "How dare you mistreat her," she chastised. "What you're doing is abusive. You married her when she was nothing more than a child. She's not just anyone. She's from a fine family, not from just anywhere, and you don't deserve her." My aunt knew Roberto was from the area where the chutus *live.*

25 Ayacucho market scene

> *"My niece doesn't want to see you," my aunt told him. "Maybe some other day, but right now she doesn't want to see you."*
>
> *He returned the next day, but my aunt already had spoken to me. "My little daughter, Hijita," she said to me. "What are you going to do in Lima? How are you going to get by?"*
>
> *"I'll stay with my sisters and they'll help," I answered.*
>
> *"You don't know how it is with two children. How are you going to work with two children? You won't be able to do anything. And besides, a husband's a husband!"*
>
> *"Ay, tía. I just want to get ahead with my two children! Just lend me bus fare to Lima," I pleaded.*
>
> *"No, hijita."*
>
> *She didn't lend me the money, but spoke to Roberto,* llamando la atención, *calling him on the carpet. "Valentina doesn't want to return to you, but I'm trying to convince her to do so. But you must never mistreat her again."*
>
> *I returned when he promised never to beat me, but I didn't believe him and was still frightened.*

Horacio Gutiérrez, like the protagonists in *Rashomon,* the classic film by Akira Kurosawa, has provided me a slightly different account of Valentina's marriage, assigning more blame to her than to Roberto for their precarious economic circumstances. Operating from a different gender and class perspective, he told me in 1967 that she had expensive taste and did not know how to manage her money. To check on the accuracy of interviews, anthropologists use participant observation and a variety of sources; what is important here, however, is not the precise story but what it tells us of marriage, gender, and class relations in the impressions of a young girl and wife as she has remembered these events many years later. Memory is notoriously fallible, but we tend to remember in ways that reflect important cultural and personal structures.[10]

Roberto undoubtedly would have a still-different assessment, although I never asked him much about his marriage. When I discussed his wedding, however, before I knew many of the details provided by Valentina, Roberto retrieved an envelope and showed me a few black-and-white photographs of the wedding. He is in a suit and *Valentina* Valentina is dressed in a white gown and veil.

Roberto bought me the cloth and veil and made me make the dress, Valentina told me years later. *I was the first person in San Pedro to wear a white dress and veil. I don't know why he did it.*

"It was probably his desire to get ahead," I commented. "He always wanted to be *gente decente,* one of the better people."

Perhaps, she responded.

I never investigated wife beating with Roberto directly. He died several years before Valentina told me about the beatings, but even so, it is unlikely that he would have discussed the matter. Roberto tended to see himself as protector of Valentina, the one who wooed her successfully and who defended her against the unjust demands of others. Valentina also acknowledges that picture, commenting to me often, *Roberto would never let my children take advantage of me the way they do. He'd defend me.* Valentina's expression of support for Roberto, and indeed her love for him, is similar to that of other Andean women whose husbands have beaten them.[11] Life never consists of simple answers, simple recipes. In 2005 Valentina still dreamed about him and each year has a Roman Catholic Mass said for him on the anniversary of his death.

Valentina had six miscarriages and six children who lived to adulthood. She and Roberto directed much of their energy to rearing their children in order to foster their economic success. At considerable sacrifice they sent them to parochial schools, which in Peru are significantly better than government ones. To eliminate the faintest accent in their children's Spanish, they punished them if they spoke Quechua—the language of their paternal grandparents. Today Valentina regrets that her children speak little Quechua.

Most of Valentina's children have done well, finishing college and securing good jobs. One daughter came to the United States on a college scholarship in 1984. She did well, graduated with a degree in computer science, secured employment, married a fellow student, and today lives in her own home in a suburban development with a new BMW in the driveway. Using her first earnings, she brought her oldest brother to northern Virginia. Undocumented, he came over the Mexican border and endured a harrowing ride through California in a false truck bottom. In Virginia he immediately began to work, and he and his sister pooled their money to bring two other brothers through Mexico.

The three brothers first worked in carpentry, using skills learned from their father in Peru. One entered college and studied computer science; another went to school to become an automobile mechanic. On completing their degrees, they regularized their immigration status and left house construction behind. It is unlikely that they would have achieved the same economic success if they had remained in Peru. It is also unlikely that they would have done so well had they not been prepared in Peru by knowledge of carpentry and by the great emphasis on formal education and the tradition of pooling family resources to help one child at a time.

Valentina's third son did not finish high school and is a worry to her. He works as a handyman and driver for a group of clients. Even with a green card, with a wife and two children, he earns little and had few prospects in 2005. *He just never wanted to study,* Valentina complained.

Two daughters remain in Peru. One is a housewife, married to an engineer employed by an international company. The other, the youngest child, although a college graduate and fluent in English, works at poorly paid clerical jobs and relies on occasional remittances from Valentina.

Valentina came to the United States as a permanent resident, brought by her daughter who is a U.S. citizen. Shortly after arriving, carrying a note written for her in English, she went door to door in the middle-class neighborhood of northern Virginia where she lived. "I am looking for work cleaning houses or caring for children. I can provide good references. Call————." She transferred the skills she learned as a young woman to her new life and built up a group of clients, but now that she is in her sixties and suffering from a bad back, she has let most of the work go.

While outwardly North American, Valentina and her children maintain significant elements of Peruvian culture. They speak

Spanish among themselves, even though her children speak excellent English. Valentina has tried to learn English but, afraid of making mistakes and teased for poor pronunciation by her children, she has been unsuccessful. Her U.S. grandchildren speak some Spanish to her, but prefer to speak English to me and other native speakers of English, a pattern they acquired after starting school.

Valentina's family remains tight-knit, much as families in Peru. She speaks to most of her children in the United States on the phone at least once a day. When Valentina's oldest daughter visited from Lima in 1999, she counseled her two brothers and sister as the oldest child. "The oldest child," Horacio Gutiérrez once told me, "is like a parent to the younger children." The family also gathers on Christmas Eve to eat a meal and exchange presents (one of them dressing as Santa Claus) after midnight, the Noche Buena. They eat Peruvian *Valentina* food and drink the national Inca Cola—now partly owned by Coca-Cola—whenever they can. At the same time, Valentina is still the unpaid servant she was in Lima. Even though she and her daughter who lives in the United States often are at odds with one another and not speaking, Valentina has cared for her grandchildren and cooked for her daughter and cleaned her house thereby allowing her to work. In recent years, however, as their relationship has soured further, Valentina rarely stays with this daughter, who resents what she considers Valentina's neglect.

Roman Catholicism and sierra practices also supply a Peruvian identity. After Valentina's oldest son was killed in a tragic accident, they held a viewing in a funeral parlor for three days. Valentina then organized the *pichqa*, the Quechua memorial for the dead that lasts from the evening of the fourth to the morning of the fifth day after the death. Just as she would have done in San Pedro, she arranged her son's newly washed clothing on a table in the shape of his body, encircled it with candles and flowers, and placed a picture of Christ at his head. I had traveled to Virginia to be with the family. Throughout the night, we talked about him and ourselves and prayed over the clothing. *His spirit,* ánima, *is in the clothing,* Valentina told me, *and it sees and hears us crying.*

At dawn of the fifth day after his death, Valentina put her dead son's clothing in a brown paper bag and cast off her everyday clothing for a black skirt, blouse, and sweater, visible signs of her grief.

A year later, we celebrated the *wata unras,* the end of mourning. Valentina laid her dead son's clothing on the table, as she had done a year earlier, and we again held vigil through the night, observing the final good-bye, when the *ánima* returns to at last realize he is dead.

25A The *Ánima* of Valentina's son on the fifth day of mourning

At dawn, Valentina put the clothing away and removed her black skirt, but to ease her great pain she continued to wear a black blouse as a reminder of her loss. She served a breakfast of *mondongo*, the hominy and *tripas* stew reserved for special occasions.

More than ten years after his death, Valentina still visits her son's grave whenever she can to speak to him and to clean and decorate it with flowers. *I still keep his clothing in a safe place as a keepsake, recuerdo,* she has confided. *He was the one who always thought of me. The night before he was killed he said, "Come on, let's get a pizza, Mom."*

Valentina and her children blame their early poverty on Roberto's concern for his birth family. *If only Roberto hadn't helped his*

brothers and sisters so much, Valentina complains, *we would be better*
off today.

Attributing poverty to individual failings is common, even though the decisions that people make and the course of their lives are shaped, to a great extent, by social and economic contexts beyond their control. This was as true for Roberto as for most San Pedrinos, who move from job to job, propelled by Peru's precarious economy.

Despite the large size of the farms of Valentina and Roberto's parents, they were not large enough to provide farms for all their children, so Roberto and Valentina were landless when they married. Farming also had become increasingly precarious. None of Valentina's sisters remained in San Pedro to farm, and only one of Roberto's brothers did, but he has complemented his farming with income from a well-stocked store on the plaza.

Valentina

Roberto and Valentina also lacked sufficient capital to tide them over difficult times. It took several years to recover from the failure of their potato crop. They also had to provide for the future of six children. Then, when they finally settled in Ayacucho City, Roberto doing carpentry and Valentina working first at her store and then in her government post, the Shining Path war forced them to move again.

Roberto's devotion to his brothers and sisters, moreover, was nothing exceptional. All San Pedrinos strive to inculcate in their children a strong sense of responsibility for one another, especially the older for the younger. This familial cohesion is a rational response to marginal incomes, for pooled resources increase the likelihood of success. One could even make the claim that Roberto and Valentina received considerable help from his siblings. They lived with his unmarried brother in Lima, who also provided space for a carpentry shop. Although Roberto helped build it, the house was far more elegant than they could have provided for themselves. Another brother took care of their home in San Pedro when they were absent.

Valentina expects no less of her own children, and she continually exhorts them to care for one another the way siblings should. The first child in the United States sent money for her older brother to come to Virginia, and he in turn sent money for his two younger brothers, and so on. They, like their father, also believe that they have a mutual responsibility to help educate one another, although they sometimes do not do this to everybody's satisfaction. Their spouses frequently resent these efforts, much as Valentina and her children begrudged Roberto's diversion of resources to his brothers and sisters, but Valentina refuses to see the parallels. She is indignant at my pointing them out to her, turning away in disgust and telling me that, in her case, it is different.

Valentina and Roberto were better off than most San Pedrinos. Their parents, unlike those of Horacio Gutiérrez and Martín Velarde, had the economic means and desire to educate them. In turn, they scrimped and struggled to prepare their children for middle-class life by forcing them to become fluent in Spanish (even punishing them for speaking Quechua) and giving them good preparatory education in parochial schools and cultural knowledge about manners and dress appropriate to the life they wanted for them.

Valentina's children visit Peru, but they have no intention of returning permanently. It is likely that San Pedro and Peru will be a distant memory to Valentina's grandchildren, much like my grandparents' Ireland is to me and my children. Valentina, on the other hand, is conflicted about where she plans to live. She loves the United States, she says, and except for her children and grandchildren in South America, would be content to remain for the rest of her life. *It's hard to believe, Billcito, but I don't miss Peru one bit.*

On the other hand, she has sent a great deal of money to Peru to build a house in a middle-class area of Lima. When in Peru she visits this house and travels to San Pedro to care for her other house, which has become increasingly dilapidated. Even though she has no intention of returning to live in San Pedro, she refuses to sell the house and has been embroiled in a costly legal battle to evict a woman who took possession and declared that the house belonged to her.

I suspect that Valentina's two houses are emotional anchors, steady places in an often-rootless life. They also remain places of refuge should something go wrong. Her house in San Pedro, moreover, is built on land that was *interés* from her father, set aside for her use, and one of the few material connections to her past and to his memory.

Valentina's life is a complex skein of conflicting beliefs and behaviors, though, like most lives, it is united by a central core. Valentina's struggle for economic independence and her love for (and desire to protect) her children and grandchildren have remained constant, guiding most of her adult decisions. *See, the baby recognizes you,* Valentina tells me, moving her one-year-old granddaughter toward me, smiling as she does so, weaving the emotional web that surrounds her family and pulls them ever more tightly about her.

SIX

Triga

GUERRILLA WAR, COCAINE, AND COMMERCE

"Yankee imperialist!"

The university student who attacked me on the street in Ayacucho City in 1967 was drunk and I was not injured. Nor did his attack reflect the way in which I was generally treated. I was never afraid for my safety, and although I usually avoided the heavily politicized university campus, I often attended the all-night parties, the *jaranas*, of the anthropology students: talking, drinking, dancing, and singing Ayacucho's melancholy music, as other students played guitar, some strumming, and some finger picking the intricate counterpoints to the vocal melody that marks Ayacucho's famous *huaynos*. But this stranger's rage, unleashed several days before a large May Day celebration at which rival student groups assaulted one another and were teargassed by police, epitomized the tensions simmering beneath Ayacucho's surface tranquillity. Such fights, demonstrations, and the political graffiti found nearly everywhere in the 1960s and the 1970s, walls emblazoned with "The People's War" and "Long Live the Armed Struggle, the Lucha Armada," were volcanic fumaroles, outward manifestations of deep troubles.

In the 1960s Peru was hurtling into a period of serious social disruption in which growing population and the declining economic value of farming created large numbers of uprooted peasants and city migrants struggling to survive economically. Many, like Horacio Gutiérrez, Martín Velarde, and Valentina Rodríguez strove to keep afloat day to day without giving much thought to the reasons for their difficulties. Some sought spiritual surcease by stressing individual moral and spiritual failure, a focus that has underlain the success of evangelical religions. Still others saw the roots of Peru's poverty in social inequality and international exploitation, and most of

26 Puna home destroyed in Shining Path war

these worked for peaceful solutions, although some advocated violent revolution.

Among the many political movements at the university in Ayacucho City, a group commonly known as Sendero Luminoso, or Shining Path, chose violent change, and in 1980 its partisans launched open warfare against the state.[1] The Peruvian military met Sendero's threat with bloody and indiscriminate repression, employing scorched-earth tactics to make peasants fear the military more than the guerrillas.[2] For a brief period my godson Triga participated in Shining Path.

Triga

"Come with me. I need your help."

I had already been in San José for several months in 1967, when my neighbor Lucio arrived at my house about 7:00 PM. He was reluctant to say what he wanted, but hurrying behind him I discovered his wife lying on the floor of her bedroom on top of a burlap sack and her newborn son covered in amniotic fluid and blood, shivering between her legs. Attended only by Lucio and his sister, the young wife, already the mother of two, had been in labor in the cold room for about five hours. Handing me unsterilized scissors, Lucio asked if I knew how to cut the umbilical cord. I did not, but I followed his directions and those of his wife. On reflection I should have steril-ized the scissors but, taken aback by the request, I was swept up by their urgency and our mutual trust, a trust that is essential to good fieldwork. I later learned that women generally cut the cord, but the baby's parents were recent migrants from a rural hamlet and women suitable for the task lived too far away.

After I cut the cord, Lucio's sister washed the infant in warm wa-ter and dressed him nicely. Lucio and I lifted the mother onto her bed and placed the baby next to her under the covers. To protect the mother from a chill, a *choque con el aire*, a piece of the umbilical cord was tied around her ankle and the rest of the cord was put aside to be buried later. The mother protected herself further while she re-mained in bed by avoiding cold water and collecting her urine in a vessel to be sprinkled slowly outside the house.

The father and I selected Triga as the infant's name, using, as was customary, one of the saints' names listed for that day on the calen-dar. Customs change, and when Triga had a son many years later, he and his wife named the boy after a character in a popular television show. In 1967, however, Triga's mother approved our choice of name, and both parents asked me to officiate at an emergency bap-tism, not out of concern for the infant's health but to solidify our relationship. Dipping a geranium into holy water, I made the sign of the cross with the scarlet petals on Triga's forehead, mouth, and chest, saying his name each time. The brief ceremony was completed when I read a prayer chosen at random by the father from a First Communion catechism to solemnize the occasion.

After the start of the Shining Path war, I lost contact with the fam-ily, but I stumbled across Triga in 1996 during a visit to Santa Anita, an industrial and working-class Lima suburb, home to many Ay-acucho migrants. Triga and I took to one another immediately. He introduced me to his wife and two children, showed me his house and shop, and invited me to eat.

They lived on the second floor of a newly built cement house on an unpaved street. Their workshop on the ground floor employed several apprentices making *retablos* and the stone sculptures known as "*piedra de Huamanga*" for international clients. Involved with de-sign and merchandising, Triga did little of the hand work himself. His wife channeled her work separately through Manuela Ramos, a Peruvian NGO that fosters women's rights, including help with craft production and sales.

The sculpture workshop, the employees, the cement house with its large-screen television, and the van parked outside boasted of economic success. But this success was recent. Like many rural villagers, Triga had a difficult time establishing his life. His grandfather, a monolingual speaker of Quechua and one of the last peasant leaders (*varayoc*) in San José, was also one of the first artisans to produce crafts commercially, and his father was one of the first teachers at the artisan school. Even though he had only completed first grade and spoke only marginal Spanish, Triga's father became a member of the new San José upper class and mayor of the town. Triga was favored by this class membership as long as he remained in the community. Once he left, his status changed to that of a rural provincial, a *serrano*, although somewhat elevated by his education, manners, and relative wealth.

I interviewed Triga over several days in 1999 while he was confined to bed after an automobile accident. "Tell him not to drink and drive," his wife asked, worried that Triga could have been injured more seriously. As his *padrino* I was expected to encourage his best behavior, which I did.

"I'm writing another book about Peru," I explained, "and want to use your life story. Is that okay?" Triga agreed and said that I could record the sessions. At the end of our interview I returned to the subject, discussed potential risks, and again asked permission to use his story. Triga was unconcerned. I told him I would change his name and disguise other aspects of his story. What name should I use? "Triga," he said, "Triga. I like that name."

In his story Triga often confused dates and time sequences. Inconsistent dates are common in oral narration. In 1983 my research assistant administered questionnaires a few weeks after my initial interviews. The sequences and dates we collected often differed, not because people were lying but because remembered time is more mercurial than written time. As an undergraduate did I take an introductory course in sociology before that in chemistry? If pressed, as would be required in answering a questionnaire, I might answer one way, then a few weeks later, another, each time taking a stab at the sequence. I confuse dates about my own life and am not surprised to find that the people of the Andes do so.

Triga's Story

"What's your earliest memory?" I began, giving Triga the tape recorder to hold to ensure that I captured his narrative. I speak loudly enough to register on the tape, but the people I interview

often do not. Propped on a metal frame bed, Triga was open and
forthright, speaking as to a friend. We were in an echo chamber,
sounds bouncing off bare cement walls, but except for brief visits
from his wife, we were alone.

My father was a teacher of sculpture in San José. I always played
with his tools and materials. It's one of my earliest memories.

Triga's early life was uneventful. He completed the five years of primary school and attended San José's secondary school for two years,
but left when he was thirteen to work on craft production. Triga has
no special memory of the beginning of the war, but three years later
he was incorporated into Shining Path, when he and five companions
went to a district two hours below the town to play soccer. It was
1983, one of the most brutal years of the war. Triga was sixteen.

We stayed in the town until eight or nine at night; there were some   *Triga*
girls we liked. It was late and the lights in the town were turned off. A
group hidden behind masks, encapuchados, *surrounded us and asked*
what we were doing. They were terrucos, *Shining Path guerrillas. They*
took us to the school grounds, away from town. They talked to us, asked
who we were, and demanded that we return to a meeting later in the
week and that we bring two friends each, but only people we could
trust. This was a strategy of theirs to get more people.

We were too scared to return without more people. The next week
ten or eleven of us went to the meeting. Two compañeros, *one of them*
armed, explained the flyers they had brought and taught us the Shin-
ing Path hymn.

Compañero is difficult to translate. The word means "companion," but this English gloss does not convey the Spanish meaning.
In the Andes, *compañero* is used to unify disparate persons and to
avoid invidious racial/class terms such as *indio* and *cholo*.[3] Shining
Path partisans described themselves as *"compañeros"* (as well as *"ca-*
maradas," or comrades), but well before Shining Path usage, friends
were *compañeros(as)*, as were lovers (a better term than the English
"partner"!) and members of the same group. During the war, displaced people frequently called one another *compañero*, doing so
not to claim membership in Shining Path, which would have been
fatal, but to create a group identity as *desplazados*. In the context of
his story, however, Triga used *compañero* to refer to Shining Path
partisans.

The compañeros *told us that they were fighting to make the leaders*
of Peru more responsible to the poor. The class lasted about three
hours. Later we joined the Party, and I was a member for a good while,
long enough to learn the hymn and the slogans. We attended meetings

about twice a week: one day a meeting and the other a patrol, a vigi-lancia. On some days we attended practice maneuvers, the prácticas. I think that they intended to draw us in little by little. It was like school. Although we didn't get to this point, they selected people according to their capabilities. Some, the bloodthirsty ones, los sanguinarios, *were assigned to killing, others to question a person, others to plan, study, and investigate. They were well organized.*

We were in the group for about six months, learning how to make household bombs [Molotov cocktails], using gasoline, nails, and a fuse, and practicing how to light and throw them. We also helped hijack trucks coming from the tropical rain forest on their way to Ayacucho City. There were a lot of us. We never took a truck directly; only the leaders, the jefes, *did that. We were the lookouts, the* vigilancia, *spread out in the hills. We carried the household bombs. If there were police, we had to let the others know. Everything was well thought out.*

The head of our region was called Martín. He was in charge of vari-ous groups from this zone. Martín was young, but he was smart, knew a lot, and spoke Spanish perfectly. You could tell he was from the univer-sity. The second-in-command was a woman, María. She had finished secondary school, but I don't know if she was getting ready for the uni-versity. She wasn't as capable as Martín. In 1984 María was captured, ambushed at her house, and the military found propaganda materials and notebooks with information about our cell. Even though we all had false names—mine was Julio—they soon began to uncover who we were one by one.

"How did the military come to discover the group?"

I don't know. It was either intelligence work or my cousin, who might have revealed the names of people in the group when he was drunk. In the end they disappeared María. I think she was found after a while, but she was dead. After that Martín was disappeared. We didn't know where he lived. He just disappeared and we never saw him again. When we discovered that Martín and María had been disappeared we left the movement. There was nobody left to insist that we remain.

Disappearances were common during the war. First used in Latin America to describe political murders in Argentina (1976–1983), then later in Chile and Guatemala, the term "*desaparecido*" has taken on ominous meanings.[4] In Peru the military would detain someone, often denying that it had done so, and the person was frequently never heard from again. Some of the disappeared were involved with Shining Path but others were not.

"Why did you leave Shining Path? Why didn't you look for an-other group?"

I didn't think I was ready for these things. And besides, the leader-
ship wasn't very good. Nobody came to urge us on, and this just in-
creased our doubts. And then some of the muchachos *had left, saying*
this and that, labeling people as terrorists, terrucos. *I kept my mouth*
shut, but others in my group were saying I was a terruco, *and damn it,*
that meant I was dead. It was like a joke to most of them. I saw this and
thought, "Things are going nowhere!"

Besides, the group only had a pistol and household bombs, and with
this you couldn't do anything. I said to myself, "I'm not going to be able
to defend myself or be able to escape." I suspected that the group was
going to fall. When the military found the information on the group in
Maria's house, I figured that they had leads to investigate, even if they
didn't have exact names. I had a lot of doubts and decided to escape.

I left for Ayacucho's tropical forest with a friend to play soccer and   *Triga*
live off the winnings. After three or four weeks we discovered that the
owner of the pensión, *the boardinghouse where we were staying, was a*
drug trafficker, making and selling the coca paste used to produce co-
caine. We decided to do the same. We were young, needed money, and
planned to buy a big car. We bought coca leaves and other ingredients
with our soccer earnings, but just when we were ready to make and sell
the paste, Argentine mercenaries, mercenarios, *showed up in a boat*
along the river. They had killed four buyers of coca paste that they had
found in the river port, decapitating them and cutting off their arms
and legs. Then the mercenaries sent out an official notice ordering
everyone to gather in the port the next day or be killed. The notice went
to everyone, to the towns, to the hamlets. Everybody was crying.

"Do you really think they were mercenaries?" I asked. "From
Argentina?"

I really don't know. That's what they told everyone.

"Could they have been Peruvian military?"

Maybe. They told us they were from Argentina, but they could have
been Peruvians too. Some of them told us that the leaders were the
bloodthirsty ones, the sanguinarios, *and that the rest had to obey or-*
ders. I really don't know what the truth is.

"Did they have Argentine accents?"

Just the leaders. There were two or three of them. The rest were local
military. The leaders could have had accents, but I really don't know. I
didn't talk to them directly, but the majority who participated in the
massacre were Peruvian soldiers.

The belief in mercenaries was widespread among Ayacuchanos
during the war, and Triga uses the phrase again later in his narrative
to describe killers who attacked San José. Many rural people believed

the mercenaries were accompanied by *pistacos* sent by the Peruvian government to kill peasants in order to render their fat and send it to Lima to pay the foreign debt (see Chapter 1).[5]

Deciphering the identity of the mercenaries is complicated by the fact that a variety of armed groups have operated in the drug-producing areas of Peru. In 1984, when Triga was there, the Peruvian army, marines, counterinsurgency militias, police, Shining Path, and drug groups were fighting brutal battles.[6] To further complicate matters, Peruvian military forces were being advised in counterinsurgency techniques "by US, Israeli, and Argentine experts," and in 1983 "Argentine police officers were reported to have visited Ayacucho."[7] Both the United States and the drug cartels also have employed private military (or mercenaries) in the Andean drug-producing areas,[8] and in the 1980s the militias reported a confrontation with agents of the American Drug Enforcement Agency.[9]

It is likely, however, that the Peruvian military called themselves Argentine mercenaries to obscure responsibility, a common practice during the Shining Path war, often making it difficult to know who was doing what to whom. Petty thieves claimed to be terrorists in order to extort a car or money. Peasant militias sometimes killed an enemy and left evidence that suggested Shining Path had done it. The Peruvian military also killed witnesses to their crimes and blamed the killings on Shining Path.[10] Moreover, people in the Apurímac Valley, where Triga was located, called Peruvian troops "mercenaries" in the belief that "Peruvian soldiers [could not] be so cruel and bloodthirsty."[11]

Whoever they were, the "Argentine mercenaries" terrified Triga. *Do we go to the meeting where we could be killed? Do we stay away? But then we could be killed for not going. I had lost my documents just a few days before. They weren't going to believe me because I had no documents. And even worse, I'm an Ayacuchano and from San José, and the military would think that made me a terrorist.*

Not to carry documents in Peru is much like driving without a license in New York. I make a copy of my passport, letters of introduction, and materials identifying my Peruvian affiliations. One must produce such documents on entering buildings, at police posts along highways, or whenever asked for them by officials. Even with documents there can be problems, but without them it is a certainty.

We decided to flee. But how? We didn't have a boat, car, or money. We had to escape on foot. It took us four days to get back to San José, leaving the tropical forest over footpaths through the sierra, crossing rivers, ravines, and freezing passes.

I was afraid to be without my documents. My friend went ahead; I followed, ready to hide if he warned that the military was on the path. We left at eight at night and arrived at the last house in the tropical forest, the montaña, *around eleven. We knew the people and spent the night there, leaving at 4:00 the next morning. The woman in the house helped prepare food for the trip. We carried everything in two backpacks. This was the day that the mercenaries were holding the meeting that everyone had to attend under pain of death, so the woman went down to the meeting and we walked up the mountain, over a narrow path in the opposite direction, heading into the sierra.*

On this first day, we ran into two Shining Path guerrillas, terrucos. *They were walking really fast and had a hard look about them. We asked ourselves, "Do we tell them what happened or do we keep quiet?" Since they were in a bad mood, we decided not to tell them and continued our journey. But a woman with several mules far behind on the path told them about the mercenaries. The* terrucos *came back after us, finding us after several hours, around 7:00 pm. They were furious that we hadn't told them about the mercenaries and the meeting. We were afraid they were going to kill us, but they lectured us and let us go.*

Triga

We slept in caves, but after three and a half days we arrived at a hamlet in the puna *just above the provincial capital. Because about fifty terrorists had left the hamlet just a half hour or so before we arrived, the people thought we also were* terrucos *and treated us well. We took advantage of the confusion and spent the afternoon there, but we couldn't stretch our luck because the* terrucos *might return. We traded the coca leaves we had brought with us for potatoes. The coca leaves served us well. In the high mountains money doesn't help that much. It won't get you anything.*

We continued on foot to the provincial capital but were worried because the town quartered military and intelligence personnel. How are we going to get into town without being discovered? At the outskirts, we bought Indian caps, chullus, *and rubber-tire sandals and entered town dressed like* indios. *I was too scared to head toward the town center without documents, so I circled around and headed up toward the highway to get a ride out of town. My friend had his documents and went into the city. He even sold his potatoes there. But the military captured him and held him for a night. There had been a roadblock, a* batida, *to check people and documents, and maybe he had been drinking with the person who bought his potatoes. I don't know what happened, but he was taken. Since he had his documents they let him go the next day. If it had happened to me, they wouldn't have let me go.*

I caught a truck on the heights above the town, practically in the puna. The truck was by itself. The driver thought I was a terrorist and stopped to pick me up. At that time it was easy to be confused with a terruco. Even though I was dressed as an Indian, a chutu, *my different face wasn't going to fool anybody.*

It would not have been Triga's face, however, but his manner and speech that would have betrayed him. Triga has the same dark skin, eyes, and straight black hair that people often associate with *chutus*.

The driver asked where I was going and I told him, "Just above San José, but I'm not going into the town."

"Ah, very good, come on in," he said to me.

As we descended into San José, I saw my father and brothers cutting firewood and collecting it into a truck. I told the driver, "I'm getting off here."

"That's strange," he said. "You're getting out here?"

"Yes, right here. How much?" I asked.

"Nothing," he replied. "That's okay." He thought I was a terruco *because I got off in the* puna. *What was I doing there?*

My father took me in his truck the rest of the way to San José. I showed him the coca paste, the paste used to make cocaine, that I had brought with me in my boots. It was only a little, just enough to show my mother and father, to tell them where I had been, how it had been.

Triga interrupted his account to accept a wheat, potato, and mutton soup from his wife. I took a bowl as well. "Gracias, mamita," I thanked her as I finished and she took my empty bowl. I turned to Triga.

"What made you think of selling the *droga?* My question is this. You had an occupation, your father had one, and so did your mother. Making *retablos* and sculptures. Why did you think of doing something else? What was your goal?"

We were invited by a friend to go to the tropical forest to play soccer and maybe to win, Triga answered matter-of-factly, his demeanor unchanged. *They paid for transportation, housing, and food. But when we got there we saw that they were making* droga, *every day: harvesting coca leaves, buying, and preparing. In that moment the idea entered our minds to make easy money, the ambition of young people. If we do this we can buy a new car. It was a* locura, *a crazy thing. It lasted only a few months, no more than two. It was an illusion: if we do this we can buy a car that nobody else has. But we didn't think of the consequences. We didn't think about it much, didn't analyze it. It was a* locura.

"How old were you?" I asked.

I was sixteen.

"And your friend?"

He was seventeen or eighteen. He was a little older than I was.

Triga's desire for a car that nobody else had is not surprising. Many Peruvians want fancy cars, computers, and other symbols of material wealth, aspirations not unfamiliar in other areas of the world. His decision to enter the cocaine trade, moreover, was not as outrageous in the Andean context as it would have been in my New Jersey neighborhood. Cocaine use is frowned on, but it is seen as a North American problem, not an Andean one. Triga and most peasants believe that the cocaine trade is wrong, against the law, and dangerous, but they reject the North American interpretation of the problem. Coca chewing and coca use are legal in Peru and are integrated into rural religious and ceremonial life. Pablo de la Cruz, for example, traded coca leaves (Chapter 1). Because of American pressure, however, *Triga* people in the coca-growing regions suffer military repression and the aerial spraying of chemical defoliants to eliminate the coca crop; because of the inherent difficulty of precision spraying, however, these defoliants scatter, endangering people, animals, food crops, and water sources.[12] From an Andean perspective, American policy is equivalent to an international campaign to force the United States to eradicate tobacco production through the defoliation of farms in the Carolinas and Virginia in order to eliminate cigarette smoking worldwide, which, like cocaine use, is a serious health problem; the difference is that the coca leaf also has useful functions.

Triga's adventures were not over.

Fifteen days after I returned from the tropical forest, masked enca-puchados, or soldiers, appeared in San José around eleven at night. They began to patrol the town, looking at the houses, telling everybody that they were Argentine mercenaries. They spent the night on the heights around San José. I became suspicious, thinking that they might be preparing to attack, as they had in other towns, but nobody paid attention.

"I'm innocent," my older brother James said. "I haven't done anything. Why should I worry?"

The next day, about four in the morning, shouting below my window woke me up. I was sleeping on the second floor. The soldiers were beating the social studies teacher who lived next door. They were still masked. A few minutes later they started banging on our door with their boots. I looked out the window to see what was happening. As soon as the soldiers saw me they shot at me. Pum! I knew then that they had come to kill. I told my brother Alejandro, who was upstairs with me, to escape with James. "I'll stay," I told him. "I'm a minor and nothing will happen to me." Alejandro agreed and went downstairs to wake James, but James took his time getting dressed, even as the soldiers pounded the door. "I'm innocent," he said, "inocente."

My two brothers were taken captive, but I escaped through the window. As I started to climb out I saw that the house was surrounded. One of the mercenaries yelled at me, "Hey, kid, chivolo*, come on down." I took off, jumping from the second floor into the yard of the next house. The soldiers fired at me and I jumped onto a wall covered with cactus, leaping through the cactus spines. I went from house to house and escaped. I tried to let my friends know what was happening, but they had been taken prisoner. The soldiers followed me, but I escaped into the countryside, heading toward my aunt's house. She hid me and helped pull the cactus spines out of my feet and hands. I*

sneaked back to town in the afternoon to see what had happened to my brothers and friends. But there was no information. The soldiers had placed my brothers on a truck with six other men. They drove the truck up and down the roads around San José, trying to confuse our families.

Desperate relatives contacted officials in Ayacucho City, but they refused to help, as did the local police and military, who refused to leave their barracks. The masked soldiers were operating with at least the acquiescence of the military, if not under its direct command.

That night we didn't know anything about what had happened until my brother Alejandro showed up at the house. He told us that as the truck climbed for the last time to the heights above San José, one of the soldiers began to kick the schoolteacher. Alejandro protested, demanding to know why they were doing that to the teacher. They should do it to him instead. They beat Alejandro until he fainted, then tossed him out of the truck, firing at him as he rolled down the ridge. But he didn't get hit. The slope was steep but his fall was broken by underbrush, and at the bottom he scampered into a tiny hollow to escape the bullets.[13]

The next day people from the town scoured the hills looking for relatives. One of them stumbled on a pile of bodies far above the town. Nobody could believe it, but we all went up in a truck to get the bodies. The person who took us was a friend of my brother's. He told me, "Let's go; I'll accompany you." He took me and we all went; it was practically a dump truck to carry so many bodies. I was shocked when I saw the mountain of bodies, saw all of them; I couldn't scream, couldn't cry. Nothing. I never had a brother die. My friend just grabbed me and held me and said, "Tranquilo, sssh, be calm, cálmate." He did nothing but hold me. I was stupefied, couldn't cry. And I saw everything: knees all over the place, hearts cut out, brains and tendons gone, hands and feet tied with their own clothing.

Triga

27 Widow walking to Rumipata war protest (see p. 160)

We brought the bodies to the medical post in town. I don't remember how we got there. It was terrible. My mother fainted, so did my father. It was chaos. Nearly the whole town was there. It might have been different if it had been only one body, but nearly all the families were there, feeling desperate, everyone crying. Little by little the families took the bodies to their homes for the wake, the velorio. *My mother never stopped crying when I was at her side. She desperately wanted me to go to Lima. "You're going," she told me, "you're going." I remained for the five days of the wake, the* pichqa, *but was frightened that the soldiers might reappear. They often attacked when people were together, but they didn't return.*

"If I were there," I told him, "as your *padrino*, I too would have made you leave."

Like Triga, I am horrified by the great cruelty of the massacre. It was actually two days of mayhem. According to various accounts I have obtained, the military had roamed through the district the day before, torturing and murdering young people in the hamlets. The next day they attacked the central town, killing their captives in the massacre that Triga describes, murdering a total of fourteen young men in those two days.

I had known a number of the dead. Some were involved with the guerrillas but others certainly were not. Triga's brother was guiltless of any participation in Shining Path, an assessment made by every resident of San José whom I have asked. He erred only in his belief that his innocence afforded protection. He did not even live in San José but was visiting his family. A year before he was killed I had spoken with him at a fair in Lima, where he had won a prize for his *retablo* depicting the famous slaughter of eight reporters who had traveled to the community of Uchuraccay on foot to investigate claims that peasants had repelled a group of *terrucos*.[14]

Much later in the interview I asked Triga, "Did the military come to the town because of your earlier activities in Shining Path?" It would have been far too crass and unfeeling to have asked this question immediately after his description of the massacre. Nor could I have done so personally. I wept as I translated Triga's account for this book, and tear up every time I read it, still shaken by the cruelty so many years later.

No, the mercenaries came looking for young people who were playing soccer and who were sharp. A lot of people who were not involved were captured too.

I do not know what caused the military to raid San José. It could have been the result of information about Triga's destroyed Shining Path group, but it also could have been a random tactic of the dirty war.

The social studies teacher was also innocent, Triga told me. *His younger brother was involved with the movement, but the teacher wasn't. The teacher was a neighbor and came by my house and played the guitar almost every afternoon. He spoke to me and my brother about school and how we should conduct ourselves. He was like another father. But he never spoke to us about Shining Path. Never.*

Because Shining Path had controlled the teacher-training program at Huamanga University, teachers were a special target of the military. "Do you think the social studies instructor was killed because he was a teacher?" I asked.

It's possible that he might have been fingered because of his social studies course in the high school, but he never said anything to me about Shining Path or communism.

The massacred San Josinos are among the 10,561 Ayacuchanos killed in the war between 1980 and 1983, two persons out of every 100. Like similar tragedies, the massacre spurred even innocent survivors to flee. The day after the funeral, Triga left San José for Santa Anita with his future brother-in-law. Shortly afterward, his parents and remaining two siblings went to live on the coast in Cañete. Triga and his family became one small fragment of the more than 600,000 people displaced by the war and its violence.[15]

Traumatized by such repression, many Ayacuchanos still speak emotionally of the murders, the disappeared persons, and the arbitrary brutality. Before 1985 the military, especially the marines, were not much interested in guilt or innocence, but focused on terrorizing the peasantry, making them more afraid of the military than of Shining Path. The goal was to eliminate the sea (the peasantry) in order to eliminate the fish (Shining Path). "The police do not know who the *senderistas* [Shining Path cadres] are, nor how many there are, nor when they are going to attack," the minister of war, Gen. Luis Cisneros Vizquerra, candidly told the Peruvian magazine *Que Hacer* in 1982. "For the police force to have any success they would have to begin to kill *senderistas* and non-*senderistas* alike, because that is the one way they could ensure success. They kill 60 people and at most there are three *senderistas* among them and for sure the police will say that all 60 were *senderistas*."[16] Unfortunately, these were the very policies that the military also employed when they entered the war at the end of 1982.

The police and military, however, were not the only institutions responsible for the dirty war. Vladimiro Montesinos, the head of Peru's intelligence services and perhaps the country's most powerful person during the war, called for "an Argentine solution," a reference to the dirty war in Argentina, saying that it didn't "matter if 20,000 die, and 15,000 of them are innocent, as long as we kill the 5,000 terrorists."[17] In an excellent and nuanced book on the violence, Gonzalo Portocarrero traces the military's brutal strategy at least partly to U.S. counterinsurgency policy, as does the Peruvian historian Nelson Manrique, especially as taught at the United States Army's School of the Americas.[18] "Training manuals used [at this] special school for Latin American military and police officers in the 1980's recommended bribery, blackmail, threats and torture against insurgents."[19] American Special Forces Mobile Training Teams distributed similar manuals "to military personnel and intelligence schools in Colombia, Ecuador, El Salvador, Guatemala, and Peru."[20]

As we will see in the story of Anastasio Huamán (Chapter 8), Shining Path was also brutal, summarily executing informers (*soplones*), alleged exploiters of the people, development workers, and anyone who refused to join. And, like the military, it attacked and slaughtered whole villages, killing children as well as adults. The peasantry was forced "between the sword and the wall," between Shining Path and the military.[21]

Like Valentina Rodríguez, Triga does not define himself as a *desplazado*, although if questioned on the matter, he will say that he is one. His flight from San José, however, led to major life changes.

In Lima, my [future] brother-in-law gave me a place to stay and work in his artisan shop. He also recommended me for a program sponsored by Peru and the Interamerican Development Bank to improve artisan production. I spent a year in the program, earning a salary and receiving room and board. I improved my technical skills and learned how to run an artisan cooperative. I also studied language and mathematics. Some people didn't take advantage of the school, but for me it was fundamental, helping me change my thinking. You couldn't just go on working in the same way as in San José.

In 1985 my parents returned to San José, and I followed about six months later. After about a year, I took a job at the artisan school teaching students the new techniques that I had learned in Lima. Because the program was funded by a foreign government, I started at a higher

salary than older teachers with lots of experience, even though I was only nineteen. A lot of the students also were older than I was; the program gave them food and a small daily wage. I remained at the school for four years, and in the last year was practically its head, given responsibility for nearly everything.

"Weren't you afraid to return to San José after what had happened?"

Things had calmed down enough so that we felt more secure. But like the other teachers, I had to be careful to speak only about artisan production and to avoid politics.

By 1985 military tactics had changed. The army replaced the notoriously brutal marines. Instead of generalized repression, the army was more selective in dealing with the peasantry, a change facilitated by the fact that, unlike in the marines, many army soldiers were from the sierra and spoke Quechua. Shining Path, moreover, had extended its operations to other areas of the country, lessening its impact in Ayacucho.

In spite of the improved political situation, however, Triga and the other teachers began to receive anonymous threats. "Who sent them? The people of San José?"

Yes, some were sent out of envy, envidia. I don't think they were sent by terrorists; I don't think so. I think they were from people who didn't want me to work there. I was very young for the job, earning two or three times as much as the older teachers. It was almost like a scholarship, causing a lot of envy.

We also received letters from the Rodrigo Franco Command [a death squad aligned with the American Popular Revolutionary Alliance (APRA) political party]. *They were killers, against the* terrucos, *and against the people. They were a paramilitary group, and after a while we realized they were tied to the government, the military. They also* *wrote vague threats on the walls of the school, saying such things as, "We'll take measures if you don't get rid of the students in Shining Path," things like that. One of my students was a* terruco, *but he was protected by the terrorists. I couldn't do anything. I was the head of the school. What do I do now? I was so worried that I almost resigned. There weren't only one or two letters, but lots. We were scared to travel to and from the school, the path was so isolated. If they killed us, who would know? We were very frightened. None of us could take it, but there was not much else to do. We were working, I was studying, attending high school in Ayacucho City. I just had to be careful.*

Triga was unnerved by the threats, but they did not drive him out of San José. Instead, it was the time that he had to devote to the peasant militia that did so, because it prevented him from manufacturing his sculptures.

The Ronda Campesina, the peasant militia, was formed in the last months I was teaching in San José. At first, I tried to just deal with it: the vigilancia, patrols, *and the miserable nights. About twice a week they announced a* vigilancia *by blowing their whistle or ringing the church bell. Everybody to the plaza, especially the young people. We had to be there in a line. And they went through the list, marking who didn't come, who came late. Pum! There were a variety of sanctions. We assembled at the hour they wanted: nine, eight, or ten o'clock at night. Sometimes even twelve midnight. Nearly everybody went. There was a lot of fear. You had to go with your blanket, your whistle. It was a very military life. They would tell us we had to go to the mountain on patrol, and we had to go. "There's an accident on the highway," they would say, and we had to go there. The main responsibility fell on the young people, but there weren't many of us. Unarmed, we were always afraid that we would run into some* terruco. *We had only a flashlight; there was nothing else.*

They had made some watchtowers, some torrecitas. *Because I was mostly in the tower, I patrolled the countryside only three times. I went on one patrol after someone had been killed in one of the hamlets. It may have been Shining Path, I don't know, but someone had killed one of the officials. The young people were told, "You, you, you are going." And we went. But when we arrived there was practically nothing. It was dark and we could hardly see. Then the police arrived.*

We never even had a skirmish, an enfrentamiento. *Sometimes the* terrucos *lit up the mountains, making the hammer and sickle and other designs with kerosene-soaked rags placed in small evaporated milk cans. "Go after them," the young people were told whenever that happened. But we never met up with them, and I never had a head-to-head*

28 Watchtower

29 Sunday muster of peasant militia

fight. We always arrived afterward and never tried to ambush them. We went making a lot of noise with our whistles so that they would leave. They were armed and we had nothing! What were we going to do? One or two soldiers followed us in the rear, and they were the only ones with weapons! It didn't make any sense.

I had just begun to live with my wife. I felt pressured by the Ronda
and was making fewer sculptures, and we were now two people. I de-
cided to leave and quit my job in August, 1990.

The early 1990s was a period of renewed political violence in
Ayacucho, initiated by Shining Path, the military, and many newly
formed peasant militias (see Chapter 7). Triga, however, could not
have chosen a worse time to leave his job, because a few days later, on
August 8, Peru's new president, Alberto Fujimori, announced dra-
conian neoliberal economic measures that abolished most food and
utility subsidies and that effectively devalued the currency, causing
prices to rise stratospherically (see Chapter 9).

*I had bought out my contract, Triga said, but Fujimori's economic
shock reduced my buyout compensation, my* liquidación, *to nothing.
I had no money, so I returned to my old job in San José but stayed for*   *Triga*
*only two or three months. I gave up my job for good, sometime in No-
vember, 1990. I had a pretty good salary in San José but I couldn't take
the pressure of not being able to produce sculptures for sale. And being
there also increased my risk. It was dangerous, a time of many murders. I spent Christmas in San José, but was in Santa Anita by the New
Year of 1991. I arrived at my brother-in-law's again, the husband of
my wife's sister, and began to work for him. He had a little land nearby
that he had bought for another brother-in-law, but I asked him to rent
it to me so that I could build a little hut, a* choza, *on it. "There's no
problem," he told me, "It's up to you."*

*I built a house of reed mats and lived there for a year and a half. I
followed the advice of the artisan program I had attended in Lima and
simplified my designs so I could produce six sculptures a day instead of
one. My sales were good, and I earned a lot of money pretty quickly.
After about a year I was able to buy my own house of adobe.*

*I was very contented. Living and working on my own made me a
little more independent, and I entered a San José artisan cooperative in
Santa Anita.*

I was astonished when I visited this cooperative in 1996 to find a
bookkeeper, a secretary, and three employees to package the products. Established with the help of an NGO, and part of an umbrella
group of artisans, the cooperative sells to international clients
through e-mail and the Web. When Triga was born in 1966, San José
had no electricity or piped water.

Triga credits the skills he learned in the Lima artisan program for
much of his success, but not everyone who attended that program
has benefited as much. His prosperity also derives from his willingness to innovate, a capacity for risk taking also evident in his narrow

escapes from both Shining Path and the drug trade. He has tried to explain his new techniques to other members of the artisan cooperative, but most have resisted.

They don't think an artisan can teach them anything. And you can't force them. The decision is theirs. You need to make new designs that have a market and take care of the client, making sure that the quality is good. Many artisans don't pay any attention to these matters. If an object is a little rough, they'll still send it, saying, "What's it to me? It'll pass." But it's not like that. Instead, I guarantee the product, selecting this one, yes, that one, no, selling the poor stuff in Lima at a discount. Because of this care, I can triple my orders the following year. Clients tell me that I send only good products.

Like most Peruvians, however, Triga also has depended on his kin network. His parents taught him how to make *retablos* and sculptures, providing him with a ready-made business to supplement farm production in San José and the basis for his entrepreneurial future in Lima. His extended family has provided him shelter and economic help; at key points his brother-in-law has given Triga shelter, food, knowledge, and a network.

If I hadn't had the help of my brother-in-law, it might have been more difficult and taken more time. We had clients, but they weren't enough. My brother-in-law knows the market and how to calculate everything, measure it very well.

Someone without kin totters on catastrophe's edge. One young man from Huancayo told me that he "has nobody." He ran away from an abusive foster home when he was eleven years old, lived on the street, but went to school at night and obtained employment. Nonetheless, he is always in danger of falling back into life on the street because, unlike Triga, he has no kin to shelter and help him in time of need.

Triga looked at me incredulously when I asked if he had become a capitalist.

No, I don't think so, he laughed. *Why do you ask me that?*

"To know what you're thinking now. You had been in Shining Path and I want to know how you have changed, nothing more."

I'm a socialist!

"But you're also a small entrepreneur, a *pequeño empresario*, no?"

Yes, but I still think the same way. The poor still suffer. At times I struggle to survive, and many others are at a much lower economic level. I'm concerned about these people. I'm not so much for capitalism; I'm more for the social part.

Nonetheless, Triga also believes that others remain poor because of some character flaw. Pressing to discover his attitudes, I asked, "Then you continue thinking about those who don't have anything?"

Yes, he responded, *a little, but not so much, because there are people who refuse to struggle. They sit and don't think about what they can do, and people are a little lax, instead of going out and doing something. There's a lot of work, but we have to knock at the doors. It's a question of sacrifice.*

"But, Triga," I challenged, "you had the luck of learning a good craft from your parents. Many don't have this skill and they don't know what to do."

It's been fundamental, he agreed, *a hand that's been at my side. Without it I would have to think, "Now what do I do?" If you don't know what to do and you can only think, then you're out of luck. Then* *maybe you can't take the risk.*

I quizzed Triga in several interviews in 1996 and 1999 to understand why, even though initially coerced into Shining Path, he was also in some ways a willing participant. Like most rural Peruvians, Triga believes that society and government are corrupt and allow the rich and powerful to exploit the poor. Unfortunately, day-to-day experience often bears them out. Responding to this inequality and poverty, rather than to the specific social vision of Shining Path, Triga and many others believed initially that Shining Path would right these wrongs. As one man asserted in a conversation with a policeman in 1966 about an earlier guerrilla insurgency, "a person in the countryside who says he's a communist is not necessarily a communist, for he knows nothing of communism. He's simply a hungry man who has accepted the premises of the communists."

I liked many of Shining Path's ideas, Triga told me in various ways and times. *Shining Path was fighting for the poor and against exploiters, fighting to make Peru's leaders more responsible and moral, making sure that they did not abuse their power. They were fighting corruption and administering justice, punishing rustlers and thieves. They did not just go and kill, but first tried to find out what had happened and then went to speak to the guilty person, giving him an opportunity to reform. They would kill someone only if the person continued to do wrong.*

Nonetheless, reflecting on the matter as an adult rather than as a sixteen-year-old, Triga also expressed reservations about some of Shining Path's methods, doubts he says that he had while in Shining Path. *I didn't want to be doing what I had been doing, but I liked that they were fighting against poverty and for poor people. All of that. I liked those ideas, but not how they were implementing them.*

Triga may have slanted his views to please me, but I don't think so. Many *serranos* held similar views. They supported the guerrillas at first, believing they would ease their poverty and end moral decay, but as the war proceeded, they rejected Shining Path's brutality.[22]

Triga and his friends also remained in Shining Path partly out of fear. *If we didn't do what the* terrucos *wanted, we were afraid that they might kill us. From the beginning we knew that we had to meet with them and to bring someone else. If we hadn't gone, we were afraid that something would happen to us. We had to say, "Yes, this is okay, I agree, I'm on your side and will belong to the Party." But I wasn't sure about what I was doing. They pressured us. "We'll kill anyone who doesn't participate," they told us. We couldn't leave.*

One of my friends in the movement had been talking to the police. One night the terrucos *came and killed him, hammering a nail into his head, not wanting to waste a bullet. When Shining Path put that nail through my friend's head, I left the group in my mind, saying, "No, no." It was the bloodthirsty ones, the* sanguinarios, *who wanted to do these things.*

The prohibition against speaking to others also isolated Triga from adult counsel. "What did your parents think?" I asked.

I didn't tell them. The leaders threatened us, demanding that under no circumstances were we to tell our parents. We were afraid what would happen if we did so. They might even have killed us.

When Martín, the leader of the group, was taken, I left and didn't want to know anything more about it. There was no reason to stay. I was in danger and so was my family.

"Who did people fear most," I asked, "the military or the *terrucos?*"

More than anything, it was the military. The terrucos *weren't a terrible problem. They would enter your house, ask for food, and then say good-bye. If you had a young boy, they wouldn't just take him as a recruit but would speak to the parents and explain what they were doing. They also might ask you to explain your behavior. They always tried to warn people, to get them to change, killing a person only if he didn't change and if they had concrete proof. They even investigated my uncle when he was mayor. There were a lot of problems about the eucalyptus plantation, that the trees were being sold improperly. They spoke to my uncle three or four times, but he explained that he had nothing to do with the trees, that they were under the control of the president of the community. If he hadn't been able to explain himself, they would have killed him, no?*

But with the military it was different. They never really tried to *get people to change. They would just arrive and kill without any explanation.*

During the interview I neglected to point out to Triga that the *terrucos* had not spoken to his parents to "explain what they were doing" when they recruited him. When I review my tapes, I sometimes find that I have not asked a logical follow-up question. But I did challenge Triga about Shining Path's brutality. "But your mother told me that in 1981 she saw *terrucos* killing the officials of Rumi Sonqo. The way she described the killings made them seem very bloody."

I guess so, he responded defensively. *I didn't see the killings, but I heard stories about them. But again, these village officials had been misbehaving. The* terrucos *would first ask questions and investigate and then execute them. And they held public executions in front of* Triga *everyone to make people afraid to misbehave. The people who liked the military are a minority,* he reiterated.

"But," I countered, "I have spoken to people who are very much opposed to the *terrucos.*" I named some of the people he knew who favored the military.

Yes, there are people like that, but I think they are in a minority. I think that in the final analysis the terrucos *have made the country better. I think that if we hadn't had the terrorism, we would be in even worse shape now.*

"You mean morally?"

Yes.

Triga and many peasants emphasize a lost but glorious past in which the Inca made people behave morally, an ideology codified in the well-known saying attributed to the Inca, "Don't steal, don't be lazy, and don't lie, Ama suwa, ama qella, ama llulla." [23] I think his defense of Shining Path in part reflects this ideology. He believed that by punishing bad behavior Shining Path made officials behave with rectitude. Such attitudes were fairly widespread; many women supported the guerrillas initially because they punished men for drunkenness and domestic violence. [24]

As the guerrillas became increasingly brutal, however, most peasants rejected them in disgust. Triga admired Shining Path's vision of eliminating corruption and alleviating poverty but at the same time was repelled by the brutal murder of his friend and his own forced participation.

Triga's account raises many conflicting emotions in me. I am uncomfortable with his justification of Shining Path and the nonchalant way he discussed executions. And yet I like Triga. Prompted by these feelings, I commented, "I don't know what the solution is. Officials certainly have committed a great many abuses in the past. But the *terrucos* were abusive as well. I don't think the solution is war."

No, he responded, perhaps slanting his views to please me, *I don't think so either. Killing is not the answer. Perhaps some form of punishment, but not killing. That just brings more killings, no?*

"Look what happened to you," I said, "to your brother, to your parents."

Yes, all of this still lingers psychologically. It was a kind of craziness. I remember once in San José when I was on my way to work, a little girl left her schoolbag unattended for a moment on the steps of the church. A cop came by and asked if the bag was mine. I told him it wasn't. He stepped back, raised his machine gun and Phhhhhhh! He blew the bag to pieces, thinking it might be a bomb. When the girl came back, she cried, "My book bag!" Really, to live like this is truly traumatic, it definitely is.

SEVEN

El Comandante Tigre

THE PEASANT PATROLS AND WAR

Mitchell, before we begin, my daughter and son aren't baptized and I want to be your compadre.[1]

I was startled by this request as I entered the house of El Comandante Tigre, Commander Tiger, the head of San Pedro's militia. *Do you agree to it or not?* **Allinchu o manachu?** *Will you be their godfather? When can we do it?*

I hesitated briefly, then responded, "I'll do it, Allinmi."

Inwardly, I was troubled. People I had known for many years told me that he had killed twenty-three San Pedrinos in order to burglarize their homes and avenge personal disputes, even shooting one young man in the back as they patrolled together. I had already visited isolated archeological ruins where another youngster had been dragged from a truck and murdered by men in ski masks, the site marked by a lone metal cross. "El Tigre killed him! El Tigre and the militia!" several people had told me, killing him, they claimed, just because the kid had bad-mouthed El Tigre and the mayor. Whatever the truth of the allegations, they unsettled me. How could I become *compadre* to a possible murderer?

I had met El Tigre only a few days before. I returned to San Pedro in 1996, two years after the last violent incident in the town, although guerrilla remnants were still active a day's journey away in Ayacucho's tropical forest. Wanting officials to know me, I had introduced myself to the military command, the police, and the mayor. A week and a half later, I spoke to the peasant militia during its regular Sunday meeting in the municipality. I had not been to San Pedro for sixteen years, so they were mostly strangers. I addressed them first in Quechua, but I had seldom spoken the language since 1980, so I shifted to Spanish. Surprised at my knowledge of Quechua and San Pedro customs, the men were pleased that I had come to learn how San Pedro had fared during the war.

Afterwards, I chatted briefly with El Comandante Tigre, who, like other militia leaders, went by an assumed name. He invited me to visit him at his home. I accepted with a mix of apprehension and impelling curiosity to hear an account of the militia different from the ones I had been getting.

I was surprised when I arrived at his house a few days later not only by his request to stand as godparent to his children but also by his congenial manner. We sat in the front room, functionally similar to the American family room, but with adobe walls, hard-packed earth floor, and crude handmade wooden benches and tables instead of plush couches. It was simple but clean and pleasant. Attired in rubber-tire sandals and old clothes instead of the nattier clothing he had worn on Sunday, El Tigre struck a humble appearance, but had deep-set, expressive eyes and spoke excellent rural Spanish. Hands are seldom idle in San Pedro, and he fashioned *retablos* throughout the interview. His wife, busy preparing the meal we later ate together, joined us whenever she could. Their young daughter and son played nearby, murmuring in the background. At more than ten thousand feet above sea level, I was cold and wore a jacket. Because the house was located close to the highway at the edge of town, the noisy trucks climbing the final, steep ascent into the plaza frequently interrupted our conversation.

El Tigre said I could record the interview, and I set my tape recorder near him on the floor as he began to speak. As he spoke, I became convinced that he saw me as a respected outsider, a gringo doctor and professor, and that he wanted to impress me in order to clear his name. He had done nothing wrong, he emphasized over and over, but was an unsung hero who had helped halt a guerrilla insurgency. His job was to defend the community against Shining Path assaults and to prevent people from aiding the guerrillas, either because they favored the insurgency or because they were coerced. As head of the militia, El Tigre told me, he also fought cocaine traffickers and rustlers.

Terrorists and drug traffickers are the same thing, he said. *They help each other,* a view at variance with those of Peruvian anthropologist Ponciano del Pino, who found that in the Apurímac Valley (the drug-producing area of Ayacucho) the drug trade was allied to the peasant militias, unlike in the Huallaga Valley, where they were tied to the guerrillas.[2]

El Tigre was born in 1951 to a poor family of artisans and spent much of his early life away from the village. As a teenager, he lived with uncles in the eastern jungles, harvesting coffee and manufacturing *trago,* Peru's cheap rum. He enlisted in the army at twenty-one and served for two years, an invaluable experience for the future commander of the peasant militia. After leaving the military in 1973, he moved back and forth between San Pedro, various coastal cotton plantations, and the guano islands (where he mined bird-dung fertilizer), seeking the menial work in Peru's export economy that Martín Huamán and many San Pedrinos had sought before him. On the guano islands he took the nickname El Tigre, inspired by a fish he admired, but a name that people later associated with the deadly land animal.

El Tigre settled more or less permanently in San Pedro in 1979, when he was twenty-eight, living off *retablo* sales and farming. He and his family lived there peacefully, he told me, until the 1980s, when San Pedro began to feel the impact of the Shining Path war, the "subversive delinquency, the *delincuencia subversiva,*" as he called it.

Some peasant communities had organized peasant militias to combat Shining Path in the early 1980s,[3] but San Pedro was split over whether or not to form one, a nearly decade-long disagreement that was so divisive that I had heard about it in Lima. Some charged that the militias were themselves predatory and killed innocent people, while others extolled them as crucial defenders against the insurgency. Some were frightened because the very formation of a peasant militia often elicited Shining Path reprisals. El Tigre favored the militia; he also believed that only Shining Path partisans were opposed to forming one.

The army and neighboring militias decided the issue for San Pedro. The military had conflicting views of the militias, sometimes supporting them, sometimes opposed, but in the early 1990s it began to require them in Ayacucho as part of a major offensive against Shining Path. In 1990 militias from the neighboring districts of Rumi Sonqo and Patampampa occupied one of San Pedro's hamlets. Wielding a list of names, they accused ten people of having participated in an attack that had left forty-two dead in Patampampa a year or two earlier. According to El Tigre, these ten people had left their identity cards at the scene of the assault, thereby confirming their guilt. The men were seized and San Pedro was labeled a "red zone," a zone that supported Shining Path.

The two militias marched to the central town, lined up the residents in the plaza, and organized the San Pedro militia, giving El Tigre command. He and other leaders acted quickly to organize militias in outlying rural hamlets. They lined up the people in each of the hamlets, as in San Pedro, and, with the help of a captured member of

30 Presenting arms during Sunday muster of peasant militia

Shining Path and a list of accused partisans provided by the neighboring militias, arrested those accused of terrorism.

As El Tigre told me these accounts, I flinched inwardly, for it was likely that many of the suspected guerrillas were later tortured and killed. The war had been brutal; both sides had murdered the innocent as well as the guilty, sometimes on only the slimmest suspicion. It was also hard to believe that ten men had discarded their identity cards during an attack on Patampampa. Identity cards are mandatory documents that all Peruvians carry carefully and, like Triga (Chapter 6), are wary of losing. The loss of the document by one man? Possibly. Ten men? Impossible. At the same time, I was aware that people were fighting for survival and that under such circumstances, moral issues are not always as clear as when people's homes and lives are not at stake.

Each militia guarded a defined perimeter, using whistles, shouts, gunshots, and passwords to communicate with one another. Sentries in adobe watchtowers, *torreones de vigilancia*, guarded strategic crossroads. All heads of households over eighteen were obligated to participate, preferably a man, but a woman if a man was unavailable. They took turns patrolling the community for one night, then waiting for their next turn. As in other communal corvées, rich people hired a substitute in lieu of participating themselves or paid a fine, the money used to provide the watch with coca leaves and rum to help ward off the cold and exhaustion of the night.

Composed largely of poor peasants, the militias in some ways protected the interests of the state and the wealthy, but in large measure they were defending their own farms and lives. Shining Path wiped out entire villages, especially those of the high-altitude herders and potato farmers who refused to support the guerrillas. They imposed a strict, authoritarian rule on many other peasant communities, killed opponents, and took children like Triga into their ranks. Lacking an understanding of peasant lives (or not caring), the guerrillas killed development workers, peasant leaders (such as the *varayoc*), and government officials (see Chapter 8), many of whom were related by ties of family to the rest of the community. Following the Maoist strategy of strangling the cities, they strove to prevent peasants from selling food to the cities, a significant impediment to peasant survival.

According to El Tigre the number of families in a hamlet determined how often each head of household had to participate in the watch, but generally it was about once a month. Other San Pedrinos, however, told me that they had to participate more often, too often, they said, cutting into time needed for work, adding to the general anxiety, and encouraging many to flee to Lima or other areas of the coast or to the tropical forests.

El Comandante Tigre

Each Sunday the militia mustered in the central plaza, lining up to present arms and salute the flag, ceremonies clearly directed at forging a national identity in rural communities beset by guerrilla war. In many ways, the militia replaced the *varayoc*, native leaders who once operated like a police force under the command of town authorities (see Chapter 1). The *varayoc* too had lined up in the plaza every Sunday to receive orders for the coming week. Unlike the *varayoc*, however, the militia had few ritual ties to local hamlets.

The militia worked under the military, not the police, El Tigre told me. *The police were unreliable and sometimes they refused to leave their quarters when there were problems. I went to the police post to ask for help during an incursion into the Urin Saya barrio in 1992. "Señor Capitán," I asked, "please help! There's going to be an attack." At that moment shots went off, everything; bombs and grenades were falling. "My men are dying," I told him, "and we don't have enough weapons. What can we do, Captain?" But the police didn't want to leave the safety of the police station. I said to them, "Señores, even though we may die, we have to protect our people." So the Ronda set forth on its own, but it was already too late. People had been killed, and the subversive delinquents had fled, leaving six people dead.*[4]

Naming some of the dead and commenting on the roles two of them played in the militia, El Tigre sorrowfully remembered his

31 Homemade rifle of peasant militiaman (face obscured to hide identity)

compadre, a fellow commando: *They killed the poor man with a grenade. A grenade! Blowing him up into small pieces. That's how it is, señor.*

Although considered a major defense against the insurgency, the Ronda at first had no arms other than homemade rifles, slings, lances, and knives. It was only around 1993 that the government gave them Winchester rifles; when I interviewed El Tigre in 1996, they had a stockpile of 163 government-issued Winchesters.

After organizing San Pedro and its hamlets, El Tigre and the militia set out to form militias in other Ayacucho communities, *always working for complete pacification,* la pacificación definitiva. *I was wounded on one of these trips; I fell while deactivating a trap, causing a nail to rip through my hand. Nearby we found a pamphlet saying "ronderos . . . don't mess with us because at any moment we'll cut you to dust."*

In 1992 and 1993 the militia forcibly resettled people from the isolated areas of San Pedro, the dispersed *estancias,* to the central town and the four newly created hamlets built to house them, a resettlement policy similar to the *reducciones* of Viceroy Toledo early in the colonial period and the more recent strategic-hamlet policies of the United States in Vietnam. The high-altitude grazing lands were emptied of people and animals, farms were abandoned. Even families from remote areas of the maize zone were resettled, although many from this zone continued to walk the long distances to and from their fields each day.

To save our children, our families, we had to group them together, putting watchtowers at the four cardinal points in the hamlets, guarded day and night to warn of anything suspicious so that people could defend themselves rapidly.

"Did they get any government help for the relocation?"

No, not then, but in 1995 the government at least donated some aluminum roofing, calominas. *Before that they received nothing, absolutely nothing!*

"Were some of the people opposed to moving?"

Some were opposed, but we explained the reasons for the resettlement, and they had to heed us.

"Surely some of the old people didn't want to leave their houses."

That's true, some didn't want to go, although some of the old people were among the first to leave, constructing a rudimentary shelter to live in. But we had to respect the old people, just like children, because we wouldn't abuse the old. There were young people, though, who were insolent terrucos. *If they didn't pay attention, we lashed them with a* chicote [*a stiff three-pronged, braided leather whip*]. *That was the way we had to keep the community in line. That's what we did. There was no other way.*

In 1996, even though the settlers were now living in adobe homes rather than rudimentary shelters, they were petitioning the militia and military for permission to return to their rural homes. The war had ended and they resented the long daily trek to their fields and their inability to keep animal herds in the towns. Most also wanted to retain their new homes, especially those in the central town, a favored location convenient to the Sunday market, transport, and central schools.

Except for sporadic fighting by a Shining Path faction under the leadership of Camarada Feliciano, the war had subsided when I interviewed El Tigre in 1996, but he, like many others, was still cautious. *There still are threats and rumors that Shining Path is leaving the montaña jungles well armed. Only a week or so ago an old woman saw two terrorists here at the Sunday fair. She didn't tell anyone because she was afraid that after the police arrested the terrorists, they would bribe the police to release them and then go after her.* A *soplón*, or informer, was a favorite target of Shining Path.

Juan, the brother of Anastasio Huamán (Chapter 8), also pointed to signs of possible Shining Path activity when we traveled in 1996 to the abandoned hamlet of Rumi Puquio in the high *puna* above San Pedro. Pointing to debris suggesting that people were sleeping in the ruined houses, he asked, "Who would do something like that?" Only Shining Path partisans would risk their lives sleeping in such an isolated area, he speculated.

In spite of such ominous signs, El Tigre believed that, unlike at the start of the war, San Pedro was prepared to deal with any threat. *I'm confident,* he told me, *that the population won't welcome Shining Path the way they did in the past. Because we're organized, we're no longer afraid. We continue patrolling to locate thieves, rustlers, and drug traffickers. We're not letting our guard down and we'll catch any Shining Path guerrillas before they can strike.*

Peruvian anthropologists Carlos Iván Degregori, José Coronel, and Ponciano del Pino are correct that the Ronda Campesina, or militia, was a major factor in the defeat of Shining Path,[5] a conclusion shared by El Tigre. *The Ronda played a very important role in the war against terrorism,* El Tigre maintained. *We've been able to analyze the situation among ourselves. We know who is who, and what they're doing, so that we've been able to stop the subversives.*

"But isn't it difficult to determine who is a subversive, a *terruco*?" People often collaborated with *terrucos* out of fear, not conviction, as many have told me in San Pedro and Huancayo, I elaborated.

We've done it without punishing the innocent, El Tigre responded defensively. *We're not like the army, which might come to a community and punish an old woman who helped the subversives out of fear. The self-defense committees,* comités de autodefensa, *are aware of their neighbors, so that we don't punish the innocent. Nonetheless, if all the evidence indicates someone is guilty, then in good conscience we have to punish the person and bring him to justice.*

Distinguishing "the good guys from the bad guys," however, is never simple, especially during war. Knowing "who is who" can

easily lead to settling old scores rather than uncovering guerrillas.
Often racked by internal and external disputes, peasant towns are not romantic exotics but are filled with tensions and self-interest as well as care and cooperation. People have always vied for control of government and other resources in San Pedro; I know of no year in which this has not been so. Neighboring communities also are frequently at loggerheads over boundaries, the rustling of sheep and cattle, and the theft of ripening crops during the night. The militia was able to take sides in these disputes as an agent of the state, thereby imposing its will and labeling the other side as "terrorists." In San Pedro opponents of the mayor and militia were quickly so labeled. In the name of fighting terrorism, moreover, some militias began to use their power for personal ends.[6]

"It wasn't the entire militia that killed," those twenty-three people, *El Comandante* señor Ricardo told me, "but a group of *sanguinarios,* perhaps ten or *Tigre* eight people under the control of the mayor." Señor Ricardo is a partisan and sees events through partisan eyes. I never interviewed the mayor about señor Ricardo's charges, and those of others, so the accusations are difficult to assess. Most San Pedro mayors I have known have been accused of serious malfeasance by opponents.

Early in our conversation, El Tigre had protested, *Because of our offensive, our* lucha frontal, *against terrorism, I'm accused of killing twenty-three people. But justice and an investigation have established that I'm not responsible, and the accusations were officially shelved,* archivados. *I'm an honest and tranquil person, and they haven't found one proof. I'm clean.*

Probably aware that I had been hearing the widely known stories of the killings, he made this protestation spontaneously, not prodded by a question. Still later in our conversation, after describing the daily patrols of the militia, he praised its success in pacifying the countryside.

And is there any thanks? he wanted to know. *In spite of all our efforts, in spite of all we have done, I'm called an assassin, a thief, everything! But I haven't paid any attention to it. That's how it is.*

I had visited Rumipata, a hamlet in the lower reaches of San Pedro, before my interview with El Tigre. People in the hamlet had been killed by the militia and others had been threatened. They were a major source of opposition to El Tigre and the mayor. "I'm headed to Rumipata," Raúl Ramírez, a community activist and native of the hamlet, told me as I ran into him in the streets of San Pedro. "They suffered a terrible hailstorm yesterday (see Chapter 4). Do you want to come?" I knew Raúl, having met him thirty years before, when he was a young boy. He also had been mayor of San Pedro during one of my visits. "Yes," I told him, unaware of what was to take place and unaware of Rumipata's special place in accounts of the killings, "I'd like to go." Much of the best ethnography comes from such unplanned events.

Fortunata Vega (Chapter 8), my *comadre* and a supporter of El Tigre, admonished me later. "Raúl's a terrorist." Was he? I had no idea, but I was impressed with Raúl. He related to me his own distressing story of escaping from the *terrucos,* who destroyed his home and farm in the tropical forest. In my experience of him (admittedly narrow), I considered Raúl a community activist (as I consider myself), one strongly motivated to rectify poverty. He took me on a tour of the central school, showing me its wretched condition and need for repairs. "The high school students come here on foot from far away, yet the high school doesn't give them any food and the parents don't have enough to give them food to take with them. I'm the only one to protest that, not for my children but for all the children."

Raúl also sought to publicize and seek justice for what he considered the horror that the militia and El Tigre had inflicted on his hamlet. He also was an implacable enemy of the mayor, accusing him of taking donated clothing and milk to reward his allies and to sell for profit, thereby subverting their intended distribution to the poor in Rumipata and other distant hamlets. "Truth is Justice," he proclaimed. "What do you think of that, Doctor?" asking me to comment on the slogan he planned to use to tell the world what had happened. "It sounds pretty good," I assured him. I also was aware that I had to keep in mind that Raúl was a partisan in a bitter community feud. I could not take what he had to say at face value.

We left San Pedro center, descending some two thousand feet over rugged terrain. We returned late that night by a different route, a safer but equally strenuous one. "Doctor, do you want to rest?" he asked as he waited for me. Panting, I dissembled. "I'm in good shape, just not acclimated to the altitude." Raúl had paid for two video cameramen from Ayacucho City to videotape his interviews and the faulty water system, doing so with the express purpose of producing evidence that the mayor had used poor materials in its construction.

Rumipata lies well below San Pedro center and has long suffered from poor irrigation and dirty drinking water, a matter of considerable concern when I visited the hamlet in 1966. I had spent the night at a *wata unras,* the end of the mourning period (Chapter 5), and it was a chill morning as I departed for home after a hearty breakfast of *mondongo,* a stew. Before I set out, however, several people took me to see the dirty, contaminated water in their cisterns, debris and insects floating on the surface. This demonstration was repeated in almost the same way thirty-three years later. It was astonishing to see what looked like the same debris floating on top of the water.

They had a new potable water system, residents told me in 1996, built with money from the government program known as FONCODES (Fondo Nacional de Compensación y Desarrollo Social— National Fund for Social Compensation and Development),[7] but it did not work. The system was indeed poorly constructed, cement falling apart, fountains inoperative. Water could not and did not arrive. They still had to drink from the dirty water collected in their cisterns. "See," Raúl told me over and over, as he pointed to one fault, then another, "the mayor claims he has built a potable water system, but nobody comes to check on him. Nobody, not even the municipal officials in San Pedro, wants to walk this far to check what was *El Comandante* done. The mayor has used inferior materials while billing for superior ones, and we have nothing!" *Tigre*

Residents also accused the militia of murdering several young people, threatening others, and forcing many to flee. "See, Doctor," Raúl proclaimed, as he pointed to a house, "nobody lives here; look at the adobe bricks sealing the entrance!" a refrain he repeated with slight variations throughout our trip. A survey he completed for me later showed that 27 percent of the eighty-six homes in this hamlet were abandoned during the war, most of them during 1991–1993. Some residents had been sent to live in the concentrated settlements, but many young people in fear of their lives fled to Ayacucho City, Lima, and the tropical forest.

The old people who remained were distraught because they were not strong enough to dig, hoe, and plow their fields alone. They missed their children, who even in 1996 were afraid to enter Rumipata itself. Roaming the isolated footpaths and fields still posed too great a risk for these refugees, so they caught only rare, furtive moments with their parents along the highway.

"Many of our houses have been abandoned, Doctor, so many of our young people left because of the war," complained an old man, his face wrinkled by the sun and years of hard work. "The young people have gone, but the rest of us who remain, how are we doing? A little advanced in age, without work. When we look for work in the fields, or on something else, the owners tell us, 'You're not able to do the work' and they don't give us any. So we stay here, always suffering."

Raúl arranged an assembly, an *asamblea*, a few days after my initial visit so that people could tell me about the war and the killings. About forty women and a few old men gathered in an abandoned Roman

32 Women displaced by the war

Catholic chapel, the sun shining through the back where the roof
should have been, a decay caused not only by the chaos of the war, but
also by lack of interest in repairing it because of poverty, the scarcity
of young men to do the work, and the general decline of Roman
Catholicism. Rural Peruvians, even the most humble, are accustomed
to public oratory, to making speeches at public assemblies and other
occasions, doing so with elaborate introductions and rhetorical flour-
ishes. During the *asamblea,* people took turns, one speaking after the
other. Each person added her or his sentiments, some in Quechua
and others in Spanish, often repetitive, voices frequently competing
with one another, but very powerful in their cumulative impact.
"We want justice!" they called, recounting their stories with passion,
speaking about these events to an outsider for the first time. During
the war, they risked being killed as "terrorists" for speaking. Now
they felt more secure and wanted me to tell the outside world that
their children and husbands were innocent victims threatened and
murdered by the military and the peasant militia.

El Tigre was defensive about these and other accusations. Partly
to combat them, he emphasized the destruction caused by Shining
Path, thereby trying to provide the violent context in which he and
the militia were operating and setting forth the necessity for his work.

*I've seen towns that have been completely destroyed, but we orga-
nized the militia in San Pedro just at the right time to defend ourselves.*

Many towns are a disaster, señor Mitchell. It is something to cry about, to see a woman by her ruined little hut, her chocita, *sleeping there. They have little food. How they cry, lacking food even to pick at! These poor people have had to leave their homes and farms and come down from the mountains to live in town. They once had everything but now nothing. What do they eat? Where do they get even a little bit of maize? I have seen these things, both here and in Uchuraccay. I've tried to help them, and I've given them a little of my own land.*

"How they suffer!" his wife interjected.

El Tigre's assessment of Shining Path destruction is attested to by many others, including Anastasio Huamán (Chapter 8).[8] Peruvian historian Nelson Manrique quotes a moving statement of a resident of a successful agricultural cooperative associated with a Jesuit developmental program that was attacked by Shining Path in 1988: "So [Shining Path] saw anyone who did not obey them as the black sheep whom they later killed with rocks as [they did] to many brothers who today rest in peace, and others they burned alive with gasoline. What a sad and lamentable time we passed, wondering desperately which day we would be killed."[9]

In order to eliminate terrorism completely, we have to eliminate poverty, but governments have rarely reached the most distant areas and the poorest people. Only rich people benefit from the Agrarian Bank, Banco Agropecuario. I've applied for a loan from the Agrarian Bank but was unable to get anything. There were too many papers to complete, which costs money, and then there was my travel. It cost too much in money and effort for such a small sum.

El Tigre had little empathy for anyone he considered to be on the other side. His vision was Manichaean: there were the forces of good, of which he was part, and the forces of evil, represented by Shining Path and communism.[10] El Tigre allowed for little ambiguity or nuance, a risky predilection for someone who has the power of life and death over others. He believed anyone opposed to him or the militia, or who had fled after the militia was formed, had to be a supporter of the guerrillas.

Perhaps 50 percent of San Pedrinos were in favor of Shining Path, he told me. *The people who accuse me of having murdered anybody are* terrucos, *communists!* El Tigre expostulated angrily.

"But what about señor Ricardo?" I asked. "He's one of the premier capitalists in San Pedro."

Don't believe it! He's a communist! How else could he have operated his store throughout the war? Only Shining Path sympathizers could do that. We have proof that he gave food and money, cupo, *to terrorists in*

El Comandante Tigre

33 Rumipata assembly (faces obscured to hide identities)

San Pedro. He was against the creation of the militia, and only a terrorist would take that position. Besides, he was on that list of Shining Path partisans that the militia from Patampampa gave us.

Señor Ricardo was a fierce opponent of the mayor and El Tigre, one of those who accused the militia of murdering innocent *campesinos*. He had accumulated voluminous materials that he believed documented his claims. His charges are difficult to judge, because he was frequently embroiled in community disputes in which he defamed his opponents as they defamed him. Having known the man, a former mayor of San Pedro, for thirty years, however, I doubted El Tigre's claim that he was a Shining Path militant. The owner of a store on the plaza and another on the highway, señor Ricardo was known as a skinflint, a *maqlla*. A leader of the faction opposed to the agrarian reform in the early 1970s, he had advocated vociferously in favor of private landownership (Chapter 4). A relatively rich man, he had much to lose in the society envisioned by Shining Path. Did he give Shining Path money in the 1980s, pay it the protection money known as *cupo* to operate his store? Probably, as did most people under threat who had something to give, but that contribution did not mean that he approved of Shining Path. He was and is a pragmatist, one of the persons who quit the town at the hint of a guerrilla attack just before I arrived in 1966.[11] He also fled from San Pedro when the Shining Path war intensified in 1983 and settled in Santa Anita near Lima, terrified of the killings, telling me that he feared for his life. He thought Shining Path might win, not a happy outcome for him. They would take all he owned if they won, he thought.

El Tigre resented the government's help to encourage refugees to return to their communities.

The militia has borne the brunt of the war. Why should we receive nothing while the refugees get government help? We used our own resources to fight the war and never earned a cent, nothing! When we went on patrol we had to take our own food, coca leaves, cigarettes, and rum. Nothing was provided us. We patrolled the mountains without blankets, without anything, risking our lives. Some of us were killed, but we still had to work to get bread for our children, even working in the fields earning seven soles, five soles. And with this and the little we earned from making retablos we have fed ourselves. Nonetheless, we stopped the subversion.

El Comandante
Tigre

"Nothing! Nothing!" his wife exclaimed. "For six years, papito, you have done this without earning anything!"

"Six years!" I interjected.

More than six years, El Tigre responded. *Sometimes sad, sometimes laughing, but prepared for action at any moment. We even fought in Ticlio, the high pass over the Continental Divide on the road to Lima. I was in eight battles!*

"Eight!"

Thirty! Thirty! But thank God I never got a bullet. They've only skinned me.

We've asked the government for help, but we get none. But the displaced people returning to their towns, yes, they get government help. The government must think that because we are here we have money and food and salt. But we've been punished and are left with nothing.

"Do people resent the refugees, the *desplazados?*"

No, we have no problem, but maybe there might be some resentment, no? The government is giving them cattle, food, and economic help, but for those who remained, who suffered in the war against subversion, we're not getting anything. Nothing, nothing. Maybe that small discrepancy has caused the threats in other pueblos against the refugees who are returning. Perhaps that's why there are threats. Yes, that's it! They didn't do anything, but left, worked peacefully elsewhere, and ate well while we remained, fighting terrorism, spending our own money, and in spite of that, we get no help!

"My husband fought everything," his wife added, "and for that reason they call him 'the Tiger.' He policed the area, fought well, more than anyone. Too much!"

"Isn't it time to forgive everyone," I asked, "and allow people accused of terrorism to return home? The old people in Rumipata cried when I visited them the other day because their children are afraid the militia will attack them if they return. The hailstorm destroyed their harvest and they need their children's help."

Only a few people fled Rumipata because they had been accused of terrorism, El Tigre responded unsympathetically. *The two, three, or four leaders, the* jefes principales, *but nobody else. I don't know why the others left. They must have gone to seek education and work. They're free to return. Most haven't wanted to, but not out of fear. They're living elsewhere.*

El Tigre's resentment at the government's poor treatment of the militia is widely shared, and *ronderos* have marched on Lima demanding help.[12] Militia members were poorly prepared and armed, some recruited by force, but they nonetheless fought a determined enemy, often taking more risks than did the police and the military. In some areas they received compensation, but in San Pedro they received none, even though they had to neglect their farms and forgo earnings from cyclical migration and artisanal production. Various people (Triga, Chapter 6; Anastasio Huamán, Chapter 8) fled to Lima in part to escape militia service because it interfered with earning their livelihood.

El Tigre still regarded himself as being in danger in 1996, a reasonable notion, since the heads of militias were often targeted by Shining Path. *Now that we've pacified things a little, we're hearing rumors that some people are saying that they're going to assassinate the people who have worked on the self-defense committee, especially the principal leaders. They're now threatening us. About a month ago, we came across a newly painted rock in the* punas *that said,* "Ronderos *and Soldiers, Desert Your Posts, Kill Your Chiefs, Join the Armed Struggle."

As we ate the meal his wife had prepared, El Tigre continued to speak. *The job of eliminating terrorism is only half done. It's as if we've built the walls of the house but have neglected to put on the roof. We've stopped before we definitely eliminated terrorism, but now that we're organized, we can immediately stop whatever subversion we find. But we can't let our guard down.*

Throughout the interview, El Tigre, to buttress his claims to innocence, protestations echoed by his wife, emphasized that he was close friends with the military commander of the region and with Archbishop Juan Luis Cipriani of Ayacucho, himself a controversial figure accused of whitewashing human rights abuses during the war.[13]

In 1995 the Fujimori government approved a general amnesty, pardoning soldiers, police, and the militias for any offenses and aborting any judicial proceedings already in process. Showing me his official amnesty, El Tigre expostulated, *Look at this, I'm innocent! I'm an honest and tranquil person and they haven't found any proof. I'm clean of any wrongdoing! The military authorities have investigated the complaints against me and dismissed them. Because there's been no firm proof, we've not had a single sanction taken against us. There have to be at least photographs or witnesses, no? Someone who will say, "Yes, when I was with him, he killed," but nobody has been able to say that. If we weren't conducting ourselves correctly, they would immediately send us all to jail.*

"You were sent to jail as a result of denunciations?"

Yes, but the authorities hadn't yet examined the matter, and I was in jail only for three or two days, and as soon as it became clear that there was no firm evidence, I was released conditionally. I was arrested again in September and was in jail for thirteen days, but I was released again. Why? Because the accusations were false, so that any prosecution has been definitely shelved. But I don't complain about the injustice. Clearly, some people hate me and want to blackmail me without any reason. In the other world, God knows what I have and have not done. Archbishop Cipriani of Ayacucho, however, helped me when I was in jail. I was the general's man, and the archbishop and others told him he had to help me.

The fact that El Tigre was denounced by others and spent time in jail should not be considered evidence of wrongdoing. Horacio Gutiérrez was jailed briefly for inquiring at the police post about the possibility that a radio he had bought had been stolen (Chapter 2).

Early in the interview I had asked El Tigre, "Who do you think killed these twenty-three people?" Many were from Rumipata, the same community where I attended the *asamblea* denouncing El Tigre.

I've thought about that, he replied, *and to my way of thinking, they were killed by subversives, not the militia. My brother and another relative,[14] among others, were wiped out before the Ronda was organized. How can they accuse me? The same was true after I became head of the militia. It was the subversives, not the peasant militias, that killed people.*

The subversives killed those people we're accused of killing. Why? Because they'd grown tired of giving the food and money that the subversives demanded and were collaborating with the military, with the police. They didn't want subversives in their pueblo and had informed on them. On discovering this, the subversives killed them. This was the first knowledge we had of the terrorists, and it led to our organizing. It was a group of aniquiladores—a special group of Shining Path killers—that murdered them. They were from Chungi, a town in the tropical forest montaña, but we caught them red-handed in Rumipata. One of them was carrying a list naming the people they had killed.

The accusations against us are totally false. During some of the killings, the subversives even left behind flyers that said, "We're going to kill El Tigre; we're going to kill him," and the entire leadership.

Earlier in the interview, El Tigre gave what appears on the face to be a different account of the killings in Rumipata, but it is unclear if these two accounts refer to the same or to different events. In any case, he denied responsibility here, too, concluding with a laugh that, even though he has been blamed for these events because he was head of the militia at the time, he was out of town.

Did El Tigre murder the twenty-three men in San Pedro? It is difficult to answer that question, for anthropological methodology is not designed to probe guilt or innocence. Nonetheless, many San Pedrinos attribute the killings to him. One informant whom I trust echoed many, telling me that the killings "were the work of the militia. The objective of the militia was to stop terrorism, but some *ronderos* took advantage of this" and used the militia as an excuse to steal. "I think the militia went too far," he said. My informant had been in San Pedro when the militia had been formed and remained there for much of 1990. He then fled to the coast to escape the mandatory patrols, but remained in contact with events in San Pedro.

"Then you think the militia has been engaged in vengeance killings, in *venganzas*?" I asked.

"Yes," he responded. "I was in San Pedro and heard much of what people had been saying, and they told me that it was the militia, the Ronda Campesina, not the *terrucos*, who did the killings. If someone spoke against them, they killed him. . . . I know the guy who killed the kid buried near the archeological ruins. The killer was a friend of mine when I lived in San Pedro. He drove a jitney, a *colectivo*, for years and had some economic problems with the kid, something about passengers, who was to leave first.[15] I believe he was drunk when he got the militia to kill this kid. It was revenge. . . . The guy who did it was my friend, but who is going to accept what he did? Phff! To do something so extreme. It's too much! I can accept fighting over the matter," but to kill? "I believe he should have done something else to solve the problem. Maybe talking about it. The killing was really ugly. Nearly everyone knows this story, both here in Lima and in San Pedro."

"But people here in Lima don't involve themselves in these matters do they?" I asked.

"Not very much. San Pedrinos rarely talk of these things in Lima."

"Why?"

"I don't know . . . People always limit what they say; they prefer not to talk, not to involve themselves."

"It certainly must be fear," I commented.

"Yes, I do think it must be that, fear for themselves or for their family in San Pedro. . . . They also say that the mayor of San Pedro had much to do with the militia and these killings, that he was their intellectual author, the one who directed things. He was president of the Ronda Campesina. I also think he was involved." But these murders have led to others; "the *terrucos* have retaliated by killing relatives of the *ronderos*."

El Comandante Tigre

Some of these assessments were foreshadowed in another interview I had in Lima in 1985 with Valentina Rodríguez's husband, Roberto Quispe (Chapter 5). He had just returned from San Pedro and Ayacucho City, where a soldier stole his watch (a gift from me), blatantly taking it in plain view of everyone, near the university's student housing complex. Roberto stood mute, fearing he would be accused of terrorism if he protested. In recounting this event and other stories, he told me that the militia from Patampampa, a neighboring town to the south, had murdered a family that lived in the heights above San Pedro. I had interviewed the family briefly in the 1970s.

"Why did they kill them?" I asked, after expressing my dismay.

"Surely out of envy or to steal their animals. Nobody knows."

"But couldn't the killing have been done by the Special Forces, the Sinchis, or by *senderistas*?" [16]

"No, it was the militia [the Ronda]."

"How do you know?" I probed.

"The people who escaped recognized the killers and knew that they were from Patampampa."

"San Pedro and the town are enemies?"

"No, it's just that as soon as the militia was formed in Patampampa they began to persecute their own people ferociously, the people from their own town. This militia and the others are trying to make San Pedro form a militia too, but San Pedro doesn't want to."

"Why doesn't San Pedro want a militia?" I queried further. At this time, in 1985, neither Roberto nor I knew of the troubles to come.

"Because it's not necessary."

"Why?"
"San Pedro has its own police, its own *policía*."
"But so does Rumi Sonqo. They have their own police force and a militia."
"The people of San Pedro are sure that nothing will happen to them," Roberto responded. "And they are certain that there are very few *senderistas,* very few guerrillas, in San Pedro."
"Are San Pedrinos afraid of the *ronderos*?"
"No," he answered. "It's because the *ronderos* don't do anything to help the pueblo. . . . And, besides, they themselves commit a lot of robberies, assassinations, and so many things, just like the Sinchis. Sometimes they're even worse, raping women, stealing animals, killing people. That's why San Pedrinos are resisting; they don't want

to go to that extreme. Is a San Pedrino going to kill another San Pedrino? That's not good, and they've decided against it. The militia is useless. People have to serve in it day and night, for nothing. The police, the Guardia Civil, not the militia, are responsible for watching over the town. That's what they get paid for. What's the Guardia going to do if the militia is responsible for security? Nothing! But it's only San Pedro that's against the militia. Militias are everywhere else."

Roberto, the man who gave this interview, was a close friend, someone I knew better than most San Pedrinos. He was opposed to the militia, but I could never believe he was a terrorist. I know that almost as well as I know that my wife is not a terrorist, even though she is opposed to violence by the state as well as by guerrillas.

Anthropologists are neither prosecutors nor judges. Nor are we supposed to take part in communal disputes, as this clearly was. But we are also moral beings. Cultural relativism is a research methodology, not an ethical system. It is often misunderstood, sometimes, I believe, deliberately so as to create a convenient target for conservative critics, who claim that the principle means we can make no ethical judgments. To the contrary, even Melville Herskovits, a major proponent of cultural relativism, acknowledged that it does not prohibit moral claims.[17] It is, instead, a research strategy in which we distance ourselves in order to understand people and their society better. Like the physicist, who does not criticize the atom she studies, or the biologist studying typhoid, the anthropologist focuses on understanding behavior and belief rather than condemning them. At the same time, like the physicist who opposes the manufacture of atomic weapons, or the medical researcher concerned about the quality of health care, anthropologists are moral beings and citizens who can make informed ethical judgments.

*El Comandante
Tigre*

34 War orphans at communal kitchen

How could I ignore the killing of twenty-three men? I could not. I am aware that El Tigre was fighting a terrible war that tore apart community after community. He was defending his town and his men. In 1990 an armed Shining Path column entered the village, killing eight members of the militia, his companions and neighbors. Some San Pedrinos, some out of fear, others out of conviction, certainly were involved with Shining Path and some may have been leaders. It certainly had to be worrisome for El Tigre to live among people he suspected were planning to kill him.

El Tigre portrayed himself as a good man doing essential work, but I think these statements were partly self-serving. By the time the militia was formed in the 1990s, much of the initial peasant enthusiasm for Shining Path had waned, even as the truly committed still pursued the war.[18] Too many people, moreover, have provided me so much detailed information that I believe El Tigre killed at least some innocent people, even though his outward appearance and humble home seem to belie accusations that he enriched himself significantly. El Tigre certainly did what was asked of him in organizing the military defense of San Pedro, an area that was a center in the war, but he also added to the violence for personal and evil ends. At the same time, he was abetted in his actions by the military, while the Peruvian state not only ignored the murders committed in the name of fighting "terrorism" but also encouraged the violence.

I have complicated feelings about my interview with El Tigre. As I review my tapes I ask myself, "Why was I so pleasant to a man I believed to be a murderer?" Just before we sat down to eat the meal his wife served, I even thanked him for the interview and used the very affectionate and typically Andean "Muchas gracias, papacito." The obvious answer is that I was there to interview him, not to judge him. Janet Malcolm has suggested that interviewing is in part seductive: we cajole our informants through our manner, charming them to tell us about themselves and the world in which they live, something I do unconsciously.[19]

The process of seduction is mutual, and El Tigre was using charm to convince me of his beneficence. In great part he was successful, and I believe I would have liked him if I had not known about the

killings. In retrospect, I am reminded of the phrase "the banality of evil," which Hannah Arendt used to describe Adolph Eichmann, one of the engineers of the Jewish Holocaust.[20] I did not meet "the monster I anticipated."[21] If I had had no foreknowledge of the accusations, I would have spent a very pleasant midmorning with El Tigre. Robert Jay Lifton uses the term "doubling" to refer to a killer's ability to maintain both a normal self and one outside normal bounds, thereby allowing the torturer to come home to his family and friends after mutilating the enemy.[22] "There's no art," Shakespeare tells us in Macbeth, "to find the mind's construction in the face." Evil exists in evil acts, not in someone's visage, no matter how pervasive our images of Hollywood villains.

But why did I agree to godparent his children? My answer is complicated. In the first place, I tend to accept godparenthood requests from informants, to give something back in exchange for the information they give me. Some might criticize this acceptance on my part, but it reflects who I am and the kind of anthropologist I wish to be. Ethnography is such a personal enterprise and skill that no two ethnographers will behave the same way. We bring to the field different psychological needs and strengths. I surround myself with people I care about. My compadrazgo relationships have created a Peruvian family that has not only helped in my research, but that has also been a source of pleasure and affection. As I revise this in 2003, I have just come off the phone with several godchildren, telling them of my forthcoming visit to Peru. Their delight in anticipating my visit is genuine, as is mine to see them. "The cuyecitos are waiting for you," a goddaughter said, inviting me for a festive meal of guinea pigs.

I also accepted because I was afraid of el Comandante Tigre. "What would he do if I said no?" I was traveling in the isolated

countryside, where men had been murdered, sometimes accompanied by his declared enemies, and interviewing people who claimed
to be his victims. My children were also planning to spend a night in
San Pedro, making a bonfire, camping next to the home of a friend.
I was concerned for them. These thoughts, feelings, really, flew
through my mind in the few seconds I hesitated before agreeing to
his request.

I immediately regretted my *yes* and hated what felt like cowardice.
I suspected that El Tigre wanted to use me to help cleanse his name. I
arranged to hold the ceremony at the end of my stay, wanting to postpone it as long as possible. He said he would ask his friend Archbishop
Cipriani of Ayacucho to baptize the children and that he would let
me know about the arrangements. We drank a *brindis,* a celebratory
drink, and I left. When I got home that night, I told my family what
had happened. They were glad I had said yes, but I was unhappy. A
"real man" would have had his shootout at the OK Corral. As much as
I have tried to shed their embrace, I am still constrained by learned
conceptions of masculinity. I also felt untrue to myself because I had
hidden my feelings about El Tigre, even though I sometimes hide my
feelings about other matters (food, for example) without experiencing similar guilt.

*El Comandante
Tigre*

Several weeks went by and I had no news from El Tigre. Then I
met him in Ayacucho City. *I haven't spoken to the archbishop yet,* he
told me, *but I will and will let you know the date.*

El Tigre never contacted me. Perhaps he had similar ambivalent
feelings, I thought. Perhaps he resented my questions in the latter part
of the interview, suspecting that I did not believe him. I continued to
work in San Pedro, and my interviews continued to point toward his
guilt. I could not be his *compadre.* Two weeks before I was scheduled
to leave the Ayacucho area, I sent El Tigre a note telling him that as he
had not contacted me, I did not know what the arrangements were,
but my university had suddenly asked me to return and I had to leave
immediately. My wife and children were happy, but I was not. I do not
like subterfuge.

In 1998 the militia killed the young man who ran the public telephone in the plaza. I had spent a day with him in 1996, interviewing
him as we walked in the countryside. He was a reflective and gentle
person and had taken a tempered position in the dispute over the
militia, struggling to see and understand both sides of the issue. But
he also thought that El Tigre was guilty. I was told that he was killed
when he remained out after the curfew hour, returning from a visit
to his mother-in-law. By this time in the war, however, many people

ignored the curfew, as had I when returning from Rumipata and other long trips.

According to the victim's cousin and other sources living in Lima, the *ronderos* contended that they had not recognized the man, but others contested this claim, asking, "How could they not have recognized him? He ran the public telephone in the plaza and was known by everyone." These people, among them, his mother, say that he was killed because he was an enemy of the mayor; perhaps he had heard things as people spoke on the telephone, some allege. Others say that it might have been a vengeance killing arranged by his first wife. It also is possible that the killing was in error. Under conditions of heightened security and fear, such errors are predictable.

Whatever the truth, the killing further alienated me from El Tigre. On subsequent visits to San Pedro I have avoided his home, even when I have visited a family of his supporters nearby, people I care about, even though they too were complicit in the evil of this terrible war. In a brief visit in 2004 I was told that El Tigre had repented of his past and had become an evangelical Protestant.

Social order is extremely fragile. Under consistent stress, as it was in Peru, life can easily descend to the proverbial war of brother against brother. Not all members of the San Pedro militia participated in the murders, nor were all militias implicated in abuses. Accounts elsewhere in Ayacucho give a more positive picture of the militias than that presented here. Militias differed significantly from place to place.[23] Some were formed freely by peasants to defend themselves, but others were imposed on communities by force. As in San Pedro, a militia imposed over significant community opposition can easily descend into lawlessness, into might sweeping aside justice.[24]

No matter their successes, moreover, even the best militias were vigilante groups that took "law enforcement into [their] own hands,"[25] and as in the tragic history of American lynching, vigilante groups that act as both police and jury are poised for abuse.[26]

As we shall see in Chapter 8, Anastasio Huamán, an opponent of Shining Path who cooperated with the police, presents a darker picture of the militia than do most scholars. Those militias formed by the military also duplicated the traditional relationship between the government in Lima and the sierra, replacing the *hacendado* and the caudillo, the traditional strongmen used to maintain order at whatever cost. In collaboration with the armed forces, they imposed that order, and like the *encomenderos* of the early colonial period and the *hacendados* more recently, some exacted payment in return.

The issue for many of us is how to maintain order while securing justice and our freedoms. I am certain that the way is not initiating preemptive attacks on presumed and real enemies, a cruel parallel found today in the international arena. The militias were decisive in ending the war, but it was their policies of patrolling and self-defense combined with the peasantry's disaffection with Shining Path and the capture of guerrilla leaders through effective police work that really put an end to the violence.[27]

Repression may be effective in the short term, but Shining Path discovered its bitter legacy when peasant rejection of its brutality led to defeat. The war is over, but the pain and anger caused by the violence remain, seeding the very resentment that facilitated the initial rebellion—a resentment continuously fertilized by the poverty found throughout Ayacucho and Peru.

El Comandante
Tigre

Anastasio

FLEEING SHINING PATH

The Huamán Family

"Miguel, do you know anyone I can interview in the *puna?*"

"Sí, tío. Anastasio Huamán. He lives in Rumi Puquio."

In 1974 I employed Claudia Velarde's grandson Miguel to take me around the district in order to study the way San Pedrinos utilized their diverse mountain environment. Leaving San Pedro, Miguel and I crossed the upper maize fields to enter the deep-green eucalyptus plantation, the town's only wooded section. Abandoning the pungent tree cover, we climbed higher. The air grew colder, and fields gave way to unpopulated communal pasturelands surrounded by dense shrubs and scrub, which provided much of San Pedro's fuel. Devoid of houses, the landscape appeared wild, but the scrub was kept low by grazing cattle as well as the high-altitude cold. Tutapa ravine plummeted sharply to our left.

"Careful," Miguel cautioned as the path narrowed. An irrigation canal alongside the path funneled fast-flowing water from the Tutapa River to fields far below; its tumult muffled our conversation. As we entered the silent world above the irrigation system, an area subjected to cold days and frequent night frosts, the brush disappeared abruptly, replaced by the low bunch grasses characteristic of Peru's *punas*. Rumi Puquio lay straight ahead, just over a sharp rise. As we entered the narrow hanging valley that sheltered the hamlet, the ground leveled and our climb eased. We arrived about five hours after our start; alone, Miguel would have made the climb much more rapidly.

Located above the tree line at about four thousand meters, a little more than thirteen thousand feet above sea level, Rumi Puquio is one of the highest settlements on earth—and one of the most beautiful.

Stone crags, one shaped like an old man, pierce the sky, guarding a half dozen stone houses in the small basin, but blocking our view of the many isolated homesteads, or *estancias,* nestled among the great rocks. San Pedro and the Ayacucho Valley lay far below. We made our way carefully through marshy spring-fed areas crowded with small lily-like plants. A few plowed fields had been readied for potatoes, but most lay fallow. Like most residents of the *puna,* the people of Rumi Puquio were agropastoralists, dedicated to both farming and herding. Their burros, horses, and llamas grazed in the distance, looking like the animal figures in the background of a nineteenth-century landscape painting.

Anastasio Huamán was stomping bitter potatoes, using his bare feet to remove the skin. Interrupting his work, he gave us a wry, charming smile and, as is the custom, politely extended his wrist in greeting, his hand too dirty for a handshake. After Miguel briefly explained my work, I introduced myself in Quechua. Anastasio responded in fluent highland Spanish, reflecting his primary and secondary schooling in San Pedro and Ayacucho City. He accepted the coca leaves that I always carried as a gift, but put them aside without chewing them. He told me that he had seen me in the *pueblo* and said approvingly that I was *Pablopa churin,* Pablo's son. I told him about my research, and he readily agreed to tell me about his farming and herding and granted me permission to record the conversation on tape.

"What're you doing?" I asked.

Making freeze-dried potatoes, he responded, "chuñu."[1] After he removed the skin from bitter potatoes, a separate species from the white potato, he put them in diverted stream water for fifteen days, subjecting them to alternating freezing at night and thawing in the day, then set them to dry in the sun. Freeze-dried potatoes will last for several years and are eaten in stews and soups. They are delicious, although their chewy texture takes getting used to. Being so high, Rumi Puquio is too cold for most crops, and farmers grow only potatoes and other tubers unknown outside the Andes: *maswa, olluku,* and *oca.* Andean potatoes come in many more varieties than elsewhere in the world. Anastasio named and described the thirty-six varieties grown in Rumi Puquio and did the same for the other tubers.

In 1974 I also was gathering data on interzonal trade. Unlike other regions of the world, where one must travel far to obtain foods from different environments, the equatorial Andes hosts a range of ecological zones close together. One can walk down from cold Rumi

Puquio to abundant orange groves in the warm, subtropical valley in less than half a day.

"What do you exchange with the people in the lower zones?" I asked. Anastasio told me about the wool trade and the barter of tubers for the maize grown lower down.

"Tell me about the saints and *cargos*. What saint do you celebrate here?" I was not specifically collecting data on religion, but like most ethnographers I cast a wide net. I never know what information I might want to use later.

Anastasio described the cross celebrated in the local chapel, but did not elaborate. *We don't have a* santo *in the chapel,* he said, *just a cross.*

Anastasio introduced me to his wife, Fortunata Vega, and showed me their new restaurant, a truck stop in the sky. Set beside an unpaved highway, the restaurant consisted of a rectangular room at the front of their house. Several tables, their rough-hewn construction hidden by bright plastic tablecloths, stood on an uneven, but scrupulously clean, earthen floor. Small triangles of waxy paper napkins jutted from a glass on each table. *Sit down, Siéntense,* Anastasio said to the two of us as he pointed to the homemade chairs. Like most Andean chairs, they were a bit too small for my frame, and the edges dug uncomfortably into my buttocks and back.

Fortunata served a delicious lunch of stewed beef, maswa, and chuñu. Because it was a restaurant, I asked for the bill, but they refused money. *Would you and your wife be Beatriz's godparents at her baptism?* Anastasio asked. Their daughter was eight months old.

"I'd be delighted," I answered. I planned more research in the high-altitude grazing zones and was glad to establish the formal relationship. "Come into San Pedro and we'll schedule the baptism with the priest together," I suggested.

No, Anastasio countered. *I want to hold the baptism in Ayacucho City. I'll arrange it when I'm there.*

Giving the matter little thought, I presumed that he and his wife preferred the prestige of a city baptism.

A cold wind told us that it was late afternoon, time to leave if we were to avoid descending in the dark. Night devours day quickly in the tropics. At the last minute, Miguel and Anastasio arranged to exchange freeze-dried potatoes for maize. *I'll let you know when I come down to the Sunday market with them,* Anastasio said.

"They're really nice people," I confided to Miguel as we began our descent. We passed the spot where, years later, the military would murder my godson Smiley and his companions, but in 1974 Rumi Puquio and San Pedro seemed very peaceful. The August wind, the *agosto wayra* that rakes the mountain at that time of year, pushed us down the slope, its force diminishing only as we approached town. We traveled by moonlight for the last few miles, but the slope was gentle and we were often on the graded road, so that the route was not as dangerous as it would have been higher up. In San Pedro, I hopped on the back of a truck to Ayacucho City.

Several weeks later Anastasio and Fortunata arrived at our Ayacucho City apartment accompanied by the infant Beatriz and Anastasio's parents. I was surprised that nobody else came for the baptism, but I assumed it was too far to travel. My wife (Daphna Mitchell) dressed Beatriz in the white baptismal dress we had bought, and we set off for the Church of San Francisco. "It's Beatriz," not my son, Sean, "who's being baptized," I had to remind the priest.

Returning to our apartment, Fortunata prepared food she had brought. Anastasio produced a liter bottle, filled a shot glass, and passed the bottle to me. *Salud,* he said. He drank, emptied the dregs, then handed me the glass. I filled it, toasted him, and drank. I nearly choked! Sweet cherry syrup! Neither my wife nor I said a word as the six of us finished one bottle of syrup, then another.

"They're from the *puna,*" I later speculated, "country hicks from the high altitudes. They probably don't know the difference between syrup and wine." Was I mistaken (and ethnocentric)! Years later, I discovered that Anastasio and Fortunata had converted to Protestantism shortly before the baptism. Though Protestants, they were choosing which customs to follow. By baptizing their daughter in the Roman Catholic church, they obtained *compadres,* but avoided criticism by doing so in Ayacucho City. They complied with the evangelical prohibition of alcohol by serving syrup instead of wine. It was because of his hidden Protestantism that Anastasio had accepted but did not chew my gift of coca leaves at our original meeting and had evaded my questions about religion.

He had reason to be careful. In the 1970s the Catholic majority still belittled the small but growing number of Protestants: armed, drunken men had even attacked Anastasio's congregation. The religious climate changed gradually, and by the time that Anastasio finally spoke of these matters in the 1990s, Protestants made up half the population of San Pedro and practiced their faith openly.

I sponsored the baptism of another daughter, Luisa, when I visited Anastasio in July, 1980. During this brief visit he told me that guerrillas had attacked the town of Chuschi and other areas of Ayacucho. He was worried, but I paid little attention. He was the only friend who made much of the attacks; they were far from San

Pedro, and an earlier revolutionary offensive in 1965 that had led many San Pedrinos to flee their homes had been quickly repressed, a panic still talked about when I arrived in 1966.[2] I also was blinded by an unconscious supposition of social stasis: a belief that life would continue in much the same way as it had yesterday and that change is gradual. I should have paid greater attention to Anastasio, for these attacks marked the beginning of the Shining Path war.

I lost track of Anastasio and his family during the war, but in 1996 I came upon them again in Santa Anita, the gritty, crowded suburb of Lima where I had gone searching for San Pedro migrants. The family was living in several rented rooms on a crowded, unpaved street cut into the bone-dry desert. Instead of the rural quiet of Rumi Puquio, they lived a few blocks from the central highway, a polluted torrent of screeching trucks, buses, and cars. Dust was kept at bay indoors by vigilant women armed with damp rags and precious water to dampen and tamp down the street.

The family now made *retablos,* the colorful wood and ceramic shadow boxes sold to tourists. Anastasio was painting figurines when I arrived. He washed his hands before offering a handshake. Shy after such a long separation, we chatted about general matters. He invited me to lunch the next Sunday. I returned with gifts. Fortunata had cooked a meal of chicken, beef, pork, potatoes, sweet potatoes, yucca, broad beans, and *humitas* (seasoned corn meal wrapped in the husk). It was a variation on the celebratory earth-oven meal, the

35 Anastasio Huamán's destroyed village

pachamanca, but cooked on the stove using a kind of Dutch oven
covered with moist towels to provide steam.

After the meal, we relaxed around their narrow table. I reminisced. "Do you remember when I visited you in 1980, compadre? I had brought a friend from New Jersey and he thought Rumi Puquio was the most peaceful place on Earth. Do you remember him, compadre? He had a beard. How is it that nobody lives there today? What happened?"

Anastasio's Narrative

Anastasio began a long narrative, one he repeated to me again three years later, in 1999, under almost identical conditions. He is a *Anastasio* great storyteller, the best I have encountered. His rural but fluent Spanish possesses the emotional power and poetic cadence of his native Quechua. His older children, Beatriz, Luisa, and José, remained to listen to his story, while his wife, Fortunata, joined us from time to time as her work in the kitchen permitted. The children were as engrossed in the story as I, even though they had certainly heard it many times. They interrupted often to make sure that their father did not forget important parts of a history that had become a family epic of great emotional power.

Compadre, we were peaceful and knew nothing of violence. Nothing! Nothing! How would we have heard of it? Day and night we could go into the countryside, taking our crops to town, leaving at three or four in the morning, loading our animals, just doing our work. We lived together like a family in Rumi Puquio, not fighting among ourselves. That's how I remember it. There was no violencia then, not in San Pedro or in any other town.

In spite of this peaceful opening, Anastasio immediately tells of several incidents before the war to suggest that life was not always idyllic.

When I started to build my house in Rumi Puquio and open my business in 1974, San Pedrinos were suspicious and told me to my face that I must be involved in the cocaine trade. "How else is this man going to get ahead and build a large house? He acts like a millionaire. He must have some secret helper."

This was just envidia, *envy, but two* guardias *arrived to search the house.*

San Pedrinos often complain that people behave badly toward them out of envy over their success, wealth, or good fortune. I have heard numerous attributions of envy to others, but have never heard anyone say he was envious.

"Where have you hidden the truckload of coca?" the policemen wanted to know. People saw you unloading a red truck and have filed an accusation against you."[3]

"I'm a law-abiding person and don't get mixed up with these things," I told them. "I don't do anything that would harm anybody. You can go into all the rooms and look them over."

They didn't find anything, not even a piece of coca leaf.

"What is the license plate of this truck that was supposed to be here?" I asked them. "Who denounced me?"

I demanded that they take me to the police post and provide proof. Before we started out, however, they whispered to me, "Tell us where the coca is. We'll buy it from you, but just tell us. We're not going to the police post. Do you understand?"

"Are you crazy?" I said. "I'm not going to say yes. Why would I do that? I built my house and restaurant through my own effort. I sold my field in the tropical forest to buy the materials, but before that I had earned money in the coffee cooperative, selling my harvest from the field every year. I have the papers to prove it!"

I showed them my papers, receipts, how much money I had received, from whom and in what year, everything with the date and signatures.[4]

We went to the police post. I told the chief what had happened and asked to see the complaint against me.

"What?" he said. "Who brought you?"

He knew nothing about the matter. Just at that moment an evangelical pastor I knew arrived from Ayacucho and spoke in my behalf. The chief turned to the two guardias and spoke to them harshly. They had been bribed by envious food sellers in San Pedro afraid of competition from my restaurant. I told the chief that I was going to lodge a complaint in Ayacucho City, and he begged me not to, telling me that it would make them look bad and that they would punish the two men themselves. He apologized and set me free.

In another incident, armed and masked men suddenly attacked the San Pedro police post, maybe in 1974 or 1972, surprising everyone. The guardia pursued the men, firing at them, but they got away. One of our neighbors had been in San Pedro during the attack. He thought somebody was celebrating a fiesta, setting off fireworks. While he was returning home with his animals, traveling late at night by the light of the moon, the guardia came from behind in a car and stopped him, asking if he had seen anyone. He told them he hadn't, but they detained

him, an innocent campesino, *saying he must have seen them. He kept*
telling them that he hadn't seen anything, and the guardia *finally set*
him free. He told us what happened when he got home.

Nobody knew where the attackers came from or who they were or
where they went. They disappeared like smoke. Everyone thought they
had been common criminals, but the police thought differently. My
son's godfather is a guardia *who visited us often. During one visit he*
asked if we had seen the fleeing men.

"They couldn't have been thieves," he told us. "Were they going to
rob the police post? Are we bankers or a business with a lot of money?"
He made sense, but he didn't tell this to anybody else.[5] Over time we
forgot what he had told us and again came to think that the attackers
had been common thieves.

Years passed, months passed. Peacefully. Nobody knew what was to   *Anastasio*
come, the violence we were going to face. It was peaceful and I was
planning to add a gas station to the restaurant, selling gasoline and car
parts. I thought about starting a trout farm.

We were working well, but little by little, we began hearing rumors.
We heard of marches, of protests. When I was traveling to the tropical
forest, the selva, *to visit my parents, we passed through a town where*
nearly everyone, men and women, were in the street protesting, march-
ing with Peruvian flags and white flags demanding their rights, calling
for peace, insisting that the police protect them from the communists.
Some passengers on the truck said that they had heard that there were
violent communists in this community and in other pueblos as well.
They said the marchers were heading on horse and by foot to Uchurac-
cay to protest the communists.

Everyone on the truck began to talk about violence and commu-
nism, wondering what might happen, saying that all the towns might
become communist.

These were among the first rumors of trouble that I heard, back in
1974. I didn't know what communism was, nor did any of the people
on the truck. But the incident left me thinking, thinking. "Something
might happen. Maybe we won't have any trucks on the highway and
customers for our restaurant."

In the early 1970s the agrarian reform program of the left-wing
Velasco military government was a source of intense debate in many
rural communities, provoking pro and con street demonstrations
(see Chapter 4). In San Pedro those opposed to the agrarian reform
called those in favor "communists." Anastasio may be referring to
such marches rather than something involving Shining Path.

When I returned home from the tropical forest I told my family what I had seen and heard, but they knew nothing about it. "This must be a problem for those other people, not for us. We're peaceful here." Years passed. We heard of other incidents, of violence in other towns, in Tambo, in Uchuraccay. We heard rumors that the communists were everywhere, in all of the pueblos. My customers and friends began to tell me things. Matters might get worse, they said. It might be a good idea to move to the city.

"What? Are you crazy?" I answered.

One night around midnight, in 1981 I think, a truck pulled up to the restaurant.[6] It was the rainy season and raining hard. Men got down from the truck. They looked like they were in disguise, wearing ponchos and chullos [an Andean hat that resembles a ski hat], *clothing used*

only by people of the puna, *people who would not be driving a truck. I was pretty surprised by their appearance, but thought they must be traveling to the tropical forest for the coffee harvest.*

They came into the restaurant and ordered food, but they spoke like soldiers, yelling, "Damn it, serve us quickly!"

"How strange," I thought, surprised because our waiters, our muchachos, *were very quick.*

Lots of men came into the restaurant and began eating. They were armed and placed guards at the door to watch for the guardias, the police. "We're comrades, compañeros," *they told me. They were* terrucos.

"They say you serve food to the guardias. *Take care, you're a marked man, damn it, and you'd better stop serving those shits. Pretty soon we're going to bomb your restaurant. You'd better escape before something happens."*

They ate quickly and refused to pay. "Forget the check!" they said.

"Forget the check?"

"Yeah, we're like that! Forget the check!"

I left it at that and told them, "Help yourselves."

Then they left. They didn't take more than five minutes to eat. Just five minutes. The leaders yelled at their men to hurry up. "Get into the truck," they shouted. That's how it was, compadre. *They left with those words to stop serving policemen.[7]*

From the moment those men threatened me, I was upset, thinking, thinking. The police guarding the TV antenna on the mountaintop came into the restaurant every afternoon for lunch. "This is a public business and I have to serve everyone!" I thought to myself. "Maybe my business will be destroyed. What will happen? Where can I go?"

"They were always killing people in restaurants," Fortunata interjected, "always."

That's right, they killed people in other restaurants and also along the roads. I knew I couldn't remain in that place. It was painful to leave my business, but I value my family more. I might have to go barefoot, to wander without anything, I thought, but my life and the lives of my wife and children were more important. My business was nothing in comparison. I was also afraid that my children might get caught up in terrorism.

I decided to go to the tropical forest and look for something there. I left on an exploratory trip and bought some land. When I returned I told my wife, "Don't worry. We'll move our business to the selva *and be okay." But before we moved the war broke out in the very area where I had bought the land. The military demolished the place, killing lots of people. I had bought the land for nothing.*

My wife's parents had a farm in another part of the tropical forest **Anastasio** *and I said to my wife, "Let's stay with them and we'll see what we can see." We went to help them in the coffee harvest, but my little ones weren't accustomed to the climate and it hit them hard. Beatriz almost died. She was sick, very sick. Her little body began to swell. We were very worried, worried for our children, anxious. We took her to the medical post, but it was closed.*

"Maybe we're going to lose Beatriz."

"I couldn't walk," Beatriz interrupted. "I just stayed in bed."

My kids were used to eating the food in our restaurant, steak and cheese, but the tropical forest food was too different. My little José, he was just a little kid. He cried and wouldn't eat.

"I wanted steak," José laughed, "and we had finished the case of crackers we had brought. We had no bread left! I didn't want to eat."

They all joined his laughter, grateful to have survived. José's expectation of steak is unusual for Andean children. Few rural adults, not to mention children, eat steak, crackers, or bread. Instead of eating a slaughtered animal, most peasants sell the flesh for cash to purchase medicines, clothing, school supplies, or staples such as noodles, rice, beans, or coca leaves. José and Beatriz were children of prosperous restaurant owners and herders.

I wasted a lot of effort and money trying to escape from the terrucos back then. I just kept spending money for nothing. We had heard that San Pedro was calm, that Ayacucho had returned to normal, but I still worried about our safety. I thought of my children more than anything. My customers wanted us to reopen the restaurant, but the terrucos had warned us to stop. But we were worried about Beatriz's health.

We returned to Rumi Puquio sometime in '82, after only about three months in the tropical forest. We had left our things in Rumi Puquio, cared for by my father. Life was peaceful, but I still worried. I continued to hear rumors that the terrucos *were organizing local communities.*

"Maybe they'll come here," I thought. "Maybe we should go directly to Huancayo or to Lima."

My customers told me, "Don't pay attention to these rumors. Just work, that way you'll get ahead."

But I was uncomfortable. After we had been home about three months [probably early 1983], *a young neighbor by the name of Víctor began to organize a Shining Path group. His brother, who lived in the puna above Tambo, was involved with the communists and took Víctor to their meetings. Víctor became a supporter and returned to Rumi Puquio, infecting our neighbors with ideas. At first one, then another secretly went to the meetings near Tambo. Víctor finally told us that he wanted to organize a group in Rumi Puquio, that he wanted to fight for our community, for our Peru. I was opposed. He was an uneducated* campesino *and hardly spoke Spanish. He knew nothing and was capable of believing anything.*

"How old was he?" I asked.

About twenty-eight or thirty years old. Shining Path made him a leader of the group in Rumi Puquio. I didn't know them, but terrucos *came to supervise him, to see what was happening. One of them came to live in Rumi Puquio and began to hold meetings almost every afternoon, first in Víctor's house, then in the house of his cousins. At first only a few people attended, but little by little everybody joined except my family.*

I was lieutenant governor, teniente gobernador, *the chief government official in Rumi Puquio. The post put me at risk.*

"There won't be any more officials," they said. "Nobody is going to tell anyone else what to do because we are the new leaders." *They taught the people this, planting the idea. Neighbors began to look at me suspiciously, thinking I might do something against them.*

The terrucos *wanted me to join them, to become a leader in their group, the president of the communist* barrio. *I began to think, "They want me to lead the group, but I'm opposed to it. I don't want to be part of a group that's against my neighbors, against humanity. That's not me!" I'm an evangelical Christian. For me God is ever-present. God wants a* pueblo *to be peaceful and tranquil. I can't be against anybody—because I am a Christian and have to respect my Creator, God.*

"But what made you decide differently from your neighbors?" I asked. "Weren't they evangelicals too?"

Momentito, compadre, just a minute.

Rushing to the rear of the house, Anastasio returned with a tract in Spanish from the Watchtower Society, the publishing arm of

Anastasio

36 Bible study: learning to read in Quechua (and Spanish)

Jehovah's Witnesses. Opening it, he pointed to a section of biblical excerpts that the pamphlet claimed demonstrated that communism is evil. He read various passages of the Hebrew and Christian Testaments, including Isaiah, Chapter 10, verses 6–7, that rail against sinful rebels. After a long biblical discussion, which I found tedious, he continued.

There it is, compadre. I consult the Bible, the word of the Lord, for advice on everything, and the Bible says communism is wrong, a product of Satan. My neighbors in Rumi Puquio were ignorant campesinos, unable to read, easy to convince. I would tell them that these groups do not come from God, but come from humanism, from the devil. They didn't listen to me until it was too late. Some were evangelical converts, but not fully, not with all their heart. Perhaps if I hadn't received the word of the Lord fully, I too would have fallen to these groups.

Anastasio had first converted to Presbyterianism in San Pedro in the 1970s, but in 1999 he attended the Assembly of God church in Santa Anita. I did not tell him that the Bible long predates modern communism and could not have any comment on it, but even if I had, he would not have believed me. To Anastasio the Bible represented authoritative truths that dealt with the present and future, as well as the past. He had no doubt that the texts referred to communism in general and to Shining Path in particular, beliefs that also sustained resistance to Shining Path in other areas of Peru.[8]

The terrucos *didn't leave anybody in peace. They held meetings three or four times a week, inviting my neighbors, inviting me, and trying to make me do what they wanted. I avoided the whole thing by going into San Pedro and other places. Only my wife and children remained at home.*

I spoke to my wife and told her to go to the meetings in order to see what they were up to. "Make yourself agreeable to them," I told her. She attended with my son, who was still a child, only six years old. She went night after night, feigning interest. "My husband is ill," she told them. "He has a bad case of food poisoning; that's why I'm here instead of him."

At first they believed her, saying, "He'll have to come himself when he's better." Then they sent emissaries, comisiones, to tell me I had to attend, but I pretended to be sick, walking as if I were sick. The emissaries became very forceful, but I remained calm, the way I usually am.

"I'll go to the next meeting," I told them, trying to put them off. "I'll go to the next meeting."

When I didn't join or attend the meetings, they began to see me as a rival, an enemy, and began to mobilize people against me, against my parents, my cousins, the whole Huamán family. I heard this through gossip, through people talking. I warned my brothers and sisters not to get involved with the terrucos, that we couldn't let ourselves be coerced by their words. I organized my family, spoke to my mother, my father. I had to convince them.

"No," I told my father, "we can't stay here. I remained here for you and the rest of the family. I would've gone to Huancayo or Lima if it hadn't been for that. However I manage it, I have to elude the terrucos, going from here to there to confuse them, skipping around like a goat. These people are convincing our neighbors. They know we disagree with them and are giving us looks. They're planning to seize us to try and make us join their group. We have to leave the house at night."

We pretended to be sleeping in the house, but began to sleep in the fields, moving from ravine to ravine every night. My little ones were with us. They couldn't cry; they had to be silent. It was the rainy season. We covered ourselves with plastic and a tarp, one of those used to cover the back of a truck, trying to keep ourselves dry and warm, but it was still cold, often close to freezing. Just before daybreak we returned to the house, acting as if we had awakened normally, getting ready for the day as if we had slept there. That's how it was, night after night, suffering like that, trying to escape. We kept moving around, doing one thing after another to fool them. We hid our valuables in a hole dug into the side of a ravine, making the opening so narrow that neighbors could never find it.

Moved by her father's account, Beatriz, very animated, cut in. "The rain made the way very slippery, padrino," she said, turning to me. "We hid whenever we saw the lights of a truck. We thought, 'It's the *terrucos!* They'll see us!' We covered ourselves with plastic when it rained. That's how we slept, my dad making little huts in the night, all of us waking up at 4:00 or 4:30 in the morning, taking down the hut, and returning home to sleep in order to fool our neighbors who came to spy. 'It's true,' they would think, 'they're sleeping in their house.' But it was a lie, and the next night we'd be sleeping somewhere else again. That's how it was, padrino! That's how it was!"

Refugees living in the city of Huancayo had told me similar stories of sleeping in the fields at night to escape both Shining Path and the military. Moved by these memories and Beatriz's account, I exclaimed, "Horrible! Horrible! I can't imagine it."

The organizers of the group had set a final date for me to come to their meeting, Anastasio continued, pleased with Beatriz's comments. *But the Lord helped me escape. On the very day they had appointed as my final day, I went to get firewood and, on my return home, I fell and injured myself. I was walking along a narrow path at the side of a steep ravine, lugging a full load of wood on my back, carrying it in a shawl, a* manta, *the way we usually carry such a load. A piece of the wood knocked and loosened a huge boulder, causing me to lose my balance and to slip down the slope. I hit my head against a pointed rock, but God saved me from falling into the ravine. I was just a foot or so from the abyss, but the axe I had tied to the load caught in the earth and stopped my descent.*[9]

I lay there, dizzy and in shock. After a bit I realized I was lying on top of my own blood and that it was pouring out of my forehead. I still have the scar, Anastasio said, pointing to the visible evidence of his story on his forehead.

I also ripped open a leg bone. My dog was at my side, my companion, licking my blood, cleaning me up, taking care of me. I got up, all cut and broken, blood falling like water, exhausted and dizzy at the edge of the precipice. I untied my load, leaving most of the firewood, and slowly limped home. I frightened my wife. She cried when she saw me.

The Lord devised this plan to save me. That very evening I was supposed to go to the meeting of this group of communists. They had appointed one of my neighbors as an emissary to take me to their meeting, using force if necessary. They thought I might be faking my illness, but when the emissary arrived, he found me in bed.

"It's true! You're in a bad way! What happened?"

"See how I am," I told him, "all covered with blood. I fell into a ravine and can't go to the meeting, but my wife can go."

He believed me. "Until you're better, you have to stay home."

Anastasio

The head of the group had told him to bring me to the meeting, say-
ing that they were going to make me a leader in their group. That's
what he told me. The accident was my salvation. I thank God. He saved
me by making me fall and injure myself. The emissaries kept returning
to see how I was healing. A friend of ours had begun to tell us every-
thing they were up to, so we knew their intentions.

I thought, "When I get better, they'll come back, take me captive,
and make me go to their meeting. I can't do that; I can't be involved
with them. I have to get out of here." I thought and thought and de-
vised a plan. "I'll leave here and tell them I went to Ayacucho City."
That's what I said to myself.

I reached an agreement with my wife while our children listened.
"I'm going to leave and stay with my padrino, my godfather, in a ham-
let near San Pedro," I told them. "Tell everybody that I got much worse
and went to the hospital in Ayacucho City. If those men come looking
for me, tell them that, but I'm really going to our padrino's house."

I left for his house around 1:00 in the morning, traveling at night
to keep people from seeing me. Nobody saw me leave, nobody, not
even the cats and dogs. I was carrying an unfinished shawl to weave.
As I reached the steep drop on the path, the one farthest from my house,
the moon disappeared and a fog covered me and everything else, turn-
ing the night pitch black. I couldn't see the rocks or trees and could
walk only by imagining the path. The wind began to blow, whistling
through the trees, growing fierce, howling everywhere, lifting up the
earth.

I carried the Bible in my hand, the words of the Lord giving me cour-
age. That's how I made my way. "Nothing will happen to me," I thought,
gripping the Bible to my chest. "The angels will take care of me."

Anastasio's fear is understandable. Night brings not only darkness, but also deceitful shadows that heighten the risk of negotiating
narrow mountain paths wrested from steep precipices. In 1983 rov-
ing bands of soldiers, guerrillas, and thieves increased the danger,
making the trip very scary indeed.

"All your hair stood on end," José added, laughing.

That's true, compadre. I felt terrible, my hair standing on end, my
face tingling, looking monstrous. I thought a phantom might be com-
ing along the path and remembered what my mother had told me
about the phantoms that existed in the time of our ancestors.

"You have to be very astute when you encounter night phantoms,"
she had told me. "You need to take precautions. They travel only along
the regular path, so whatever may happen will happen only on the
path."

I quickly jumped above the path, and at that moment thunder crashed all around me, thunder so great that it flattened the sand and the rocks. It was like a hurricane. My skin and face tingled even more. It felt like my body had changed form. I knelt to the ground, turning my back to the path, grabbing my Bible to my chest. I prayed, reciting the "Our Father," asking the Creator for help. I prayed and prayed and prayed. The thunder grew closer, passing right behind me. Everything shook, like the back of an old burro. This phantom, this corpse that travels at night, nearly carried me with him, but I remained praying, praying, praying. Keeping calm in my faith.

Before the thunder began, an animal that we call huejocho, *a bird that travels with the phantom, whistled loudly three times. I don't know how it makes the sound but it makes the body tremble. This is what happened to me.*

Anastasio

By "phantoms" Anastasio was surely referring to *manchachicos,* feared by everybody. San Pedrinos draw on a rhetoric of *manchachico* encounters (see Chapter 5), and Anastasio's account makes use of that tradition here.

Little by little, the wind and hurricane died down. The birds began to sing and whistle in the fields. As I continued down the path, just below where I had been, I found two bodies behind a little tree, a bush, really. A man and a woman! Dead! Shot! I was stunned once again. I passed to their side, saying good-bye to them, and continued my journey. I don't know what happened that night, what took place. I was alone in a peaceful area of San Pedro, a place where nobody lives.

Were they killed by *terrucos?*

Compadre, it's probable that some terruco *killed that night, but I don't know. We later heard that two men had fought and one of them killed the other man and the woman, but I don't know what happened.*

Anastasio's account of the storm and phantom and two dead bodies is absent from his 1996 version of the story, a surprising omission. My guess is that he had combined two separate events into one, a fairly common trick of memory.[10]

I continued my journey and finally arrived at the hamlet just as the cocks began to crow. I felt a little braver. I reached the house of my padrino *very early and knocked at his door.*

"Papá!" I called out.

"Who is it?" he asked. "Anastasio? Is that you?"

"Yes, Papi," I answered. "Open the door! Wake up!"

"What happened?" he asked as he opened the door. "What are you doing here at this hour? You must be crazy to come here so early. You frightened me."

"Yes, Papi, I'm here very early. I brought a shawl, a manta, to weave. Let me sleep a bit and I'll tell you what happened."[11]

He told my madrina *to fix a bed for me and I went to sleep. When I awoke, I told my* padrino *what was happening.*

"I can't stay in Rumi Puquio, Papi. Things are very bad there, evil, especially for my family, for my parents, for my cousins. I came here to rescue them. I can't stay in Rumi Puquio. People know me there; I have lived there so many years. They know that I'm an honest man, a sound man, tranquil and peaceful, someone who doesn't cause any problems, but now I hear the opposite. They want to kill me. I'm thinking of escaping to the city of Huancayo."

My padrino *began to cry. He was like my father and I was like his son. I always helped him whenever he asked. And here I was at his side and he cried. My* madrina *cried. "Where are you going to go, son? You have a family, children! You can't leave. I'm insisting on this. I'll help you. They'll have to kill me first before I let them harm you. I don't want you to take even one step away, not to Ayacucho City, not to Huancayo. Stay here with us."*

"That's why I'm here, Papi," I told him. "People are looking for me, and I want to hide out in your house while my wife and I arrange our escape. We have to get all our things out of Rumi Puquio before we can leave. We also need to harvest our potatoes." The crop was still in the ground, and more than anything I was concerned about all our work in planting and caring for the potatoes. We weren't going to abandon the crop for somebody else's benefit. We had to wait for the harvest.

"You can stay here," my padrino *told me, "but you can't work in the fields. You have to stay inside the house."*

"I have a shawl to weave."

So I remained in my padrino's *house, working on the shawl, staying inside. Sometimes I helped him. My family remained in Rumi Puquio. When they visited, they told me what was happening. My wife came on Sundays. The situation was getting worse, she said. Our friend continued to keep us informed of the* terrucos' *plans.*

The emissaries kept asking my wife how I was. I was in the hospital in Ayacucho City, she answered, asking them to help her with money, since we didn't have any. They believed her and raised some money through a levy for my hospital stay. But they were angry that I had left. "We have our own hospital and would have taken your husband there," they told my wife. "We have medicines." But they also came looking for me in San Pedro, thinking that I might be hiding. They didn't find me.

There I was at my padrino's *house, weaving the shawl, waiting until we could rescue our possessions and harvest our crop. I also was*

thinking about what to do. Day and night I was thinking, sketching out
plans. "How am I going to rescue all my family?"

My padrino *didn't want us to go to Huancayo, so I decided that I first had to find a place to live. I finally found a house in San Pedro and sent word to my mother that I wanted to see her. "I've found a place to buy," I told her when she visited. "If you can help pay for it, help me, but if not, I'll do whatever it takes to buy it. I can manage."*

"Whatever I have I'll use to help you," she answered.

My mother gave me a small part of the money and we bought the house. My father didn't know what we were doing. My father! When my mother told him about the house, he didn't believe it, but he's living in that house right now. Anastasio smiled at the memory.

I still needed to rescue our belongings, our things. I thought of a friend in San Pedro with a truck. He was from my class in school. Anastasio
"Friend, do me a big favor," I asked. "I want to move my things to San Pedro and I could use your help. Can you do me this favor?"

He accepted my request and asked when I needed his help. "I need it done," I told him—here Anastasio paused for dramatic effect—*"at midnight!"*

I laughed uproariously along with Anastasio, his wife, and children at the absurdity of the hour. "Did your friend know why you wanted to move, *compadre?*"

No! I told nobody. Nobody knew what I was up to. I'm telling this story for the first time right now. My friend did it just as a service; he didn't know what was happening, what was taking place.

Anastasio's statement that he is "telling this story for the first time right now" comes from his 1999 narrative. Because Anastasio told me a version of the story in 1996, the claim could not be literally correct. The assertion that this is "the first time" he is telling the story can be true only once. His subsequent use of the claim is a rhetorical embellishment, a formula, embedded in his narrative.

We arrived at Rumi Puquio around midnight.[12] One of our neighbors was a spy. Even though she was a relative, she had been placed to watch us and let them know what we were up to. I knew this and planned to remove our things after she had gone to sleep, but she heard us anyway. We knew then that her group would know the next day that we had loaded or unloaded something in the night. We decided to work rapidly. My father helped stow my stuff on the truck and we took some things from his house as well.

It rained and hailed a lot that night. There was lightning, everything. We had to work in the rain and cold. A stream had washed out the road just before San Pedro. We couldn't cross and we had to get out of the truck, take off our pants, and go into the freezing water to make a path for the truck. The driver didn't have a pickaxe or shovel, so we only had the cover of a pot to dig out the rocks and debris. And it was still raining! The truck entered the water but stalled in the middle. We got out to push, making every sacrifice, using wedges to free the wheels from the mud.

"Give it gas! Give it gas! ¡Dale! ¡Dale!" we yelled.[13]

We were soaked, freezing, our hands icy. Just the three of us: me, my father, and the driver. We suffered a lot that night.

My mother was living in the house we had bought,[14] *so my* padrino *told me, "You'll go to live in your sister's house in San Pedro; that's where you'll take your things." She was in the tropical forest with her family, and her house was empty.*

By referring to his own daughter as Anastasio's "sister," the *padrino* was incorporating Anastasio into his familial network, a common Andean practice for godchildren and other ceremonial kin. I am called "tío," uncle, by the children of my godchildren.

We got to San Pedro to the little square in front of her house, looking like a traveling circus, all our pots and pans hanging from the truck. The guardias *had heard rumors about trouble and were on watch. One of them blew his whistle when he heard us and signaled the others with his lantern. They surrounded us, all of them well armed. "I'm from here," I told the commandant. "I'm moving my things from Rumi Puquio. I have a restaurant there and I want to set up a branch in town. Please understand."*

Employing what Peruvians call "*palabreando*," the quick-witted use of convincing arguments, Anastasio persuaded the suspicious commandant that he was not a *terruco*. He told him that he had good intentions, was an official in Rumi Puquio, a friend of the *guardias,* and wanted to collaborate with them.[15] Anastasio had learned that the *terrucos* were planning to attack the San Pedro police post and he opposed the attack.

This is my country, my patria! *I was on the side of the police. I let the commandant know about the attack, telling him that the police had to be careful, that the* terrucos *planned to kill all the* guardias. *At that time, the police weren't taking the proper precautions but were sleeping peacefully without posting a guard.*[16]

"Why are you so careless?" I asked. "Groups came to my hamlet, forcing me to move to the central town to escape their clutches," I told him. "The guardias *have to build a tower and keep watch."*

The commandant believed me and told me to unload my cargo. I had gained another friend. The next day I invited him to my house for a beer and told him what was happening in Rumi Puquio. He assured me that the police would protect me and that I should let them know what I heard.

Dropping his voice to a whisper to emphasize the danger, Anastasio revealed his collaboration with the police: *"What are those shits, those cojudos, up to?" the police asked when they came to visit. "Do you know anything?" And I told them what I learned from my family. My younger brothers were little and overheard what was taking place. They're doing this thing, that thing, they would tell me.*

Days passed, weeks passed. After one or two months the people in Rumi Puquio knew that I was a fugitive, that I was not in the hospital. They were furious. "How are we going to make the family pay?" they thought. "We'll begin by liquidating his parents and killing them one by one until the last one's dead."

Anastasio

"How terrible! These were your neighbors?"

Yes, even our compadres were threatening to kill my parents!

English has no easy way to convey Anastasio's meaning. He was saying that the children of his parents' godparents (for their marriage) were threatening to kill his parents. Because these children and his parents referred to one another as *primos*, or cousins, their death threats were especially reprehensible, made all the more dire by the great respect accorded marriage godparents.

"That's true!" José called out, still outraged. "I heard them telling my grandfather, my *abuelito*, that they were going to kill him. I began to cry. They had dynamite in cans, weapons in their ponchos, I was terrified."

Everyone cried, Anastasio continued, *my mother, my cousins, but my cousin stopped the killing. "Why are you going to kill my aunt?" he asked them. "She's your family! You're compadres, all from the same barrio! You don't even know what communism is! How can you possibly kill her? If you even try, you'll have to kill us too, because we'll fight you to the end! Kill me, if you're a man! Sooner or later everyone will pay!"*

His words turned things around. They voted against killing my mother right then. But the leader of the terrucos, the jefe máximo, who had come to supervise the wiping out of my family, the aniquilación, convinced them to kill my family that very afternoon.[17] *My wife, mother, and children escaped by bringing our harvested potatoes into San Pedro on a truck. My brother had already come to town to tell me what had happened. He had slipped out while herding his sheep, not letting anyone see him. Nobody was left in Rumi Puquio.*

"Who was this leader?"

We don't know who it was, or whether it was a man or a woman.

I told the police commander that the terrucos *were planning to kill my family and that their chief was hiding below the hamlet, waiting to take charge of the attack. I pointed out the hiding place and advised the commander what to do.*

"If you're really for the pueblo," *I told him, "you have to take immediate action."*

The chief called the main military base, the cuartel, *in Ayacucho. They sent a helicopter, and the local* guardias *left for Rumi Puquio in a car.*

"The Vietnam War!" José interjected laughing.

My wife and mother passed the guardias *on their way down from Rumi Puquio. The police were masked; they were* encapuchados. *Because the* guardias *began to fire too soon, the* terrucos *escaped, but the* guardias *prevented them from killing my family or doing something else. This was the first confrontation of the* guardias *with the* terrucos.

I continued to let the police know what was taking place in my pueblo. *One day, Rumi Puquio organized a soccer competition, inviting teams from nearby towns. A lot of* terrucos *and their leaders were going to be there. They were planning another execution, another* aniquilación.

"Who were they planning to kill?" José interjected.

Who? Anastasio asked, surprised by the question. *Who?*

He reflected on the query for a few seconds, almost as if he were so tied to the stream of his narrative that he had difficulty interrupting it, but he finally replied, *Who? Why, they were going to strike against our uncle Vicente, against our uncle Eleaso, against our family, against everyone. They wanted to make up for their failure to kill us previously. They thought to themselves, "The others escaped, but this time we'll get someone!" People told me this.*

I told the police what the terrucos *were up to, that they were planning to attack San Pedro and that there were going to be a lot of them at the soccer match. "You've got to do something," I told them, "at least scare them. People are coming from all over, and you can surprise them. Go on! Take them! Then you'll trust me."*

They believed me, and the military and police set out in cars and a helicopter, but most of the terrucos *escaped. The* guardias *captured only the* terrucos *from Rumi Puquio and the innocent people who stayed behind.[18] They brought them to San Pedro and questioned them one by one, but these people were really obstinate and said nothing. The* guardias *punished them and made them carry sacks of sand to build a bunker at the church tower but freed them afterward.*

My neighbors returned home wondering, "How could the guardias *have known? They stopped our execution once before. This is the second time. How could they have known that we were going to attack the guard post in San Pedro? Who's giving them information? Who's letting them know? They're not letting us get even one step ahead!"*

"You were an intelligence service!" laughed José.

Yes, I was an intelligence service in San Pedro, but the terrucos *didn't know it. They thought I was hospitalized in Ayacucho City![19]*

We all laughed.

After these things, days passed, weeks passed. I kept thinking, "How am I going to save my family still in Rumi Puquio, my parents, brothers, uncle, and cousins?"[20] My family can't live inside that terror! I can't abandon them!" I developed a plan. "Just as I brought down my things at night," I told my younger brothers and sisters, "I'm going to do the same for my father." I rented a large truck, and we took everything. At night, just like before. We took everything! We brought down my cousins, my mother, and all their possessions![21]

My father didn't want to leave. "I want to die in my home," he said. "Where am I to go? Where can I bring my animals? Where can I plant my crops? Let them kill me, let them do whatever they want, I'm not moving."

My mother and brother spoke to him forcefully. "What do you mean you're going to stay, that you're not leaving with the rest of us? We bought a place below. What can you be thinking? How can you remain here alone? We want you alive, not dead!"

Real stubborn, he answered them, "You go. I'm staying."

Anastasio laughed at the memory. "Your poor father," I remarked, also laughing. "But he was lucky to have you for a son!"

My father was really angry. He stayed behind, keeping a few cows and sheep and his dog. There wasn't anything else, just a small pot to cook in.[22] My old man woke the next morning all alone and very sad. He cried and finally decided to join us. He left the kitchen fire burning, using the smoke to fool our neighbors into thinking we were still there. Then he took his cows and sheep and met my brothers and uncle, who were bringing our herds from the high pastures. They took the animals to the lower slopes for the night, and the next day brought them to San Pedro.

When they entered the town, everyone ran from their houses to stare at all the sheep, llamas, cows, pigs clogging the streets, even horses with their young! They had never seen so many animals in San Pedro before. Everyone was crying—my father, the animals, even the cattle and pigs. My mother wept as she greeted them.

It was truly a great sight, and I had heard of it from other San Pedrinos in Lima, who had been amazed at the number of animals that had entered the town.

That night we celebrated, sometimes sobbing, sometimes laughing, embracing one another with great joy. I rescued my whole family: my father, my uncle, my cousins, everybody. The three Huamán families escaped with their animals! Nothing was left, not a thing. And our neighbors? They went into our houses and found nothing! Nothing! Only fleas!

We all laughed heartily as Anastasio said these last phrases, acknowledging his role and our great relief at the happy rescue.

We were the only ones to escape. All the other families remained in Rumi Puquio, caught up in terrorism. We heard later that they spoke against us at their meetings, angry that we had left. "Why did we let them escape?" they asked. "Why didn't we kill them when we had the chance?" They decided that if any of us returned, they would kill us straightaway, without discussion. We have not been back to Rumi Puquio since.

The days passed little by little. After we were in San Pedro about a year, they began to organize Rondas Campesinas in nearby pueblos. The town of Rumi Sonqo was one of the first to set up a militia, and once they did, they went from town to town to establish militias by force. They scoured the countryside, brutally killing people, burning their houses, stealing their animals and possessions. How many people have died at the hands of the militias, killed by knives, by sharpened staves? It was war. Everywhere! People couldn't defend themselves.

The Rumi Sonqo militia attacked Rumi Puquio. It was harvest time. Families were making freeze-dried potatoes; their houses were filled with harvested crops, the animals well fed. Everything was peaceful, so people didn't flee when the militia arrived. They remained in their houses, in their fields. They were foolish, no? I thought ahead, planning how to get out, but they didn't. They paid dearly for our tears. Nobody escaped. Everyone from Rumi Sonqo went, killing people with sticks, rocks, knives, whatever. They seized their animals, food, and other goods, taking them back with them to Rumi Sonqo. The people of Rumi Puquio couldn't defend themselves and were forced to move, brought down to Rumi Sonqo and San Pedro, made to live in foreign places without home, animals, harvest, without anything.[23] Anyone who resisted was tortured and killed. It was a massacre. God's justice is great.

After all this happened, my father finally thanked me. "You thought well, my son, taking care of your children, your family." But the people of Rumi Puquio cried. "Why did we have to suffer so?" they asked.

"Anastasio escaped but we lost everything. He lost nothing! How did he
know? His religion and Bible told him! We should have listened to him!"
That's what they thought.

"Your brother told me in San Pedro that the people of Rumi
Puquio are no longer *terrucos.*"

That's true, they've repented, they're arrepentidos. *In San Pedro,
compadre, I didn't open my restaurant as I had planned. There was too
much competition. But the food sellers thought I was going to do so and
were anxious.*

*"Mamas, Mamitas," I told them, "you're worrying about nothing.
I'm not selfish. Keep your business. I'm going to do something else."*

*One way or another, I managed to buy an electric saw, and with that
I worked in carpentry. I cut boards for houses, built tables and chairs,
made doors and lots of other things. I had a great many customers.* Anastasio
*Back then there were no other electric saws. I worked with my chil-
dren. José, he was just a little one, but he helped me a lot, just like a
grown man.*

*People came, arriving early in the morning, and I had to schedule
them: "You tomorrow, and you the next day." I was working well. People
liked my work. I cut firewood without charge for old women and orphans who had nothing.*

*"Grandma, Abuelita," I would ask, "why are you crying? Why do
you suffer?"*

*"Papi," they would answer, "my children are in Lima and my hus-
band is dead. When he was alive, I never lacked firewood. My fields
were worked. Now I have nothing, no money, no firewood, nothing.
Because of this I suffer."*

*"Here's your little grandson," I would tell them, as I showed them
José. "He'll cut the wood for you."*

*"How can I pay you?" they said. "I have nothing to give you. Surely
God sent you to do this kindness for me."*

"Don't cry, Mamita. God will pay me."

*I traveled throughout the countryside with my saw, going peace-
fully, not causing harm nor harmed by anyone. I trusted in God and
wasn't afraid, even as I stumbled on dead bodies. The military was all
over San Pedro in 1983 and 1984. These were killing years, a time of
matanzas. There were burials every day. It was dangerous, very dangerous. Mercenaries came to San Pedro...*

"Ah, when they killed Smiley," I interrupted (see Chapter 3).

*Yes, that's it. The mercenaries came and killed a lot of young people.
I saw them every day passing by my house with prisoners. One night
they took their captives in a truck up near Rumi Puquio and killed*

them. The cemetery was filled with dead bodies. It was terrible. Corpses were everywhere in 1984; people would find them along the footpaths.

I didn't want to live in the middle of that terror. I didn't want my children to see all this violence. I began thinking, thinking, and decided to go to someplace like Lima, where people weren't killing one another. Friends told me marvelous things about picking cotton on the coast, that it was peaceful, that there was work. I asked my wife, "What do you think? Maybe we'll find something better?" We went to Pisco on the coast to pick cotton.

When the violence subsided in the mid-1980s, Anastasio and his family returned to San Pedro, but conditions worsened again at the end of the decade.

San Pedro hadn't organized a militia, and in 1989 the militia in Rumi Sonqo and other towns began to menace us, saying, "We're going to San Pedro to kill people unless everyone joins the militia."

I heard that and knew that we were once again in danger. The terrorists had begun to organize in San Pedro, and I thought that the people opposed to the militia were mixed up in terrorism. Things became really oppressive. People were killed, and a lot of blood was spilled.

"I'm never going to find peace," I thought. "The same thing is going to happen here that happened in Rumi Puquio. We can't stay here. I know how to work. My hand is not broken. Even if it's just mixing clay, I will be able to get by."

My friend Guillermo arrived in San Pedro looking for peons *to work with him in Lima. I stopped him and we talked.*

"I want to work making retablos," *I told him. "I know how to do it, even if just a little."*

"Damn it," he said, "come with me. Don't stay here. The situation in San Pedro is terrible, but Lima is peaceful."

That's why I left San Pedro, compadre. I was really set with my business. People liked me, thought I was very good. Everyone knew me. But because of the violence we had to leave, and my saw is now stored at my parents' house in San Pedro.

"Let's go," I told my friend, and I took Beatriz and José with me to his place in Santa Anita. We had decided that, if we didn't like it after one or two weeks, we would return to San Pedro.

We worked day and night for Guillermo. At that time he didn't have much, not even a shop, only a room to sleep and work in. There wasn't much space. We worked at a small, uncomfortable table and slept on cardboard on the floor with only a blanket to cover ourselves. I slept in the doorway. At that time this barrio *in Santa Anita had nothing, no* electricity, no water, nothing, just rats, mice, and fleas. Sewer water passed right by us, stinking everything, giving us fevers and headaches. We suffered a lot.

We lived that way for several months. I was always thinking of my family, of my little ones in San Pedro. "How are they doing?" I wondered. My wife wrote asking for money, but I had none to send. "How am I going to manage?" I asked myself. "I can hardly get by on what I earn here, but in San Pedro they are organizing the militia and things are getting worse and worse."

We barely had enough to buy soap to clean our clothing, but I managed to save and sent her ten soles [about U.S.$3.00]. That wasn't nearly enough. We were all hungry. Guillermo discounted our meals and paid me two and a half soles a day [about U.S.$0.75]. He didn't pay José anything. José didn't know how to make retablos and didn't *Anastasio* want to do it, but little by little, we all became skilled.

By working and working we got ahead. I suggested to Guillermo that we buy a generator to work at night. We could get more done, but it was very expensive, so we arranged to run an electric cable from a friend's house. It was free! That way we were able to advance our work, earning more. We connected the electric cable to the houses of three neighbors, so they had light as well. We also ran a plastic pipe to get water from the big water canal. Guillermo began to buy the pots and pans he needed, a bed for his room.

He brought more people from San Pedro to work with us, my cousins, his in-laws, everybody. There were more of us working, but we thought it would be far better if we had an association, a cooperative, to organize, helping us get more orders. We talked about the cooperative every evening and became convinced it would be successful.

But I was worried about my family. My wife was having a hard time in San Pedro. She had a lot of expenses and was writing me for money. She also had to serve in the militia. I was unhappy. How could I bring her here to Santa Anita when I was sleeping on the floor on top of cardboard? But it was peaceful here; there was no violencia. I decided to bring my family one way or another. I told Guillermo that I was going to San Pedro to bring my wife and children and that I planned to get my own place to live.

"That's fine," he said. "Bring your wife and get your own room, but you can continue working for me."

I arrived in San Pedro the very night my wife had to go on patrol with the militia, and I went in her stead. I didn't like it one bit. It was so cold. "How can we live here?" I thought. "It's a good thing I'm taking my wife away."

But the military and militias from other communities invaded San Pedro the very next day to search for terrucos. They combed the district and made us stand in formation on the plaza, the first time I had ever seen anything like it. The plaza was full of people, from all the hamlets, from everywhere. The military went down the lines, one by one, using a list naming the infiltrators, led by guides who pointed them out. They took young men, muchachos, *right in front of me and beat them. I hated seeing that! They took them away in a car, I don't know where, but I thought they were going to massacre them, to kill them. There were so many* muchachos! *I hated it!*

I regretted not having come to get my family sooner, when things were more peaceful. "Maybe they're not going to let me leave," I thought.

I went to the governor of San Pedro as soon as I could to seek permission to leave. "I work in Lima and my children are enrolled in school there," I told him. "I came only on a visit and have to go back to educate my children. I can't stay in San Pedro but I'm not against the pueblo." He allowed me to go, and the military gave me a good-conduct pass. With that pass I left San Pedro for Lima with my wife and children.

In Santa Anita, Guillermo let us stay on a lot he had bought for his brother. It was an empty lot, but we took some adobe bricks and covered them with reed mats. It was just a hut, a chocita, *but it was our place.*

We worked for years together, Guillermo and I. We formed the association, but the first members returned to San Pedro. It was only later that we got permanent members. I finally told Guillermo that I wanted to work apart from him. "Give me the orders," I told him, "and I'll get the work done on my own, but I'll still be working for you." Guillermo didn't pay us well, but little by little we got ahead. One way or another I sent my children to school. They are now artisans themselves and know how to do the work.

That's my story, compadre. I hope it will help you in some way. That's how we came to be living here. It was very bloody in San Pedro, but we no longer see the violence, and I no longer worry the way I used to. One way or another, I have educated my children, and we have gotten ahead.

Conclusions

One of the 600,000 to one million refugees who fled the war,[24] Anastasio is rightfully proud of his successful escape from death and the rescue of his family. He clearly portrays the horror inflicted by Shining Path, its intimidation and murderous righteousness, as well as the violence of the militias. His account is filled with vivid detail

Anastasio

37 Rural Pentecostal church

and reflects the trajectory of the war and is corroborated by visual evidence and the accounts of others. I admire Anastasio's concern for his family and his steadfastness in overcoming conditions that could well have destroyed a weaker person. I feel privileged to know him.

Like most of us, however, Anastasio also exaggerates, placing himself at the center of action. He has sharpened and trimmed his experiences to make a story that he presents to others, and as in many such presentations, he reorders events and emphasizes certain things over others to prove a point.

Anastasio is telling a "war story," and, as such, his account illuminates problems in David Stoll's (1999) criticism of Rigoberta Menchú, the 1992 winner of the Nobel Peace Prize. Stoll critiques Menchú's autobiography, a widely read book and a prime factor in her gaining the Peace Prize, for not faithfully recording the history of her life or of the Guatemalan civil war that, beginning in the 1960s, devastated the country for several blood-drenched decades.[25] Like Anastasio, however, Menchú was not a historian but an impassioned advocate who elided facts and altered details to create a testimonial (*testimonio*) that appealed to a larger public, much as Garcilaso de la Vega had done many centuries before, when he created an ideal picture of the Inca Empire to protest Spanish depredations.[26] It is helpful to be aware of the historical problems in her account, but in his analysis, Stoll fails to explore adequately issues of memory (who remembers what and how) and the rhetorical changes in narratives as "war stories" and testimonials are melded into personal and political

advocacy. He, thus, commits the very error he accuses her of: the unequal marshalling of evidence to make a political argument.[27]

While I believe Anastasio truthfully reported his own actions and
thoughts as much as anyone can, I am uncertain about his assertions
concerning the thoughts of others. To what extent did his opposition to Shining Path color his assessment of his neighbors in Rumi
Puquio? Although Anastasio was horrified by excessive military brutality ("I hated seeing" the military beat the young men, he says), he
exults in his victory over his neighbors and generally privileges the
military in most of his account.

Was Anastasio paranoid in his early fears? This question, of course,
has a more general import: at what point in any society do fears of political persecution become not paranoid fears, but foresight? The gen-

eralized fears of some Jews, Romanies (Gypsies), and homosexuals in
early Nazi Germany at some point became realistic assessments of
danger and a thoughtful goad to appropriate action. Anastasio too
was perceptive, not paranoid. He was living during a period of severe
social disruption: student strikes, rural mobilization, agrarian reform, calls for revolution, and, beginning in 1980, armed rebellion.

Nonetheless, Anastasio also has created a tale with a beginning
and an end that accentuates his foresight. As we actually experience
life, it has no beginning and no end, but only appears to have a linear trajectory as we look back trying to explain how we have arrived
at the present. It is likely that, as he honed his story, Anastasio accentuated his early fears of Shining Path, ignoring other motivations
for his actions.

In the end, Anastasio was right to be worried. I was stunned by
the sight of the roofless, ruined houses in Rumi Puquio when, accompanied by Anastasio's brother, I visited in 1996. "It's still dangerous to be here at night," the brother told me. They had begun to
plant their fields, but returned to the safety of San Pedro before dark.

When I returned in 1999, again accompanied by the brother as
well as by Luisa, Anastasio's daughter, Rumi Puquio was still unin-
habited. It was midday as we explored the ruins in 1999. Our teeth
chattered in the cold, and I lent Luisa my scarf. She loved visiting the
hamlet where she was born, but was happy to return to the relative
warmth of San Pedro. And while she enjoyed visiting her grandparents in San Pedro, she was even happier to return to her home in
Santa Anita. Like many other refugees, she and her family are unwilling to return to live permanently in the rural sierra. Life is too
hard there, far from schools, medical care, stores, and other resources. They have made new friends and have a successful business

making the *retablos* that they send to international clients, using
e-mail and the Internet to place and arrange orders. Why should
they start over again? What would be gained?

I visited San Pedro again in 2004, chatting briefly with Anastasio's
parents and relying on one of their sons to translate their Quechua
into Spanish. They told me that Anastasio's sister had finally returned to live in Rumi Puquio. She repaired the tumbled walls of
their home and raised a new roof, as she once again sowed their
fields and tended their animals. Other people also had begun to return to cold and isolated Rumi Puquio, clinging to their homes, like
green lichen to bare rock, signs of hope in a sometimes barren world.

Anastasio

NINE

At the Margin of the Shifting World

In 1996, four years after the capture of most of the Shining Path leadership, I watched soldiers jog through the streets of Ayacucho City, chanting, "Terrorists, tonight we're gonna enter your houses, eat your guts and suck your blood, rip off your heads, and tear out your eyes."[1] The soldiers' chant was a chilling remainder that *Ayacucho* is a Quechua word that means "corner of the dead," the name derived from a site near the city that was the scene of a bloody pre-Columbian battle.

In Lima, three years later (May 1999), several events reminded me once again of Peru's continuing state of crisis. The first was a brief conversation with a taxi driver who was taking me home after my afternoon walk on the *malecón*, a spectacular promenade along the cliffs above the Pacific Ocean in Miraflores, a wealthy district of Lima.

"What're you doing in Peru?" he asked.

"Working on a book about Peru's crisis."

"Well," he laughed, "that book'll be very long! You'll probably die before you can finish it!"

A few days later on that same walk but on the isolated steps descending to the sea, a disheveled man threatened me with a broken bottle, yelling, "Give me your money, give it to me!" Terrified, I handed him my coin purse and he ran. Friends thought he was a drug addict, but I was not sure. He also could have been insane, a common criminal, or simply desperately poor: that same month, eleven adolescents were found living alone in a cave near the government palace, children who certainly faced a hungry and uncertain adulthood.[2]

Shortly after the robbery, I attended an elegant dinner party at the home of friends in an upper-middle-class Lima neighborhood. Like mine in New Jersey, their home exuded privilege: upholstered sofas, carpets, and art on the walls. Protected by bars on the windows and

38 Meeting of displaced people

doors, its thick perimeter walls bristling with broken bottle-glass (eerily resembling that used to attack me), and a private guard securing the street, my friend's house was very different from the children's cave and the homes of Martín Velarde, El Tigre, and most Peruvians. Guests at the dinner party relaxed, sipping pisco sours around three tables in an interior courtyard. Kept verdantly irrigated to conquer Lima's ash-dry desert, the courtyard was scented with flowering jasmine; crimson bougainvillea splashed down one wall, a sharp contrast to the menacing bottle sherds along the wall's top. "This is a special variety of pisco from an hacienda in Ica," the host commented at the end of the meal, as he handed me the national brandy served over ice made with purified water.

A distinguished elderly man asked about my book. He was a former government minister of the APRA party, the American Popular Revolutionary Alliance, which has populist roots (even if now significantly moderated) and is at least ostensibly concerned about the poor. After a brief synopsis of each chapter, I concluded by telling the five guests around the table that the militia in San Pedro had recently killed another San Pedrino and that a friend in Ayacucho City feared that various signs of rural unrest might indicate renewed Shining Path activity.

"No! I don't want to hear anything about terrorism!" the APRA official's well-dressed wife said, visibly distressed. Her husband agreed, and the conversation shifted to other topics.

I found the reaction of the woman and her husband understand-able. My Ayacucho friend's speculation about renewed Shining Path activity proved incorrect, but such rumors, driven by fear, as was the response of the woman, were common in 1999. Violence had racked Peru for more than a decade, affecting mostly the poor, but even the wealthy of Lima had been shaken by car bombs and dynamited power lines. Frequent electrical blackouts not only disrupted com-merce but also instilled a sense of general insecurity. It was frighten-ing to be caught outside during a blackout, as when dynamited power pylons on New Year's Eve in 1987 darkened the city at mid-night, sending me and other celebrants scurrying home.[3]

It was not always clear that the government would prevail. In 1983 I spent the evening on the rooftop of my temporary home in San Miguel, a middle-class barrio of Lima, gawking at the factories on the horizon set ablaze by Shining Path, the only light in a dark-ened city. As I stared at brash Lima chastened by the guerrillas, I imagined the final days of Saigon, U.S. partisans fleeing Vietnam in haste. When the police captured Abimael Guzmán, the head of Shining Path, in 1992, the country erupted in joy.

In 1999, a few nights after the elegant dinner party with the APRA official and his wife, the popular TV show *Laura en América* pre-sented a heavily advertised segment entitled "In Search of Peace." Valentina's children had urged me to see it, and we watched together. It was a retrospective of the war, providing interviews with widows, orphaned children, wounded police and soldiers, and imprisoned Shining Path partisans. Laura Bozzo, the star, called the wounded po-lice and soldiers "the heroes of the war," as well some of them may have been, but she mentioned no other heroes and depicted only Shining Path as committing atrocities.

San Pedro and San José, the many Smileys, the displaced people I had been interviewing in Huancayo, and even the complexities in the lives of those attacked by Shining Path like Anastasio Huamán and El Tigre, were being extinguished from memory. Ignored were the global demographic changes and economic policies that have so distressed the peasantry. Forgotten too were the wretched economic inequalities, the racism, and gender hierarchies that underlay the war's brutality.

Such selective forgetting often has hidden motivations and conse-quences. It is likely that "In Search of Peace" had been orchestrated by the intelligence service as part of the triumphalist government rhet-oric to equate any challenge "to its version of history with subver-sion."[4] Laura Bozzo was later placed under house arrest for having

been on the payroll of Vladimiro Montesinos, the disgraced intelligence chief of Peru's former president, Fujimori.[5] Montesinos is in
prison for corruption, and Fujimori fled Peru in November, 2000,
like Montesinos, accused of organizing secret murders during the
war and diverting public money to his own uses.

Unfortunately, the intelligence services have had some success
disseminating their views. Limeños, especially the middle classes and
the wealthy, have tended to focus on the terrorism of Shining Path,
ignoring that of the military. During and shortly after the war, many
Limeños, ignoring the costs, showed blanket gratitude to the military
for their successes. Rich and poor Ayacuchanos, however, remember
multiple versions of the war. They do not often speak of *el terrorismo,*
as in Lima, but of *la violencia,* a usage that permits a look at atrocities
on both sides. Although they refer to Shining Path partisans as *"los* *At the Margin of*
terrucos,"* the terrorists, they also speak to the brutality of the military. *the Shifting World*
"It was terrible, terrible," a middle-class woman who lived through
the war in Ayacucho City told me in 1996. "The military were the
worst of all, worse than the terrorists." She and others remember that
in the eyes of the military "to be Ayacuchano was to be guilty."[6]

Numerous human rights accounts have sustained the accuracy of
this more-nuanced view. In his preface to the Final Report of the
government's Truth and Reconciliation Commission, the president
of the commission concluded that there were two scandals in Peru:
"that of the murders, disappearances, and systematic torture, and
another [resulting from] the indolence, ineptitude and indifference
of those who could have prevented this humanitarian catastrophe
and did not do so."[7]

According to the commission, sixty-nine thousand people were
killed in the war between 1980 and 2000, a statistic that aligns Peru
with Colombia, Guatemala, and El Salvador as the Latin American
countries with the greatest number of human rights violations at the
end of the last millennium.[8] The commission attributes "54 percent
of the deaths to Shining Path, 30 percent to government security
forces," 14 percent to the militias and other paramilitary groups
such as the Rodrigo Franco Command, and less than two percent to
a guerrilla group known as MRTA, the Tupac Amaru Revolutionary
Movement. Because the militias and paramilitary groups operated
in coordination with the military, the 14 percent of the deaths attributed to them should be aggregated to those of the military, making the government responsible for 44 percent of the deaths. But
even this combined figure may be too low, for many disappearances
and murders went unrecorded.

I do not minimize the crimes of Shining Path. Its leadership employed the rhetoric of a "people's war" to consolidate power.[9] The accounts of Triga and Anastasio Huamán clearly illustrate the brutality of the guerrillas, a brutality exercised whenever they were challenged, resulting in the deaths of development workers and peasant men, women, and children. Indeed, the Truth and Reconciliation Commission lays prime responsibility on Shining Path as "the principal perpetrator of human rights' crimes and violations."[10]

Nonetheless, international human rights law holds governments to higher standards than guerrilla movements. When police forces and the military are themselves lawless, even while fighting a cruel enemy, and when they are abetted in their torture and murder by the government, that government compromises its moral legitimacy. These considerations apply as much to my own government's actions in Iraq and elsewhere as to the dirty war in Peru.[11]

The Popular Flood

The Shining Path war and other events that have shaped the lives of Peruvians are best understood as manifestations of the social revolution that the Peruvian anthropologist José Matos Mar has called the "desborde popular,"[12] the flood of people and culture that created modern, urban Peru. Spurred by rapid population growth and economic policies that impoverished them, many peasants shifted from full-time farming to more profitable commercial work, while others flooded into the cities. The accompanying social disruption, the economic inequality that became increasingly more visible and real, and the knowledge gained by formal education and shared experiences created a volatile mixture that generated support for ideologies that promised to mitigate the social chaos and personal distress.

I have always been interested in population issues, perhaps because, as one of seven children, reared in a crowded working-class home in Brooklyn, two boys sleeping in each of three small beds in one small room, I have experienced the difficulties (as well as the joys) of large families, especially problems of scarce resources. In the popular imagination, population growth is caused by individual women giving birth to too many children. That has not been the case in Peru recently, nor in much of the developing world. It may at first seem contradictory, but most Peruvian women were actually having fewer children during the rapid increase in the country's population. The cause was not that there were more births per woman, but that more newborns lived. Instead of dying in high numbers in the first five years of life, as in the past, more children lived to themselves have children, a demographic transition that began to affect Peru and the rest of the developing world in the mid-twentieth century. Because of this decline in infant mortality, similar to that which had shaken Western Europe two hundred years before, population grew exponentially. Even acknowledging problems with the accuracy of Peruvian censuses, the reported growth of the country's population from 2,699,000 in 1876 to 27,547,000 in 2004 is a spectacular jump of 921 percent, most of it occurring since the mid-twentieth century.[13] How can parents and societies provide for all these new lives?

It is necessary to emphasize that this rapid population growth has not been the threat to world resources some alarmists have proposed. A Peruvian born in the twenty-first century will consume far less petroleum and other resources and will produce far fewer environmental contaminants than will a North American born in the same century. At the same time, however, population growth has created a substantial problem within the country. As we saw with Horacio Gutiérrez in Chapter 3, Andean families have too few fields to accommodate all their children. The rapid growth, moreover, has created high dependency ratios; it is difficult to create viable futures for children when half the population is under the age of nineteen.

At the Margin of the Shifting World

Nonetheless, population growth by itself does not explain what happened in Peru. Although most of the Andean highlands consists of summits, cold high meadows, steep rocky cliffs, arid deserts, and eroded gullies, farmers could have expanded fields by building new irrigation systems and mountain terraces, technologies that Andean farmers have used for millennia to sustain fairly large populations. Unlike the Inca, however, who encouraged peasant farming, contemporary policies (both national and global) have done the opposite and have discouraged peasant farmers from expanding food cultivation.[14]

Peruvian governments usually focus policy on strengthening exports (especially the production of metals, sugar, cotton, and fish meal) and generally ignore the needs of peasant farmers.[15] With few and inadequate roads, peasants like Claudia Velarde struggle to get crops to market, often hauling produce on their backs or on mules for much of the way. As El Tigre complained, peasants cannot easily get credit to invest in new tools, seeds, and other farm technologies. Appropriate technical assistance to improve small-scale farming, animal husbandry, and local industry seldom reach them. "We'd like to start a trout farm, but need capital and help," displaced people told me over and over in Huancayo in 1996.[16]

Even the best farmers with good land lose crops to drought, hail, pestilence, and other disasters. Without capital or credit to sustain them after such losses, peasants are forced to migrate, looking for work, or to eat their seed stock and sell precious cattle and other goods, thereby destroying resources necessary for the next planting. Valentina Rodríguez and Roberto Quispe were plagued for years by debts caused by the failure of their potato crop (Chapter 5). I still do not know how the frail, elderly people, living in Rumipata managed to survive after the devastating hailstorm (Chapters 4 and 7), but it is likely that migrant children scrimped even more to send some support. It is also possible that some may have succumbed, not to starvation itself, but to diseases that can conquer a body weakened by poor nutrition.

Although focused on producing food for subsistence, peasant farmers also sell a portion of their crop to buy things they need, but the market is often stacked against them. In most years, peasant farm income has not risen as fast as the costs of the manufactured tools, clothing, medicines, kerosene, candles, and school supplies that farmers buy. On top of these difficulties, peasant farmers the world over must struggle against the unfair competition of artificially cheapened wheat, noodles, and other foods imported from the United States, the European Union, and other powerful states that subsidize farm exports and practice economies of scale.[17] Objecting to these practices of the major agricultural exporters, more than twenty developing countries walked out of the meeting of the World Trade Organization in Cancún, Mexico, forcing an early end to the September, 2003, conference.[18]

These external pressures on Peruvian peasants have been compounded by national economic policies. In the 1980s the Peruvian government also underwrote food imports, cheapening the food costs of city dwellers even more. These policies lessened urban discontent, but at a significant cost to peasant farmers, whose incomes fell. In the Ayacucho area, wheat had been a major cash crop, but Ayacuchanos could not compete against the low prices of the better-quality imported wheat subsidized by both national and international governments.

These constraints on peasant farming have affected different crops and different areas of Peru with greater or lesser force. Maize and potatoes often garner good returns, allowing peasants to sell their own crop and buy cheaper agroindustrial foods.[19] Some regions of the sierra, like the Mantaro Valley, benefit from fertile conditions, good transport, and proximity to Lima, the major market.

The poor soils and dry climate of Ayacucho, on the other hand, combine with external constraints to make farming both riskier and more difficult. Some years also have been worse than others. The 1970s and the 1980s were particularly bad for Peruvian agriculture, which suffered not only external shocks, but also political disruptions and the devastating climate changes caused by the 1982–1983 El Niño (Chapter 4).

It would have been difficult for Peru to have fed its rapidly growing population under the best of circumstances, but these international and national economic policies have scuttled any such possibility. At the beginning of the twenty-first century, Peru, once an almost self-sufficient agricultural country, imports 38 percent of its food.[20]

In addition to their economic difficulties, farmers also are aware of the better schools, markets, health facilities, and, during the Shining Path war, the greater safety of Lima and other cities.[21] In 1981 only 19 percent of Ayacuchanos lived with electricity, compared to 85 percent of Limeños.[22] Ayacucho did not have a single telephone in the 1960s. Until a new road was opened in the 1970s and asphalted in the 1980s, transport between Ayacucho and Lima was over unpaved roads, often blocked by avalanches and flooding in the rainy season. Even after the devastating Shining Path war, most government aid to the poor in 2004 went to Lima and its neighboring town of Callao, not to Ayacucho, Huancavelica, and Apurímac, the

At the Margin of the Shifting World

39 Washed-out road between Ayacucho and Huancayo

centers of the guerrilla insurgency and the departments most in need of such aid.[23]

"Stranger[s] and afraid in a world [they] never made" (A. E. Housman), peasant farmers responded to the possible and began to question whether it made sense to expand or even maintain their farms. Faced with increasing family size and declining income, they entered the commercial economy, either part or full time, or, like nearly every person in this book, sought work elsewhere. Instead of expanding irrigation canals, *serranos* have built school after school with their own labor, creating the infrastructure for the future mobility of their children.[24]

Although many remained poor, significant numbers of migrants to the coast, like Martín Velarde's parents, found relative prosperity during the 1950s and the 1960s. In the 1970s, however, they faced increasingly dire prospects, as national economic output plummeted and jobs disappeared. Encouraged by international financial capital awash in petrodollars, the governments of Peru and other developing countries borrowed heavily in the 1970s, often to purchase military technology used to repress their own citizens. These debts became a critical economic burden in the 1980s, when interest rates rose sharply (a result of tight monetary policy in the United States), inaugurating what came to be known as "the lost development decade" in Peru and throughout Latin America.[25] By the mid-1980s Peru's foreign debt payments soaked up 75 percent of its export income. Governments increasingly lacked resources for solving local unemployment and other internal needs, including the miserable economic conditions in the war zones.[26]

By the end of the 1980s Peru's economy was in free fall: 75 percent of the population was either unemployed or underemployed, and per capita income had fallen by 72 percent over what it had been in 1975.[27] As incomes deteriorated, so did health, and in 1983 eight out of ten children admitted to Lima's public Children's Hospital were malnourished, compared to half in 1971.[28] Inflation reached an extraordinary 2,775 percent in 1989 — so high that the price of food and other necessities rose in the course of a day, paid for with bundles of bills, each nearly worthless.

In 1990 Pres. Alberto Fujimori reversed his electoral promises and embarked on an extreme neoliberal economic course, embracing the International Monetary Fund (IMF) prescriptions often referred to as the "Washington Consensus." These aimed to open up trade and foreign investment. By presidential decree, Fujimori privatized government enterprises, reduced public expenditures, eliminated food

and many other subsidies, raised taxes, and increased tax compli-
ance. Prices rose on average by at least 280 percent: bread became
twelve times more costly, fuel "rose sixfold; electricity [and water]
twofold; and telephone rates fourfold." [29] Unions were crippled, the
minimum wage and rights to secure employment eliminated, and
many workers were dismissed from their jobs. Traumatized like most
people, Martín Velarde's sister-in-law (Chapter 4) spent the whole
night crying after the policies were announced, afraid that she and
her family could not cope in Lima. With typically mordant Peruvian
humor, the program came to be called the "Fuji-shock," memorial-
izing the name of the president.

After an initial recession, the economy grew strongly during
1993–2002, leading to increased trade and a plethora of international goods for those who could afford them. In the 1980s it took *At the Margin of*
years to get a telephone; they are now widespread and quickly in- *the Shifting World*
stalled, even in Ayacucho, for those with means. In Lima cell phones
are ubiquitous, even for the less well-off, who can use a phone that
charges the caller rather than the cell phone holder. Stores that in the
1980s were devoid of goods for the middle classes and wealthy now
stock national and global consumer goods: household gadgets, lawn
chairs, imported cheeses, fine wines, and Mercedes-Benz automobiles. But imported wines, fine cheeses, and luxury automobiles in a
country in which half the people are unable to feed themselves adequately is "a sign of sickness, not health." [30] The new tax burden,
moreover, fell heavily on small-scale enterprises, [31] while the rapid
growth of supermarkets in the new economy may add additional
pressures on peasant farmers, who are unable to meet such new
standards as perfectly round tomatoes. [32]

The Peruvian economy demanded reform, at the very least to
curb hyperinflation and to cut the bureaucratic inertia that blocked
the entry of numerous informal enterprises into the formal economy. [33] It is unlikely, however, that the neoliberal model of the 1990s
will improve the lives of most people, although the changes have
enabled the people at the top (including foreign anthropologists)
to live quite well. Average wages rose slightly after the reforms, but
the increase was not enough to make up for all the years of income
decline. In 1994 wages (adjusted for inflation) were still on average
50 percent lower than in 1980. [34] As Alejandro Portes and Kelly Hoffman put it, "with few national exceptions, to be a worker in Latin
America means to be poor." Social inequality, moreover, has increased, as unskilled workers have fallen farther behind and many
professional workers have been dismissed from jobs. [35]

These national and global economic and political forces have structured the lives of most of the people in this book. In the Andes, both "the poor and . . . non-poor . . . lead precarious lives,"[36] and even in the 1960s, people in Ayacucho asked me to speak to their poverty. "You will write about the poor of Peru, won't you?" Teodosio interrupted me as I danced the *huayno* during his friend's birthday party in San José in 1966. He was drunk, as one usually becomes at such events, but he was earnest and insistent. Juan joined him. "You will write about the poor, not the rich," they insisted one after the other. "Maybe then the United States will learn something about Latin America, because most of Latin America is poor, not rich."

VOICES FROM THE
GLOBAL MARGIN

When I arrived in 1966, few adults in San Pedro or San José could speak Spanish or read or write, but their children were attending school in ever-increasing numbers. Pablo de la Cruz and Claudia Velarde were economically successful as illiterate Quechua-speaking farmers, aided considerably by Pablo's trade as a muleteer and Claudia's petty commodity sales, but as the economy changed, so did the need for education. Horacio Gutiérrez suffered as a ceramicist without any formal education but managed to get by economically with Quechua and untutored Spanish. When Martín Velarde was a young field hand on coastal cotton plantations, he had little reason to seek an education, but as an adult he lacked the skills for anything but ill-paid menial work, and he fell further and further behind. Valentina Rodríguez and Roberto Quispe were among the early group of schooled San Pedrinos: formal education helped them and their children considerably. Education also underlay the success of Triga, El Tigre, and Anastasio Huamán.

The initial educational goal of most of the poor was to teach children to speak and read Spanish and to calculate simple sums in order to provide them with skills to cope as migrant laborers and petty tradespeople. The realization of those educational goals, however, stimulated desires for further social mobility, spurring children to become professionals: engineers, teachers, lawyers, government employees, and, sometimes, anthropologists. Peruvians, even the most humble, perceive education as a major route to social mobility and prestige. "He's educated—a professional," people frequently say of another, doing so in a manner that signifies both admiration and approbation.

Unfortunately, many Peruvians have been educated to perform work that has become increasingly difficult to find, especially after government work—a prime source of employment for the newly educated classes—was eliminated with the 1990 neoliberal reforms. Because of rapid population growth, most of the country is young. Even in 2001, when the rate of population growth had begun to slow, 53 percent of the population in the Department of Ayacucho and 45 percent of all Peruvians were under the age of nineteen.[37] These young people struggle to support themselves.[38] Disaffected, some were initially attracted to Shining Path, especially the depeasantized children of rural townspeople, who left relatively high rural-class positions only to encounter prejudice and economic difficulties in the cities. Shining Path, claiming that a short war would correct these wrongs, offered them and their less-tutored rural paisanos a panacea.[39]

As the economy worsened, more and more poor migrants worked several jobs, selling from pushcarts, touting lottery tickets in the streets, hawking peeled garlic cloves door to door. Unmoored by their poverty and the visible inequality around them, some of the disaffected also took to crime. Most, however, tried one brief job then another to fend off hunger. Martín Velarde's life well portrays this strategy, but Valentina, Roberto, Triga, El Tigre, and Anastasio similarly have had to jump from one occupation to another, "skipping around like a goat," in Anastasio Huamán's words, but skipping to keep the wolf, not Shining Path, from the door. *At the Margin of the Shifting World*

"Right now," Raúl Ramírez (Chapter 7) told me in San Pedro in 1996, "I'm dedicating myself to plumbing. If I have no plumbing jobs, I turn to carpentry. If there's no carpentry, I do farmwork. I do whatever I can find. If I'm in a river, I grab a boat, a yacht, a raft and operate that. If I'm on the road, I grab a car. 'I'll never be down,' I tell myself. . . . Even barbering. In Lima, when I had no other income or work, I cut hair. I didn't do it well, only so-so. That's how I've spent my whole life: going from one job to another trying just to get by. That's how it is, Doctor, that's how it is."

This upbeat statement, however, should not blind us to Raúl's pain and suffering. He could barely function when, depressed and traumatized by his narrow escape from the depredations of Shining Path and the military that had destroyed the life that he had made for himself in the tropical forest, he fled to Lima in the 1980s. Although he had rebounded psychologically, it had not been easy for him.

At first, Peru's diminished economy affected Raúl, Martín Velarde, and other less-well-educated Peruvians, but after the 1990 neoliberal reforms, the impact climbed up the status hierarchy. Educated professionals moonlighted as taxi drivers or, like their destitute neighbors, pooled the resources of several families into a single household. Many who lost work responded to the unequal international economic structure, in which Peru and other poor countries provide cheap labor and raw materials to the rich countries of the world, and fled the country for the United States, Japan, Europe, and Australia.[40] People earn much more abroad than they would in Peru. One academic colleague joked in the late 1980s about having to leave the country to teach in a foreign country in order to earn the income that allowed his return to teach in Peru. Remittances sent to all of Latin America by such international migrants constituted U.S.$25 billion in 2000 (less $2 billion in fees, for a net $23 billion), an amount greater than all the foreign aid sent to the region.[41]

Extensive commerce, migration, and education undermined other social relations in provincial towns. Farming requires community cooperation to build and maintain irrigation canals, to obtain labor ("I'll work on your farm for a day if you'll work on mine"), and to organize systems of barter and exchange. The fiesta system was central in sustaining this sense of community obligation. When labor was scarce, poor peasants preferred to work in the fields of those considered generous in sponsoring the elaborate celebrations honoring the saints.

With the decline of farming and the rise of commerce, production became far more individualized, and the fiesta system was increasingly viewed as an economic drain. How could people raise capital for commercial enterprises and the education of their children at the same time that they spent large sums on celebrating the saints? Many began to refuse to do so and to question Andean Roman Catholic tradition. Only patronal and tourist fiestas like Ayacucho City's famous Holy Week celebration have continued with any opulence, with sponsorship often undertaken by rich migrants and others seeking to sustain local commercial relationships.[42]

Those seeking to avoid costly fiesta service received support in Protestant belief, which condemned the celebrations of the saints. Furthermore, as we saw with Anastasio Huamán and Martín Velarde, evangelical Protestantism's prohibition of alcohol furnished an escape from excessive drinking while its focus on individual moral behavior provided an alternative to the social vision of Shining Path. Protestantism, therefore, offered a religious and moral alternative, another way to fashion a better society. Protestants also actively proselytized among the poor, while the Roman Catholic Church (except for the practitioners of Liberation Theology) responded tepidly. In the Ayacucho region, moreover, the Church remained tied to the old oligarchy.

In 1966 San Pedro and San José maintained rigid hierarchies. Local political officials, the police, *hacendados,* and other townspeople spoke Spanish, the language of power; peasants did not. *Hacendados* cemented hierarchy and controlled labor not only through punishment and other physical force, but also through a moral order tied to Catholicism and the asymmetrical reciprocities of godparenthood (*compadrazgo*), which linked them with the local community. "Dear godchild," the relationships implied, "I will help you, but you must help me too." In her story, Valentina Rodríguez clearly articulates the velvet glove of hacienda power, while other stories detailing hacienda control of irrigation, government, and physical force speak to its brutality.[43]

Although always constrained by limits on what priests could do ("I wouldn't dare interfere with their celebration of the saints," one San Pedro priest told me), the Catholic Church was another major source of order. The peasant leaders known as the *varayoc,* a group tied to the fiesta system and rural Catholicism, also were a police force working under the direction of the district governor to maintain order and to obtain peasant labor for compulsory work on communal projects.

As *hacendados,* the *cargo* system, the *varayoc,* and the Roman Catholic Church declined in influence, space opened for the entry of Shining Path, which promised a more just society and moral order.[44] The uniformed police, often abusive and relying primarily on force, were poor substitutes for the informal systems of control. Rural civic institutions collapsed even more during the war. Municipal governments, schools, and police posts were all but abandoned in many areas, leaving the military and the militias to reestablish order, and, as we have seen, they often did so brutally.

Peasants fled the violence, thereby accelerating the rural flight created by the economy. Between 1980 and 1991 the total number of people living in the Department of Ayacucho fell by 3.5 percent, and the decline in the farming and herding areas was an extraordinary 23.3 percent.[45] Some people left of their own volition (if one can speak of volition in a context of terror), but most fled the demands, threats, and killings of Shining Path, the military, the government-sponsored peasant militias, and the Rodrigo Franco death squad.

Conclusions

Driven by fierce demographic and economic pressures, numerous Andean peasants were forced off their land and pulled into petty commerce and migration. No longer able to live as did their parents, they responded creatively. Horacio and Benjamina devoted most of their energy to tourist-art production, supplementing their artisan income with farming and teaching; Martín left San Pedro to work as a coastal laborer; Valentina migrated to the United States; Triga tried Shining Path and the cocaine trade until he settled into petty entrepreneurship; El Tigre toiled in the tropical forest and on the guano islands and cotton plantations, then returned to San Pedro to combine farming with craft manufacture; and Anastasio fled from his "truck stop in the sky" to the tropical forest, then to carpentry in San Pedro, and finally to craft manufacture in Lima.

Life has not been easy for them. Themes of loss ("Adiós Pueblo de Ayacucho," a major departmental hymn), economic difficulty ("This year is worse than last"), dislocation ("Skipping around like a goat"), privation ("all beak and stomach"), and war and repression ("The military were worse than the terrorists") thread through their lives and those of other Ayacuchanos, many of whom, like the war widows, street children, and the elderly poor of Rumipata, have had even greater difficulties.

In *Globalization and Its Discontents,* Joseph Stiglitz, former chief economist of the World Bank, presents a damning indictment of the global inequities that have underlain much of this poverty in Peru and other developing countries. Like nineteenth-century empires, he tells us, the International Monetary Fund (IMF) and the World Trade Organization have opened the developing world to First World banking, trade, and investment in ways that ensure that the developed world "garners a disproportionate share of the benefits." In spite of the "repeated promises of poverty reduction," Stiglitz emphasizes, "the actual number of people living in poverty has actually increased by almost 100 million. . . . at the same time that total world income increased by an average of 2.5 percent annually."[46]

June Nash similarly has called attention to the ever-tightening squeeze of the global economy on peasants in Chiapas, Mexico; tin miners in Bolivia; and unemployed workers in Pittsfield, Massachusetts.[47] Gloria Rudolf has outlined analogous processes undermining the poor in Panama,[48] and in her in-depth study of the School of the Americas, Lesley Gill has traced the role of the military in sustaining these inequalities.[49] The Zapatistas in Chiapas and the fight against the privatization of water in Cochabamba, Bolivia, moreover, are just two instances of many in which people on the global margin have organized to contest neoliberal policies that are impoverishing them.[50]

On an abstract social level, we can predict that when intense economic pressures beggar large numbers of people, especially when the population is growing rapidly, then other troubling social changes are likely, including increased migration, violence, crime, and such diseases of poverty and crowding as intestinal disorders, typhoid fever, and cholera. Prediction of individual behavior requires different methodology. In the 1960s I could not have foreseen the particular trajectories of the young Valentina, the infant Triga, or anyone else. Because of social and economic conditions, they all had to do something, but the routes they took depended on opportunity, knowledge, and the confluence of life experiences and learned values that transmute into a person's character. Even so, they are not entirely free actors. Like the apothecary in *Romeo and Juliet* highlighted in the epigraph to this book, it has been their poverty—not their will—that has underlain many of their decisions to take certain actions rather than others. People "make their own history," Marx admonished, "but they do not make it just as they please; they do not make it under circumstances chosen by themselves, but under circumstances directly encountered, given and transmitted from the past."[51] So too they forge lives under circumstances dictated by the global present.

At the Margin of the Shifting World

Prospects

Like many developing countries, Peru is entering a period of demographic equilibrium. In the first decade of the twenty-first century, the number of children born each year will finally decline to replacement levels. Although the number of births will still be higher than in the 1970s, the rapid increase in population will have ended, and the proportion of young people will decline as the population ages.[52]

The open political violence (outside the drug-producing regions) that afflicted the country between 1980 and 1995 is also over. The rhetoric of Shining Path no longer captures the imagination of the young, and, by reinserting itself into local communities, the national government now fills the social vacuum that had opened with the disappearance of *hacendados,* the *varayoc,* and other local authority figures and that subsequently was occupied by Shining Path. The work of the Truth and Reconciliation Commission also has helped the country acknowledge the terrible devastation wrought by the war.

What has not changed is the unfavorable economic order that siphons wealth upward to the already wealthy and outward into rich countries mostly located in the northern hemisphere.

"Ayacucho little orphan bird/What has brought you to these strange lands?" a famous Ayacucho *huayno* laments, reflecting, like many of the department's songs, on the personal consequences of impoverishment. "Take flight," the song continues, "Let us return to Ayacucho,/where your parents weep at your absence./What were you missing/in your poor home?/Caresses and sweetness were given you in abundance./Only poverty in its irony wished to oppress you within its claws."[53]

The increasingly stark inequities that haunt Ayacucho and the global margin have stimulated not only song but also the growth of worldwide political movements seeking change. Opponents often trivialize these efforts by labeling them "antiglobalization," an inappropriate term to describe efforts by groups that actively embrace the Web, e-mail, and global travel.[54]

The term "globalization," moreover, is itself problematic. It directs attention away from the neoliberal policies that underlie contemporary economic change and creates the impression that these policies are the result of a politically neutral force outside human decision-making and control.[55] The contemporary discourse on "globalization," moreover, tends to accentuate recent economic change and to ignore the long history of global relationships. Ayacucho, for example, was incorporated into the nascent global system at least as early as the Spanish conquest of the Inca in the sixteenth century, which altered the ways in which people lived, spoke, worshiped, and died.[56] The exchange of Old and New World crops changed food habits and the distribution of population (imagine San Pedrinos without Old World wheat or the Irish without the Andean potato!). The exchange of diseases, epidemic smallpox, whooping cough, and measles to the New World and possibly syphilis to the Old killed millions. The transport to Spain of Andean gold and silver, extracted with coerced native labor, helped fund the development of European capitalism.

"'First, they took our silver, then they took our tin, they took everything,' [said] Carmelo Colque, standing outside his mud-brick home," during protests in Bolivia against the foreign sale of energy resources in March, 2005. "'The oil and gas [are] all we've got left. We Bolivians have woken up, we won't let them have it.'"[57]

Recent economic changes are not all bad: few would advocate a return to an Ayacucho without telephones and the Internet. It is not

40 Communal kitchen in Lima. Advice on the wall: How to avoid infant
diarrhea and cholera

change that is at fault, but its inequities, its damage to the poor, the
middle classes, and the environment. Today, activists in what is more
aptly called the "global justice movement" gather each year at the
World Social Forum. First held in the Brazilian city of Porto Alegre
in 2001, the forum has evolved into an annual conference focused
on creating a global system in which the needs of the poor and the
developing world are primary concerns.[58]

Just before I left Peru in 1999, I attended the anniversary celebration of a communal kitchen in Comas, a neighborhood that began
as a shantytown but that, while still poor, has been transformed by
its residents into an officially recognized district of Lima. Slogans
painted on a kitchen wall fronting a stamped-earth plaza advised
mothers on steps to prevent infant diarrhea and cholera. "Cleanliness!" was the mantra, a point emphasized by the care of the unpaved
street alongside the kitchen that had been tamped with water and
swept clean. This was the same kitchen where I had listened as women
came to agree that wife beating was unacceptable (Chapter 2).

The anniversary ceremony was to begin at four in the afternoon,
but the electricity failed. Participants were unfazed. "Drink up,
Sírvete," a friend invited as several of us shared a few rounds of beer
in an adjacent cantina, waiting as others rigged an electrical connec-
tion from a neighboring house. Four hours later, the festivities
began with lively folk songs and dances, followed by good food

and more beer. Laughing children created a ruckus, a sign of vital humanity.

The leaders of a group of displaced people from the highlands spoke of the war and thanked the barrio for its support in their struggle to obtain government and NGO assistance to help them return to their devastated homes and to establish a fund for small-business loans.

"Sing us a song," people called to me, "Canta." I sang "Swing Low, Sweet Chariot" after explaining that it was a secret hymn of freedom that North American slaves had sung to imagine a free life. People applauded. But the applause did not mean that they only imagine a better life. Like Frederick Douglass, they are not waiting for spiritual delivery but are demanding economic justice and an end to the economic roulette in which the accident of birth determines success or misery.

The devastation left by the war between Shining Path and the state has made it clear that violence breeds violence and increases helplessness. Inaction is nearly as bad. When the world looks bleak, as it does when I consider the conditions of the world's poor, I remind myself of the life-sustaining code attributed to Eleanor Roosevelt: It is better to light a candle than to curse the darkness. The members of this Comas kitchen are helping show the way, organizing to effect change, as have the activists who have mobilized in the World Social Forum and many other grassroots and transnational movements seeking social justice.[59] Rather than curse the dark, I focus on these efforts. They challenge me to action and help sustain my faith that the "orphan birds" along the global margin will someday fly free of "poverty's oppressive claws."

Notes

Introduction

1. I use "developing world" with reservations to refer to the countries sometimes called the "Third World" or the "Global South." None of these terms adequately labels the poor countries that are marginalized from centers of world economic, political, and military power and that are generally located in the southern hemisphere.

2. Webb and Fernández Baca (2002:228–229).

3. Coral Cordero (1994:23); Comisión de la Verdad y Reconciliación (2003a).

4. I worked in Peru in 1965–1968, 1973, 1974, 1980, 1983, 1986–1987, 1996, 1999, 2000, and briefly in 2003–2004. In 1983 and 1986–1987, when it was dangerous to travel to Ayacucho because of the Shining Path war, I lived and worked with sierra migrants on the coast.

5. An anonymous referee of the manuscript.

6. See Starn (1991, 1994) and Mayer (1994).

7. Mitchell (2001).

Chapter 1

1. See Ansión (1989) and Weismantel (1997, 1998).

2. See Mitchell (1976, 1991b) and Mitchell and Guillet, eds. (1994).

3. Mitchell (1991a).

4. Usually pronounced *senal* in the Quechua of San Pedro.

5. I use the Spanish *tripas*, meaning "intestinal lining," in order to avoid negative reactions on the part of readers unaware that intestinal linings are used to make sausage casings. The English *tripe* is an unsuitable gloss, as it is called *panza* in Spanish and refers to the stomach lining of cattle or other ruminants rather than to intestinal lining. *Panza*, as well as beef meat, is often added to *mondongo*.

6. Weismantel (1988) discusses food and gender in the Andes.

7. The two-part sectioning of most Andean communities has long fascinated scholars. Benavides (1988) discusses these divisions elsewhere.

8. Orlove (1988) provides the only other description of Andean suicide that I am aware of in the literature.

9. See *Daily Telegraph* (2000).

10. In other areas of the Andes, *pongo* refers to a serf or peon, a usage not found in San Pedro.

Chapter 2

1. See González-Cueva (2000).

2. *Warmi qurquy* is also known as *yaykupaku*. Millones and Pratt (1990) discuss marriage practices elsewhere in Ayacucho, and Bolton and Mayer (1977) cover the Andes.

3. I do not know if this is a recent or ancient belief. Wife beating and the patriarchal domination of women was found in the colonial and early republican periods (Chambers 1999), but women may have had more power in pre-Columbian Peru (Silverblatt 1987).

4. See, for example, Van Vleet (2002). Seligmann (2004:5) also briefly refers to the physical abuse of women.

5. The concept of "doing gender," that gender is not the property of individuals but "an emergent feature of social situations," is helpful here (West and Zimmerman 1987). Gender is not a set of qualities that resides in persons but, rather, the conceptions and behaviors that people manifest in particular contexts. An American man's behavior in front of a mirror and his conception of himself as a man, for example, generally are very different from his conception when he lectures in front of a classroom or when he is in a locker room or with his child or partner. Men and women are subjective beings who construct their gender in specific contexts and in a variety of ways.

6. Behar (2002:ix).

7. See also Allen (1988:78–79), Millones and Pratt (1990:passim), and Van Vleet (2002).

8. See Babb (1989), Bourque and Warren (1981), and Buechler and Buechler (1996).

9. Coral Cordero (1998).

10. Kandiyoti (1988).

11. Harvey (1994:74, 85). See also Allen (1988:79, 119–122), Gill (1997, 2000:108–132), González-Cueva (2000), Lyons (2002), Nencel (1996), and Winifred Mitchell (1994).

12. Bourque and Warren (1981:108–110, 141–143) describe similar difficulties for all woman, but especially single mothers.

13. See Chambers (1999) and Latin American and Caribbean Committee for the Defense of Women's Rights (CRLP) and Center for Reproductive Law and Policy (CLADEM) (2003).

14. Coral Cordero (1998). See also Seligmann (2004:5 and passim).

15. A similar dynamic is found in Cuzco (Allen 1988:79) and the United States (Bowker, Arbitell, McFerron 1988:166; and Kaufman Kantor and Jasinski 1998). See also Bolton (1973), Bourque and Warren (1981:107–108), Gill (1997), Harris (1978, 1994), Harvey (1994), Mayer (1994), Stølen (1987), Urton (1993), Van Vleet (N.d., 2002), and Weismantel (2001:136–175) for other discussions of interpersonal violence in the Andes.

16. This biological conception of race had already been actively attacked by Ashley Montagu (1942), among others, but in the 1950s and the 1960s I unthinkingly accepted it. De la Cadena (2000) and Weismantel (1997, 1998, 2001) describe the more complicated Andean notions of race.

17. This change occurred everywhere except in the tropical rain forest, where legal indigenous communities, but not peasant communities, exist (Sean Mitchell, personal communication, February 8, 2000).

18. See de la Cadena (1998).

19. "The human development index (HDI) . . . combines measures of life expectancy, school enrollment, literacy and income to allow a broader view of a country's development than does income alone" (http://hdr.undp.org/docs/statistics/indices/stat_feature_1.pdf) The index ranges from the low of 0.1 to 1.0. In 2001, the world mean HDI was 0.729, ranging from Norway's high of 0.956 to Sierra Leone's low of 0.273. Partly because of the gender components of the HDI, Peru's index of 0.752 was high in comparison to the mean for all developing countries of 0.663. The mean for Latin America and the Caribbean as a whole was 0.777 (http://hdr.undp.org/reports/global/2003/pdf/hdr03_complete.pdf).

20. Although the "one drop of blood" rule in the United States creates racial divisions regardless of color, skin color is used when people are unaware of a person's ancestry.

21. Mitchell (1979). See also de la Cadena (2002:223–225 and passim) and Seligmann (2004:129–130, 148–160).

22. "*Chino*" refers to anyone who "appears" Asian, not just to the "Chinese."

Chapter 3

1. *Tayta urqu,* the mountain god, is similar to what in other areas of Ayacucho Department is called the "*wamani*" (see Isbell 1978).

2. Dean Arnold, personal communication (July, 2003).

3. See Arnold (1972; 1975; 1983:644; 1993) for a description of Andean pottery making.

4. The use of special cups during ceremonial drinking has ancient roots in the Andes. Inca ceremonial cups were called "*keros.*" See Donnan (1976, 1978), Sabogal Diéguez (1952), and Sabogal Weisse (1989).

5. See Caldwell and Findlay et al. (1990), Caldwell and Santow, eds. (1989), Cleland and Hobcraft, eds. (1985), Durand (1967), Glass (1965), Handwerker, ed. (1986), and Kunitz (1983) for further discussion of this health transition. Bourque and Warren (1981:89–90) discuss the desire to limit births and women's birth control strategies in two other Peruvian communities.

6. Coale and Hoover (1958), Durand (1967), Handwerker (1986), Harris and Ross (1987:100–102), and United Nations (UN), Population Division (1953).

7. Preston (1985:261–263).

8. Like many *serranos,* Horacio used "Lima" to mean not only the city but the coastal area around the capital.

9. Malcolm (1990).

10. Buechler and Buechler (1996); Friedlander (1975).

11. Stoll (1993, 1999) describes similar fears in Guatemala's civil war.

12. Mitchell (1999).

1. Once known as *barriadas,* squatter settlements were renamed *pueblos jóvenes* in the 1970s. See Lobo (1982) for a description of squatter settlement life.

2. Martín actually said "a little bad [un poquito mal]," reflecting rural Spanish, which often employs the diminutive to mean its opposite.

3. Quechua speakers of Spanish often enumerate years and other numbers by starting with the highest number and ending with the smallest.

4. *Chem-News* (September, 1990). See also New Jersey Department of Health and Senior Services (2001) for the health risks of lead arsenate. Robert Topper provided these citations.

5. See Wright (1990).

6. *Primos hermanos* are the children of full siblings. Martín's and Sergio's fathers were brothers.

7. See Altamirano (1984, 1992).

8. See Touré and Compaoré (2003) and Chapter 9 here.

9. Blondet and Montero (1995).

Chapter 5

1. In the early twentieth century elite *hacendados* in Cuzco, unable to see their own abuses, similarly differentiated themselves from *gamonales,* whom they defined as rural and abusive landowners (de la Cadena 2000:78–84).

2. Elisabeta had already assigned one field as *interés* to the eldest daughter, so it was not included in the lands divided by the five sisters. With respect to these lands, Elisabeta died intestate. See the following discussion of *interés* in this chapter and in the glossary.

3. Others become *manchachicos* when they borrow an iron implement and die before returning it to the owner. To some San Pedrinos the terms *manchachico* and *condenado* refer to different creatures, the *condenado* being more fearsome.

4. See also Seligmann (2004:79).

5. See also Millones and Pratt (1990:15).

6. Van Vleet (2002:575) and Harris (1994) discuss similar marriage patterns called *warmita suway* in Bolivia.

7. Millones and Pratt (1990:13) and Harvey (1994:72).

8. In the several histories of her life that she has given me, Valentina confuses dates and sequences in her early married life.

9. Inca emperors similarly did not inherit lands and wealth from parents, but had to obtain their own, an inheritance pattern that some scholars believe underlay Inca expansion (Conrad and Demarest 1984).

10. Mitchell (2001) discusses memory and life history.

11. Van Vleet (2002).

Chapter 6

1. Shining Path's full name was the Communist Party of Peru in the Shining Path of José Carlos Mariátegui. Mariátegui was a brilliant socialist and Peruvian intellectual of the early twentieth century, an early interpreter of

Marx for a Latin American context. See Mariátegui (1959 [1928], 1971) for his most famous work: *Seven Interpretive Essays on Peruvian Reality*, as it is known in English.

2. The literature on the war is voluminous, but see in particular Burt (1993), Chávez de Paz (1989), Coral Cordero (1994, 1995), Coronel Aguirre (1996), Degregori (1986a, 1986b, 1989, 1990, 1992, 1996, 1998), del Pino Huamán (1993, 1995, 1996, 1998), Favre (1984), Fumerton (2002), Gorriti (1990, 1999), Kirk (1991, 1993, 1997), Mayer (1991, 1994), Mitchell (1999), Palmer, ed. (1992), Poole and Rénique (1991, 1992), Starn (1991), Starn, ed. (1993), Stern, ed. (1998), and Tapia (1997). Reid (1985:106–121) presents a brief but excellent review of the war's early years. Burt (1998) analyzes Shining Path's move into the shantytowns of Lima.

3. De la Cadena (2000:191, 192, 311).

4. The earliest example in the *Oxford English Dictionary* of "disappeared" in the sense of "abducted for . . . political reasons and subsequently secretly imprisoned or killed" is a reference in 1947 to "disappeared Polish officers."

5. Ansión (1987) and Portocarrero (1998).

6. Del Pino Huamán (1993, 1995, 1996, 1998).

7. Reid (1985:114).

8. Forero (2004), Kawell (1995:403), Risen and Marquis (2001), Silverstein (2001), Singer (2003:15, 206–209, 220, 298), and Van Dongen (2003).

9. Del Pino Huamán (1996:169). See Gill (2004:160–162) for a discussion of the military abuses entailed in drug enforcement in Bolivia and Colombia.

10. Bowen and Holligan (2003:97–98)

11. Del Pino Huamán (1995:377; 1996:147).

12. See Gill (2004:161–197) for a graphic portrayal of the drug war. The chemical used in the aerial spraying is glyphosate, the major ingredient in Roundup. Although the U.S. government and the Drug Enforcement Administration (United States, Department of State N.d.) claim that aerial spraying for drug control is safe, the WWF (and others) believes that glyphosate and other chemical additives in the formulation "pose potentially serious risks to human and ecosystems health" (World Wildlife Fund 2001).

13. Triga's brother has given me a slightly different version of the massacre, saying that a policeman pushed him over a cliff.

14. Uchuraccay illustrates many of the problems of assigning responsibility in the war. Blame was first placed on the peasants, but competing claims and counterclaims confused responsibility, creating suspicion that the murders had been committed by military personnel in disguise. It is now clear that the murders were the work of the peasants (Asociación Pro Derechos Humanos [APRODEH] 2003; Fumerton 2002:80–85; Vargas Llosa et al. 1983).

15. As is to be expected, the figures on the number of *desplazados* varies, but I use those of Degregori (1996:16). The figure of 600,000, however, may underestimate the numbers, as people like Valentina and her family were never counted as *desplazados*. Coral estimates 600,000 to one million *desplazados* (1994:23).

16. Portocarrero (1998:73). Fernández-Salvatteci (1986:68–71 and passim), a retired military officer opposed to the dirty war, quotes additional remarks of Gens. Luis Cisneros and Clemente Noel, among others, to emphasize their brutality. Information on military and Shining Path brutality is voluminous. See especially Gorriti (1999), the final report of the Truth and Reconciliation

Commission (Comisión de la Verdad y Reconciliación 2003a), the many reports of Americas Watch and Amnesty International, and Poole and Rénique (1991, 1992). Generals Noel, Cisneros, and José Valdivia have defended themselves against the findings of the Truth and Reconciliation Commission (Forero 2003), and General Noel (1989) has written an autobiographical apology that defends his record.

17. Bowen and Holligan (2003:119).

18. Manrique (1998) and Portocarrero (1998:76–83), but see Obando (1998:388) for a different view. González-Cueva (2000) discusses Peruvian military conscription and its association with and impact on violence. See also Starn (1999:74–77).

19. Myers (1996). See also Gill (2004:212–213), Amnesty International (2002), and copies of the manuals posted on the Web site of School of the Americas Watch (http://www.soaw.org/new/article.php?id=98). Gill's concept of "impunity" helps clarify the processes by which officials escape responsibility for murder; see 2000:149, 159, and passim.

20. Gill (2004:49).

21. Poole and Rénique (1991, 1992). See also the many reports from Amnesty International and Americas Watch.

22. See Fumerton (2002:60) and also Degregori (1998) for a similar but slightly different explanation of the reasons that the rural young were initially in thrall to Shining Path. Stoll (1993, 1999) discusses similar peasant ambivalence about the guerrilla war in Guatemala, but see my critique of some of his conclusions (Mitchell 2001).

23. The saying is also found in Otavalo, Ecuador (Colloredo-Mansfeld 2002).

24. Coral Cordero (1998).

Chapter 7

1. El Tigre pronounced my name "Mitchaél."

2. Del Pino Huamán (1996:119).

3. Fumerton (2002) gives an excellent discussion of the militias. See also Americas Watch (1992:104–113), Coronel Aguirre (1993, 1994, 1996), Coronel Aguirre and Loayza (1992), Degregori (1998), del Pino Huamán (1993, 1995, 1996, 1998), Huber (1995), Kirk (1997:23–47), and Starn, ed. (1993, 1997). Starn (1998, 1999) discusses the Rondas of the northern Andes. Colloredo-Mansfeld (2002) provides information on community justice in Otavalo, Ecuador.

4. Fumerton (2002:122) notes other instances of the military's refusing to defend or help the militia.

5. Degregori (1998) and Degregori, ed. (1996). See also del Pino Huamán (1995), Starn (1992, 1997, 1998), Starn, ed. (1993), and Wade (1997).

6. See Americas Watch (1986), Amnesty International (1985:12–18), and Burt (1999) for discussions of abuses by the militias. Coronel Aguirre (1996) and del Pino Huamán (1996) similarly acknowledge Ronda abuses. Fumerton (2002:136–137) provides another example in which "the accusation of 'subversion'" was "a cudgel for silencing opposition."

7. See http://www.foncodes.gob.pe/.

8. See Manrique (1998). See also Coronel Aguirre (1996) and Fumerton (2002), as well as the many reports of Americas Watch and Amnesty International.

9. Manrique (1998:204, 202–211). Manrique puts "[they did]" in brackets.

10. This Manichaean vision was promulgated by General Noel, one of the architects of Peru's dirty war (Portocarrero 1998:69–73).

11. This was probably the attack by members of the Army of National Liberation (Ejército de Liberación Nacional), led by Héctor Béjar on an hacienda in La Mar province (Brown and Fernández 1991:172–173).

12. See Castillo (1999). Fumerton (2002) also has excellent material on the difficulties encountered by members of the militias.

13. Archbishop Cipriani, a member of the secret Opus Dei movement of conservative Catholics, was bishop and then archbishop of Ayacucho from 1988 to 1999, when he was named archbishop of Lima and subsequently cardinal. He condemned human rights activists in various interviews, calling them "useful fools" supporting "Marxist and Maoist" political groups (*National Catholic Reporter* 2001).

14. El Tigre and his brother shared patronyms, but not matronyms. They could be brothers through a common father or they could be *primos hermanos,* cousin-brothers (first cousins).

15. Like the taxis that line up to pick up a single passenger on the streets of Lima, several *colectivos* generally compete for passengers in San Pedro, and the driver who fills his jitney first leaves first.

16. The Sinchis, who went by the Quechua word referring to Inca military chiefs, were a special counterinsurgency battalion organized and trained by the United States in the 1960s. They had a reputation for brutal ferocity and "were feared, but also hated" (Gorriti 1999:145–148; all translations throughout the book are mine unless otherwise noted).

17. Fernandez (1990).

18. Del Pino Huamán (1998), Fumerton (2002), Starn (1998).

19. Malcolm (1990).

20. Arendt (1964).

21. A phrase John Conroy (2000) uses in describing torturers in Israel, Northern Ireland, and Chicago. See also Gill (2004:18 and passim).

22. Lifton (1986:418–429 and passim).

23. Coronel Aguirre (1996), Degregori, ed. (1996), del Pino Huamán (1995, 1996), Fumerton (2002), and Starn (1995, 1998, 1999).

24. See Coronel Aguirre (1996:84). Even del Pino Huamán (1996:147–148), who generally praises the militias, reports that at least sometimes they "killed" and "mistreated the people."

25. *American Heritage Dictionary.*

26. See also Fumerton (2002:120) and Starn (1998:240–244). Sengupta (2005) describes similar human rights issues in Nepal, where peasant vigilante groups are fighting Maoist guerrillas who have modeled themselves on Shining Path.

27. Fumerton (2002:140, 215, and passim) argues otherwise, focusing more than I do on the benefits of the "extirpation" of guerrilla forces by security forces in combat, particularly the *comités de autodefensa.*

1. Although generally called *chuñu* in Peru, Anastasio and most San Pedrinos pronounce it *chunu*.

2. See endnote 11, chapter 7.

3. It is unclear whether Anastasio stood accused of bringing in coca paste or the coca leaf. Although the trade in coca leaf is legal, he would have needed a receipt from the national coca monopoly (ENACO, Empresa Nacional de la Coca) to show that he was a legal producer. Without one, a truckload of coca leaves would be presumptive evidence that he was in the cocaine trade. Ayacucho is a major producer of coca paste, *pasta básica* (see Chapter 6), the first step in the production of cocaine and usually undertaken near the source of the leaves (Drug Enforcement Administration 1993; Rick Vecchio, e-mail, September 2, 2004). Anastasio was likely accused of transporting *pasta básica*.

4. In 1974 Anastasio told me that he and Fortunata had had lands in the government colonization project of Pichari in the tropical rain forest for at least six years.

5. In his 1999 account, Anastasio says that his *guardia compadre* told him that they were organizing the people against communism and that they were placing police in all the towns to do so.

6. It is unlikely that Anastasio and Fortunata's restaurant was open at midnight, but, like the innkeepers of premodern Europe, most proprietors of restaurants and small stores in rural Peru (in both town and countryside) will open in response to a potential customer's knocking. Their alacrity in doing so is one indication of their marginal income.

7. Anastasio's account of the *terrucos* in the restaurant is omitted from his 1999 account.

8. Del Pino Huamán (1995:379–381).

9. In 1996 Anastasio attributed his fall to a piece of the firewood, in 1999, to the axe itself. He might have made this change for rhetorical effect, for in 1999 he emphasized that the axe both caused the fall and saved him.

10. Schacter (2001).

11. In his 1996, but not his 1999, account, Anastasio says that he told his *padrino* that he had come to stay for a while and would help with the farmwork because he had fought with his wife and she had hit him. But his *padrino* was incredulous. "How could you leave your business? Your family? Are you crazy?" Anastasio then told him the truth.

12. Anastasio's 1996 and 1999 accounts differ, at least on the surface. In 1999 he speaks of moving his things shortly after arriving at the house of his *padrino*. In 1996 he places the move after the military attacked Rumi Puquio during the soccer match discussed later in his narrative. I use the 1999 account here.

13. "Dale" is Spanish for "Give it, go to it," and is frequently shouted by bystanders to urge a driver on in rural Peru.

14. Both accounts are confusing about what happened to this house, and I only surmise that his mother was using it.

15. He includes these detailed arguments in his 1999 but not his 1996 narrative.

16. This statement is obviously at variance with the alert police reception to Anastasio's arrival in San Pedro.

17. Or the next day. The account is confusing.

18. There are significant differences here between Anastasio's two accounts. In 1996 he said that all the *terrucos* escaped and made no mention of anybody's capture. In fact, he said that "this group just escaped." They escaped? "They escaped," he answered, then hesitated and said, "They escaped twice. It's true! This group, damn it, lives a charmed life, arriving at night and slipping out in the daytime. But I was in favor of the police. They gave me a good-conduct certificate." I use the 1999 version in the foregoing account.

19. Because Anastasio has already told us they knew he was not in the hospital, this statement is rhetorical.

20. It is unclear from either narrative how and why his family had returned to Rumi Puquio after the soccer game attack.

21. This rescue probably took place in July or August, 1983.

22. In 1996 Anastasio says that his father had nothing, not even a pot.

23. In his 1996 account, Anastasio emphasizes the killing, but in his 1999 account, he emphasizes the loss of their goods and farms.

24. See Kirk (1991, 1995) for other portrayals of Peru's internal refugees.

25. See Stoll (1999) and Menchú (1983, 1984).

26. Garcilaso de la Vega (1966 [1609]).

27. See Mitchell (2001) for an expanded discussion of Stoll's critique of Rigoberta Menchú.

Chapter 9

1. See also Portocarrero (1998:69). Although sporadic guerrilla activity continued in the tropical forest and other areas of Ayacucho, the city was peaceful, and my two sons were able to teach English at the University of Huamanga, where Shining Path had originated.

2. Chumpitaz (1999).

3. See Comisión de la Verdad y Reconciliación (2003b) for a graphic and gruesome photographic portrayal of the violence, as well as Chávez (2003), which focuses more on the devastation of Lima than of the sierra.

4. Burt (1999). See also Bowen and Holligen (2003:331–332), North American Congress on Latin America (2002), Vecchio (2000), and Wise (2003:240–241).

5. Laura Bozzo denies the charges, claiming that they are politically motivated. And the evidence against her is unclear. Her former TV bosses, however, were "secretly videotaped by Montesinos as they took wads of cash to toe a pro-Fujimori line. Montesinos dictated the content of the station's newscasts and, on occasion, the topics of Bozzo's show" (Vecchio 2004a). *Laura en América* has not been shown in Peru since her house arrest (at least as of 2004), but since 2000, the show has been broadcast to nine million viewers in the U.S. on NBC's Telemundo network (Vecchio 2000, 2004a, 2004b).

6. Most people I have spoken with echo that the military, especially the marines, were "worse than the terrorists," but see El Tigre (Chapter 7) and Basombrío Iglesias (1998:433, 441–442) for different views.

7. Signed by Salomón Lerner Febres, presidente, Comisión de la Verdad y Reconciliación, on page 1 of the Preface: http://www.cverdad.org.pe/ifinal/pdf/TOMO%20I/PREFACIO.pdf.

8. Council on Hemispheric Affairs (2003). The report of the Truth and Reconciliation Commission is available on the Web at http://www.cverdad.org.pe/ifinal.

9. Degregori (1989), Fumerton (2002), and Poole and Rénique (1991, 1992). See Díaz Martínez (1969) for the views of a major Shining Path theoretician.

10. Comisión de la Verdad y Reconciliación, http://www.cverdad.org.pe/ifinal, Conclusions, chap. 1, p. 127.

11. See Danner (2004a, 2004b) for an insightful discussion of U.S. torture of detainees in Iraq.

12. Matos Mar (1984).

13. Webb and Fernández Baca (2002:219).

14. The following materials provide insight into the economic policies adversely affecting Peruvian peasant production: Appleby (1982), Caballero (1981), Collins (1988), Crabtree and Thomas, eds. (1998), deJanvry (1981), Ferroni (1980), Franklin et al. (1985), Gonzales de Olarte (1987), Long and Roberts (1984:60–63), Mayer (2002), Montoya (1980), Paredes and Sachs (1991), Pastor (1992), Reid (1985), Ross (2003), Sheahan (1999), Thorpe and Bertram (1978), and Wahl (1996). Meillassoux (1981) describes similar processes elsewhere.

15. Figueroa (1983) and Hunt (1996:33–34).

16. It is important to note that such technical innovations have not always been helpful to small-scale farmers. Developed-world technical help to the developing world often requires costly seeds, fertilizers, and irrigation schemes, which have fostered the dominance of transnational agroindustrial corporations at the expense of peasant farming (Ross 2003).

17. Touré and Compaoré (2003), Alden (2004), *New York Times* (2003b, 2004), *Financial Times* (2004), Mayer (2002:234, 314), Tokar, ed. (2004). In June, 2004, "the World Trade Organization ruled against American cotton subsidies in a case brought by Brazil," a landmark decision that might force changes in U.S. and European agricultural subsidies (Benson 2004).

18. Choike (2003); Elliot, Denny, and Munk (2003); Tokar, ed. (2004); and Vidal (2003).

19. Blum (1992:256).

20. Altamirano (2003:208).

21. Altamirano et al. (2003) and Figueroa (1999).

22. Webb and Fernández Baca (1990:124).

23. Chevarría León (2004).

24. Mitchell (1994, 1997).

25. Hunt (1996:18), Nash (1994), Potter (2000), Stiglitz (2003:239), Thorp (1996:64), Wise (2003:143–147 and passim).

26. Paredes and Sachs (1991:35).

27. Hamann and Paredes (1991:77–78).

28. Reid (1985:98).

29. Boloña (1996:228). See also Chossudovsky (1992:13, 52, and passim), and Iguíñiz (1996:271). Published average price increases range from the 280 percent provided by Carlos Bolaña (1996), the principal author of the neoliberal policies, to Michel Chossudovsky, a strong critic, who says they rose 446 percent.

30. Stiglitz (2003:154). For other negative evaluations of structural adjustment policies, see Chossudovsky (1992, 1997) and Ugarteche (1998) for Peru; Gill (2000) for Bolivia; and Ugarteche (2000) for all Latin America.

31. Seligmann (2004:97–100).

32. Dugger (2004).

33. See the work of de Soto (2000, 2002) and de Soto et al. (1986).

34. Ugarteche (2000:122). See also Altamirano et al. (2003:31), and, for Bolivia, Nash (1994).

35. Portes and Hoffman (2003:59). Their paper provides an excellent review of the impact of the neoliberal policies of the 1990s throughout Latin America, which I have relied on for material in this paragraph. See also Nash (1994). Mayer (2002:313–332) and Sheahan (1999) provide a slightly less pessimistic view of neoliberal changes.

36. Mayer (2002:323).

37. Webb and Fernández Baca (2002:223).

38. Chávez de Paz (1989), Degregori (1986a:37), Favre (1984), Mitchell (1999), Poole and Rénique (1992:40–41, 61–62).

39. Coral Cordero (1998).

40. Altamirano (1992, 2004), Figueroa (2001), Portes and Hoffman (2003), and Ugarteche (2000).

Notes to Pages 211–218

41. Data are from the Inter-American Development Bank, as cited in Portes and Hoffman (2003). See also *Guardian* (2005).

42. Mitchell (1991a) and Seligmann (2004).

43. See Lyons's interesting discussion of the complex use of both persuasion and coercion on an Ecuadorian hacienda (Lyons 2005).

44. Coronel Aguirre (1996) and Seligmann (1995).

45. Degregori (1986b:49) and Degregori, ed. (1996:16).

46. Stiglitz (2003:5,7, 17–18, 61–62, 71–72, 171–179, 206–216, and passim).

47. Nash (1979, 1992a, 1992b, 1994).

48. Rudolf (1999).

49. Gill (2004).

50. See Cleaver (2003) for information on Chiapas and Forero (2005) and CEDIB for Bolivia.

51. Marx 1869[1852], chap. 1.

52. The 584,000 births predicted for 2020–2025, while lower than the 666,000 births in the 1990–1995 period, are still 10,000 births more each year than the 574,000 annual births in 1970–1975 (Webb and Fernández 2002:235). Even though these births will be offset by an increase in the number of deaths as the Peruvian baby boomers age, the pressures for resources will still be great.

53. I have translated the following lyrics freely:

"Ayacuchano huérfano pajarillo/¿A qué has venido a tierras extrañas?/Alza tu vuelo, vamos a Ayacucho,/donde tus padres lloran tu ausencia./En tu pobre casa/¿Qué te ha faltado?/Caricias, delicias, de más has tenido./Sólo la pobreza con su ironía/entre sus garras quiso oprimirte." See http://www.angelfire.com/pe/huamanga/cancion.html for the lyrics of this song as well as others from Ayacucho. Poetry and music are difficult to translate; I am grateful to Barbara Jaye, Sean Mitchell, José Oriundo, Priscilla Gac-Artigas, Claire Sylvan, and Roberto Genovés for reviewing my translation.

54. Indeed, with their call for the free movement of people over national borders, such activists might be considered more "global" than the so-called globalists, who advocate the movement of money and goods but not of people.

55. I am grateful to Sean Mitchell for this critique of the terms "globaliza-tion" and "antiglobalization."

56. Crosby (1972). Andre Gunder Frank (1998) has argued that capitalism did not begin in Europe but in Asia, following the arrival of New World gold and silver obtained from Europeans in exchange for Asian goods.

57. Tuckman (2005).

58. See Graeber (2001, 2002, and 2004) and Vidal (2005).

59. Jackson and Warren (2005) describe research on Latin American indige-nous movements. Vanessa Baird (2000) lists resources directly related to social justice in Peru. Current news on Peru also is available at http://www.gci275.com/peru/lista.shtml and http://www.topix.net/world/peru. Lists of general global-justice organizations can be found on the following Web sites: http://www.globalexchange.org/, http://www.globalnetwork4justice.org/, http://www.powertothepeaceful.org/social.html, http://www.rethinkingschools.org/publication/rg/RGResource05.shtml, and http://www.freechild.org/SJforALL.htm. I do not necessarily agree with the policies of all the groups listed on these and other Web sites. One must carefully pick and choose organizations compatible with one's political philosophy. David Graeber, an anthropologist and self-identified anarchist, also provides insightful commentary on the various strands of revolutionary anarchists and Direct Action Network that are trying to create new forms of participatory democracy (Graeber 2001, 2002, and 2004; Grubacic and Graeber 2004). A liberal in temperament, I am less comfortable with these actions, even though unarmed anarchists do not threaten human life.

Glossary

acompañar: To accompany; often a hierarchical relationship in which the less powerful accompany and assist the more powerful.

alfarero: Ceramicist, the name preferred by San Pedro ceramicists. See *ceramista.*

alférez: Standard bearer, the most important and expensive *cargo* for the patronal fiesta, responsible for bringing an orchestra to the celebration.

ambulante: Street peddler.

amor serrano: Literally, "highland love," but a euphemism for wife beating.

andino: Andean.

aniquilación: Annihilation, extermination.

aniquiladores: Killers; applied to groups of killers during the war. See *sanguinarios, los.*

anticuchos: Barbecued beef hearts, a Peruvian delicacy often sold on street corners.

apra: A child born out of wedlock and adopted and cared for by the mother's mother (the maternal grandmother). Not to be confused with APRA, the acronym that is commonly used for the American Popular Revolutionary Alliance (Alianza Popular Revolucionaria Americana), a Peruvian political party.

apu runa: Powerful people, especially referring to townspeople.

arrepentido: Someone who legally repented of Shining Path activities by confessing, providing specific information on his/her participation, and informing on others.

arriero: Muleteer.

asamblea: Assembly, public meeting; organized by rural communities to resolve important issues.

Ayacuchano(a): (1) Resident of Ayacucho City; (2) anyone from the Department of Ayacucho, not just the city.

ayllu: Bilateral kindred, consisting of the mother's and father's relatives extending about two generations. In other localities, *ayllu* is given other meanings that often evoke an ideal pre-Columbian community.

ayni: Balanced reciprocity; used for the exchange of services or goods.

bajíos: The lower region of San Pedro, stereotyped by townspeople as occupied by Indians.

barriada: See *pueblo joven.*

batida: A police or military roadblock to check for documents.

buena gente: A good person; a common phrase used to say that someone is okay.

cachuelo(s): Odd job(s); used to piece together an income.

cargo: A post to organize religious fiestas or other public burdens. See also *varayoc.*

caudillo: Military strongman.

centro: Traditional clothing. See *huali.*

ceramista: Ceramicist. See *alfarero.*

chacra: Agricultural field.

chacra partición: Division of lands among children as their inheritance; done while parents are alive.

charqui: Dried meat, usually beef. The English "jerky" is derived from the Quechua word.

chicha de molle: Local beer made from the berry of the pepper tree, *Schinus molle L.*

chicha: Maize beer; *aja* in Quechua.

chivolo: Youngster.

cholo(a): An ethnic/class term of shifting meaning used to refer, often disrespectfully, to former peasants.

choque: A shock or blow; usually used to refer to a severe chill, as in *choque con el aire,* literally, an air shock.

chullo: Wool hat with ear flaps, often of alpaca wool, worn by people of the *puna.* A model for many modern ski caps.

chunchu: Native of the tropical forest. Although a neutral term in San Pedro and San José, many tropical-forest people consider it a slur.

chuñu: Freeze-dried potatoes; also pronounced *chunu.* Alternate spellings are *chuño* or *chuno.*

churi: Son; Pablopa *churin,* Pablo's son.

churiymi: My son.

Chuschi: Town in southern Ayacucho.

chutu: Indian.

colectivo: Jitney, a common form of public transport.

comadre: See *compadre/comadre.*

comedor popular: Communal kitchen organized by women to prepare cheap meals for their families and others, using donated funds and food, supplemented by the advantages of bulk purchases. Some also function as community centers focusing on the needs of women.

compadrazgo: The ritual kinship of co-parenthood and the reciprocal obligations between *compadres* and *comadres.*

compadre/comadre: Co-parents; describes the relationship between godparents and parents. Parents call the godfather *compadre;* godparents call the father *compadre. Comadre* is the term for a woman. The plural *compadres* refers to both men and women. See *compadrazgo.*

compañero(a): Companion; also used for members of the same group, including Shining Path.

compromiso: An appointment or social commitment.

comunero: Registered member of the *comunidad campesina.*

comunidad campesina: Peasant community, a formal political designation. Before the 1970s, known as "*comunidad indígena.*"

comunidad indígena: Indigenous community. See *comunidad campesina.*

condenado: Phantom. See *manchachico.*

contratista: See *enganchador.*

cortamonte: A celebration during Carnival in which a tree (the *yonsa*) is cut; planted in a set place; decorated with paper chains, fruit, bread, cigarettes, candies, and other favors; then cut by the celebrants, who stand around it and take turns dancing, drinking, and wielding the axe.

cupo: Money, goods, and services demanded by Shining Path; a system of extortion or protection.

cuye: Guinea pig (*Cavia porcellus*) bred for food; served at ceremonial meals.

desaparecido(a): Disappeared person; someone seized by a group (usually the military) and never heard from again, presumably killed.

desplazados: Refugees from the Shining Path war.

Dios pagarasunki: God will repay you, the standard Quechua thank you.

droga: Drug; commonly used to refer to illegal drug traffic, especially the cocaine trade.

Glossary

dueño: Owner; a woman's lover, with implications of patriarchy.

encapuchados: A group of masked men and, less often, women, faces covered by balaclava ski masks; used by the military, Shining Path, and the militias to hide identities.

enganchador: Labor contractor who recruits peasants to work on cotton plantations and other commercial enterprises. Also known as *contratista.*

envidia: Envy; a common accusation about others who are thought to have behaved meanly out of "envy."

estancia: A small rural hamlet, usually occupied by pastoralists.

faena: Municipal labor corvée.

gamonal: A powerful *hacendado* who controlled local political posts and benefices in the sierra. The *gamonal* class disappeared along with haciendas.

gente decente: Literally "decent people," but refers to the local upper class.

gringo: Light-skinned person.

guardia: The Guardia Civil, Civil Guard; uniformed police.

hacendado(a): Owner of an estate with peons.

hacienda: Estate with resident peons.

hijo(a) político(a): Child born in wedlock

hijo(a) natural: Child born out of wedlock; literally, "natural child."

huali: The regional Ayacucho dress for women: usually three ankle-length skirts, placed one over the other, a plain blouse, and a colorful shawl. Alternate spelling: *wali.*

huayno: Andean music style and dance.

humildad: Humility, humbleness.

humilde: A poor person who knows his or her place.

ignorante(s): Ignorant person(s); a common pejorative to refer to rural and other "lower" social classes.

interés: Inherited land, specifically assigned by a parent to a child in the *chacra partición.*

Israelitas del Nuevo Pacto: Israelites of the new Covenant, an autochthonous Peruvian religion.

jarana: Party or fiesta, carrying the connotation of "wild."

leva: A periodic military levy.

Limeño(a): Resident of Lima, Peru's capital city.

llahta: Central town.

llahta runa: Townspeople.

llamar la atención: To call someone on the carpet; to formally give advice on appropriate conduct.

madrina: Godmother.

Mamay: My Mother, an affectionate term of address for a peasant woman.

manchachico: Phantoms, *condenados;* people who die without telling their family about buried money, condemned by God to become wandering dead, seizing unwary travelers to take their place.

manta: Shawl worn by women. *Lliqlla* in Quechua.

matanza: Massacre, slaughter, killing. Ayacuchanos refer to the many *matanzas* of the war years.

maswa: Tuber (*Tropaeolum tuberosum*) native to the Andes. Alternate spelling: *mashua.*

mayordomo: The person responsible for organizing a fiesta, ensuring that all necessary posts are filled.

mercenarios: Mercenaries; frequently applied to masked killers, presumably, military or police personnel or people working for them.

minka: A festive work party given by rich peasants.

mondongo: An elaborate stew made of tripe, *tripas,* and hominy; served during heavy agricultural work and at ceremonies. The wealthy often add beef to enrich the stew.

montaña: The beginning of the tropical rain forest on the eastern slopes of the Andes, one of Peru's major ecological zones; the area for the production of coca, coffee, cacao, and tropical fruits.

muchacha: Young girl; a common term for maid. *Empleada* (literally, female employee) is a somewhat more refined synonym.

negocio: Business, often a petty enterprise that can be as small as selling eggs from a single hen.

novenante: The *cargo* (always occupied by a couple) responsible for bringing bulls to the bullfight during a fiesta.

Ñuqallaymi: "It's just me," a standard Quechua greeting.

oca: Tuber (*Oxalis tuberosa*) native to the Andes.

olluku: Tuber (*Ullucus tuberosus*) native to the Andes.

Pachamama: Mother Earth.

pachamanca: Earthen oven feast; a celebratory meal of tubers, other vegetables, and seasoned meats cooked in the earth with heated stones. Urban residents improvise the meal on the stove.

padrinazgo: Godparenthood, emphasizing not only the ritual ties but also the associated complex of mutual obligations and support.

padrino(s): Godfather (godparents).

papacito: Literally, "little father," implying great affection.

Papay: An affectionate term of address for a peasant man.

Papi: Father, but used affectionately to refer to sons, husbands, godfathers, and other close male ties.

parrillada: Barbecue, mixed grill, often organized by migrants to Lima in a commercial locale.

patrón(a): Boss, chief, patron, employer, patron saint.

patronal fiesta: The fiesta for the patron saint of a community.

pensión: Board; a boardinghouse that provides room as well as board.

peña: Music club featuring "ethnic" music and dance.

peon: (1) Any farmhand or other manual laborer; (2) indentured resident of large estate, given fields or irrigation water in return for labor.

pichqa: The Quechua word for "five"; the memorial observed from the evening of the fourth to the morning of the fifth day after a person's death.

pistaco: Mythical creature, usually depicted as light-skinned and blue-eyed, who preys on natives to sell their rendered fat to Lima. Called *nakaq* in Quechua.

pongo: Diviner; in other areas of the Andes, serf or peon.

prenda: Piece of clothing or other vestment; clothing or personal possession taken from a woman as a token of affection.

primicia: Droit du seigneur, but in San Pedro referring, not to a lord's sexual access to a bride, but to the priest's right to the first fruits of a peasant's field.

primo(a) hermano(a): Cousin-brother (-sister); the children of full siblings.

propietario: Landowner.

propina: Tip, allowance; a small sum made to a social "inferior" in payment for some service.

pueblo: Town.

pueblo joven: Literally, young town, a euphemism for squatter settlement or shantytown. Before the 1970s, known as a *barriada.*

puna: High-altitude grasslands; Andean area above the tree line.

qarawi: Songs celebrating agriculture and herding; sung by two women during ceremonies and agricultural work parties.

retablo: Colorful wood and ceramic shadow box, with fold-back doors that reveal ceramic figurines. Once carried by muleteers as portable altar, but now depicting secular as well as religious scenes, for sale to tourists.

Ronda Campesina: Peasant militia, also known as *comité de autodefensa.*

Rodrigo Franco Command: Comando Rodrigo Franco, a paramilitary death squad associated with APRA and the government of Alan García.

rondero: Member of the peasant militia, the Ronda Campesina.

saco largo: Henpecked man; literally, "long coat."

sanguinarios, los: The bloodthirsty ones; used to describe both military and Shining Path killers. See *aniquiladores.*

San Pedrino(a): Resident of San Pedro.

selva: Lowland tropical rain forest.

Senderista: Shining Path partisan.

serrano(a): Person from the Andes Mountains, the sierra; an insult when said in a deprecatory manner.

Sinchis: A feared and hated counterinsurgency battalion of the Peruvian military.

sol: The Peruvian monetary unit, its value varying significantly from year to year.

soplón: Informer; a deadly epithet that placed a person at risk of being murdered during the war.

Taytay: Honorific for a peasant man.

teniente gobernador: Lieutenant governor; the chief official of a hamlet, often attacked by Shining Path.

terruco: Shining Path terrorist.

tienda: Store; often a tiny room devoted to small sales in the front of a home.

torreón de vigilancia: Watchtower; a small adobe structure sheltering sentries guarding an important road or path.

trago: Cane liquor; the local rum, produced from sugarcane; cheap and freely available.

traje: Suit, attire; the knee-length skirt, heavy stockings, and blouse worn by townswomen.

tripas: Intestinal casings used in making *mondongo.*

urqu taytacha: The mountain god, one of the most important deities in San Pedro and San José; known as the *wamani* (alternate spelling, *humani*) in other Ayacucho communities.

varayoc: Peasant political post (*cargo*) charged primarily with maintaining order; today rarely found.

vecinos del pueblo: Townspeople.

venganza: Vengeance.

vigilancia: The peasant watch; responsible for guarding peasant communities; a Shining Path patrol.

voluntad: Wish, desire, free will; often used to describe a person's willingness to do something.

wakcha: Poor person.

wamani: The mountain god. Alternate spelling: *huamani.* See *tayta urqu,* the term generally used in San Pedro and San José.

warmi suway: Stealing the woman (bride); marriage by capture.

wata unras: Ceremony marking the end of mourning, one year after a person's death.

yanapay: Generalized reciprocity; help given without the specific expectation of its return.

yanta waqtay: Ceremonial work group to prepare firewood for a festival.

yarqa aspiy: Cleaning the irrigation system through corvée labor; consists of both work and festival.

yonsa: A cut tree planted in the street during carnival. See *cortamonte.*

yugada: The amount of land that can be plowed in one day. Many authors estimate 4 *yugadas* to a hectare, but actual field measurements average 7.7 *yugadas* per hectare.

Bibliography

ALDEN, EDWARD
2004   Cotton Report Frays Temper of US Farmers. *Financial Times,* May 20.
ALLEN, CATHERINE J.
1988   *The Hold Life Has: Coca and Cultural Identity in an Andean Community.* Washington, DC: Smithsonian Institution Press.
ALTAMIRANO, TEÓFILO
1984   *Presencia andina en Lima metropolitana: Estudio sobre migrantes y clubes de provincianos.* Lima: Fondo Editorial, Pontificia Universidad Católica del Perú.
1992   *Éxodo: Peruanos en el exterior.* Lima: Fondo Editorial, Pontificia Universidad Católica del Perú.
2003   Transnacionalismo y remesas. In *Emigración latinoamericana: Comparación interregional entre América del Norte, Europa y Japón,* ed. Y. Matsuo. Japan Center for Area Studies, Symposium Series, vol. 19. Osaka: National Museum of Ethnology.
2004   La "fuga de cerebros": Un desafío para la Pontificia Universidad Católica del Perú. Paper presented at the Reunión del KAAD (ex-Becarios Latinoamericanos en Alemania), Quito, Ecuador, February 12–14.
ALTAMIRANO, TEÓFILO, ET AL.
2003   *Poverty Studies in Peru: Towards a More Inclusive Study of Exclusion; WeD Working Paper 05.* Bath, UK: ESRC Research Group, University of Bath. http://www.welldev.org.uk/research/workingpaperpdf/wed05.pdf
AMERICAS WATCH
1986   *Human Rights in Peru after President García's First Year.* New York: Americas Watch Committee.
1992   *Peru under Fire: Human Rights since the Return to Democracy.* New Haven, CT: Human Rights Watch and Yale University Press.
AMNESTY INTERNATIONAL
1985   *Peru: Amnesty International Briefing.* London: Amnesty International Publications.
2002   *Unmatched Power, Unmet Principles: The Human Rights Dimensions of US Training of Foreign Military and Police Forces.* New York: Amnesty International USA.

ANSIÓN, JUAN

1987   *Desde el rincón de los muertos: El pensamiento mítico en Ayacucho.* Lima: Grupo de Estudios para el Desarrollo.

1989   *Pishtacos de verdugos a sacaojos.* Lima: Tarea.

APPLEBY, GORDON

1982   Price Policy and Peasant Production in Peru: Regional Disintegration during Inflation. *Culture and Agriculture* 15:1–6.

ARENDT, HANNAH

1964   *Eichmann in Jerusalem.* New York: Viking Press.

ARNOLD, DEAN E.

1972   Native Pottery Making in Quinua, Peru. *Anthropos* 67:858–872.

1975   Ceramic Ecology in the Ayacucho Basin, Peru: Implications for Prehistory. *Current Anthropology* 16:183–203.

1983   Design Structure and Community Organization in Quinua, Peru. In *Structure and Cognition,* ed. D. Washburn. Cambridge: Cambridge University Press.

1993   *Ecology and Ceramic Production in an Andean Community.* Cambridge: Cambridge University Press.

ASOCIACIÓN PRO DERECHOS HUMANOS (APRODEH)

2003   Nuevos testigos de Uchuraccay. *El Comercio* (Lima), January 27.

BABB, FLORENCE E.

1989   *Between Field and Cooking Pot: The Political Economy of Marketwomen in Peru.* Austin: University of Texas Press.

BAIRD, VANESSA

2000   Return to Ayacucho. *New Internationalist,* issue 321 (March). http://www.newint.org/issue321/contents.htm.

BASOMBRÍO IGLESIAS, CARLOS

1998   Sendero Luminoso and Human Rights: A Perverse Logic That Captured the Country. In *Shining and Other Paths: War and Society in Peru, 1980–1995,* ed. S. J. Stern. Durham, NC: Duke University Press.

BEHAR, RUTH

2002   Preface: Gender Que Pica un Poco. In *Gender's Place: Feminist Anthropologies of Latin America,* ed. R. Montoya, L. J. Frazier, and J. Hurig. New York: Palgrave Macmillan.

BENAVIDES, MARÍA

1988   La división social y geográfica Hanasaya/Urinsaya en el valle del Colca y la provincia de Caylloma. *Boletín de Lima* 60:49–53.

1989   Las vistas a yanque collaguas de los siglos XVI y XVII: Organización social y tenencia de tierras. *Bull. Institut Français d'Études Andines* 18(2):241–267.

BENSON, TODD

2004   W.T.O. Rules against U.S. Cotton Subsidies. *New York Times,* June 19.

BLONDET, CECILIA, AND CARMEN MONTERO

1995   *Hoy menú popular: Comedores en Lima.* Lima: Instituto de Estudios Peruanos/UNICEF.

BLUM, VOLKMAR

1992   Crisis social y modernización campesina en el sur andino del Perú. In *Perú: El problema agrario en debate, SEPIA IV,* ed. C. Degregori, J. Escobal, and B. Marticorena. Lima: SEPIA.

1996   The Viability of Alberto Fujimori's Economic Strategy. In *The Peru-vian Economy and Structural Adjustment: Past, Present and Future*, ed. E. Gonzales de Olarte. Coral Gables, FL: North-South Center, University of Miami.

BOLTON, RALPH
1973   Aggression and Hypoglycemia among the Qolla: A Study in Psychobiological Anthropology. *Ethnology* 12(3):227–257.

BOLTON, RALPH, AND ENRIQUE MAYER
1977   *Andean Kinship and Marriage*. Washington, DC: American Anthropological Association.

BOURQUE, SUSAN C., AND KAY B. WARREN
1981   *Women of the Andes: Patriarchy and Social Change in Two Peruvian Towns*. Ann Arbor: University of Michigan Press.

BOWEN, SALLY, AND JANE HOLLIGAN
2003   *The Imperfect Spy: The Many Lives of Vladimiro Montesinos*. Lima: Ediciones Peisa.   *Bibliography*

BOWKER, LEE H.; MICHELLE ARBITELL; AND J. RICHARD MCFERRON
1988   On the Relationship between Wife Beating and Child Abuse. In *Feminist Perspectives on Wife Abuse*, ed. K. Yllo and M. L. Bograd. Newbury Park, CA: Sage Publications.

BROWN, MICHAEL F., AND EDUARDO FERNÁNDEZ
1991   *War of Shadows: The Struggle for Utopia in the Peruvian Amazon*. Berkeley & Los Angeles: University of California Press.

BUECHLER, HANS, AND JUDITH-MARIA BUECHLER
1996   *The World of Sofía Velázquez: The Autobiography of a Bolivian Market Vendor*. New York: Columbia University Press.

BURT, JO-MARIE
1993   The Dispossessed Look Homeward: Peru's Internal Refugees Organize for Return. *NACLA Report on the Americas* 27(1):8–11.

1998   Shining Path and the "Decisive Battle" in Lima's Barriadas: The Case of Villa El Salvador. In *Shining and Other Paths*, ed. S. Stern. Durham, NC: Duke University Press.

1999   Unsettled Accounts: Militarization and Memory in Postwar Peru. *NACLA Report on the Americas* 32(2):35–41.

CABALLERO, JOSÉ MARÍA
1981   *Economía agraria de la sierra peruana: Antes de la reforma agraria de 1969*. Lima: Instituto de Estudios Peruanos.

CALDWELL, JOHN C., AND GIGI SANTOW, EDS.
1989   *Selected Readings in the Cultural, Social, and Behavioral Determinants of Health*. Canberra: Australian National University, Health Transition Centre.

CALDWELL, JOHN C., ET AL.
1990   *What We Know about Health Transition: The Cultural, Social, and Behavioral Determinants of Health*. Health Transition Series, no. 2. Canberra: Australian National University, Health Transition Centre.

CASTILLO, MARÍA ELENA
1999   Las promesas incumplidas: Lucharon a muerte contra Sendero y hoy son marginados. *La República* (Lima), May 6.

1999 "To a Company of a Man Like My Husband, No Law Can Compel Me": The Limits of Sanctions against Wife Beating in Arequipa, Peru, 1780–1850. *Journal of Women's History* 11(1):31–53.

CHÁVEZ, ENRIQUE, ED.

2003 *La verdad sobre el espanto: Dossier fotográfico de Caretas.* Lima: Caretas.

CHÁVEZ DE PAZ, DENNIS

1989 *Juventud y terrorismo: Características sociales de los condenados por terrorismo y otros delitos.* Lima: Instituto de Estudios Peruanos.

CHEVARRÍA LEÓN, FERNANDO

2004 Lima y Callao reciben más recursos sociales que las regiones pobres. *El Comercio* (Lima), August 31.

CHOIKE: A PORTAL ON SOUTHERN CIVIL SOCIETIES

2003 Fifth WTO Conference–Cancun 2003. http://www.choike.org/cgibin/choike/links/page.cgi?p=ver_indepth&id=1236.

CHOSSUDOVSKY, MICHEL

1992 *Ajuste económico: El Perú bajo el dominio del FMI.* Lima: Mosca Azul Editores.

1997 *The Globalisation of Poverty: Impacts of IMF and World Bank Reforms.* Atlantic Highlands, NJ: Zed Books.

CHUMPITAZ, ÓSCAR

1999 Sobrevivir es única meta de "los niños topos." *La República* (Lima), May 12.

CLELAND, JOHN, AND JOHN HOBCRAFT, EDS.

1985 *Reproductive Change in Developing Countries: Insights from the World Fertility Survey.* New York: Oxford University Press.

COALE, ANSLEY J., AND EDGAR M. HOOVER

1958 *Population Growth and Economic Growth in Low-Income Countries.* Princeton, NJ: Princeton University Press.

COLLINS, JANE

1988 *Unseasonal Migrations: The Effects of Rural Labor Scarcity in Peru.* Princeton, NJ: Princeton University Press.

COLLOREDO-MANSFELD, RUDI

2002 "Don't Be Lazy, Don't Lie, Don't Steal": Community Justice in the Neoliberal Andes. *American Ethnologist* 29(3):637–662.

COMISIÓN DE LA VERDAD Y RECONCILIACIÓN

2003a *Informe final.* Lima: http://www.cverdad.org.pe/ifinal/.

2003b *Yuyanapaq—para recordar: Relato visual del conflicto armado interno en el Perú.* Lima: Fondo Editorial, Pontificia Universidad Católica del Perú.

CONRAD, GEOFFREY W., AND ARTHUR A. DEMAREST

1984 *Religion and Empire: The Dynamics of Inca and Aztec Expansionism.* Cambridge: Cambridge University Press.

CONROY, JOHN

2000 *Unspeakable Acts, Ordinary People: The Dynamics of Torture.* New York: Alfred A. Knopf.

COORDINADORA NACIONAL DE LOS DERECHOS HUMANOS

1998 *Informe sobre legislación de "seguridad nacional, 23 de junio de 1998.* Lima: Coordinadora Nacional de los Derechos Humanos. http://www.derechos.net/cnddhh/.

1994   El proceso del desplazamiento en el Perú. In *III Encuentro Interinsti-
       tucional sobre Desplazamiento en la Región Central*, ed. S. Peña Guerra.
       Huancayo, Peru: Grupo de Trabajo de la Región Central sobre el
       Desplazamiento.
1995   Desplazamiento por violencia política en el Perú, 1980–1992. In
       *Desplazados: ICVA (Consejo Internacional de Agencias Voluntarias)
       consulta sobre desplazamiento y refugio en la región andina*. Lima: In-
       stituto de Defensa Legal.
1998   Women in War: Impact and Response. In *Shining and Other Paths:
       War and Society in Peru, 1980–1995*, ed. S. J. Stern. Durham, NC:
       Duke University Press.

CORONEL AGUIRRE, JOSÉ

1993   Todavía es un proceso abierto. In *Hablan los ronderos: La búsqueda
       por la paz en los Andes*, ed. O. Starn. Lima: Instituto de Estudios
       Peruanos.
1994   Comités de autodefensa: Un proceso social abierto. *Ideele* 59(60):
       113–115.
1996   Violencia política y respuestas campesinas en Huanta. In *Las rondas
       campesinas y la derrota de Sendero Luminoso*, ed. C. Degregori. Lima &
       Huamanga: Instituto de Estudios Peruanos/Universidad Nacional
       San Cristóbal de la Huamanga.

CORONEL AGUIRRE, JOSÉ, AND CARLOS LOAYZA

1992   Violencia política: Formas de respuesta comunera en Ayacucho.
       In *Perú: El problema agrario en debate, SEPIA IV*, ed. C. I. Degre-
       gori, J. Escobal, and B. Marticorena. Lima: Instituto de Estudios
       Peruanos.

COUNCIL ON HEMISPHERIC AFFAIRS

2003   *Truth and Reconciliation Commission Forces Peru to Confront Its Vio-
       lent Past*. Memorandum to the Press 03.56. Washington, DC: Coun-
       cil on Hemispheric Affairs.

CRABTREE, JOHN, AND JIM THOMAS, EDS.

1998   *Fujimori's Peru: The Political Economy*. London: Institute of Latin
       American Studies, University of London.

DAILY TELEGRAPH

2000   Obituary of Ezequiel Gamonal: Leader of a Peruvian Cult Influenced
       by the Films of Cecil B. de Mille. July 24.

DANNER, MARK

2004a Torture and Truth. *New York Review of Books* 51(10) (June 10).
2004b The Logic of Torture. *New York Review of Books* 51(11) (June 24).

DEGREGORI, CARLOS IVÁN

1986a *"Sendero Luminoso": Parte I: Los hondos y mortales desencuentros;
       Parte II: Lucha armada y utopía autoritaria*. Lima: Instituto de Estu-
       dios Peruanos.
1986b *Ayacucho, ráices de una crisis*. Ayacucho, Peru: Instituto de Estudios
       Regionales José María Arguedas.
1989   Que difícil es ser dios: Ideología y violencia política en Sendero Lu-
       minoso. Lima: El Zorro de Abajo Ediciones.
1990   Ayacucho 1969–1979: El surgimiento de Sendero Luminoso. Lima:
       Instituto de Estudios Peruanos.

Bibliography

244

1992　Origins and Logic of Shining Path: Return to the Past. In *Shining Path of Peru,* ed. D. S. Palmer. New York: St. Martin's Press.

1998　Harvesting Storms: Peasant Rondas and the Defeat of Sendero Luminoso in Ayacucho. In *Shining and Other Paths: War and Society in Peru, 1980–1995,* ed. S. J. Stern. Durham, NC: Duke University Press.

DEGREGORI, CARLOS IVÁN, ED.

1996　*Las rondas campesinas y la derrota de Sendero Luminoso.* Lima: Instituto de Estudios Peruanos.

DEJANVRY, ALAIN

1981　*The Agrarian Question and Reformism in Latin America.* Baltimore, MD: Johns Hopkins University Press.

DE LA CADENA, MARISOL

1998　From Race to Class: Insurgent Intellectuals *de Provincia* in Peru, 1910–1970. In *Shining and Other Paths: War and Society in Peru, 1980–1995,* ed. S. J. Stern. Durham, NC: Duke University Press.

2000　*Indigenous Mestizos: The Politics of Race and Culture in Cuzco, 1919–1991.* Durham, NC: Duke University Press.

2002　The Racial-Moral Politics of Race: Mestizas and Intellectuals in Turn-of-the Century Peru. In *Gender's Place: Feminist Anthropologies of Latin America,* ed. R. Montoya, L. J. Frazier, and J. Hurig. New York: Palgrave Macmillan.

DEL PINO HUAMÁN, PONCIANO

1993　Los campesinos hacen suya la organización que inicialmente se impulsó. In *Hablan los ronderos: La búsqueda por la paz en los Andes,* ed. O. Stern. Lima: Instituto de Estudios Peruanos.

1995　Peasants at War. In *The Peru Reader: History, Culture, Politics,* ed. O. Stern, C. I. Degregori, and R. Kirk. Durham, NC: Duke University Press.

1996　Tiempo de guerra y los dioses: Ronderos, evangélicos y senderistas en el valle del Río Apurímac. In *Las rondas campesinas y la derrota de Sendero Luminoso,* ed. C. Degregori. Lima & Huamanga: Instituto de Estudios Peruanos/Universidad Nacional San Cristóbal de la Huamanga.

1998　Family, Culture and "Revolution": Everyday Life with Sendero Luminoso. In *Shining and Other Paths: War and Society in Peru, 1980–1995,* ed. S. J. Stern. Durham, NC: Duke University Press.

DE SOTO, HERNANDO

2000　*The Mystery of Capital: Why Capitalism Triumphs in the West and Fails Everywhere Else.* New York: Basic Books.

2002　[1989] *The Other Path: The Economic Answer to Terrorism.* New York: Basic Books.

DE SOTO, HERNANDO, ET AL.

1986　*El otro sendero: La revolución informal.* Lima: Editorial El Barranco.

DÍAZ MARTÍNEZ, ANTONIO

1969　*Ayacucho: Hambre y esperanza.* Ayacucho, Peru: Ediciones Waman Puma.

DONNAN, CHRISTOPHER B.

1976　*Moche Art and Iconography.* Los Angeles: University of California Press/UCLA Latin American Center Publications.

1978 *Moche Art of Peru: Pre-Columbian Symbolic Communication.* Los An-   245
geles: Museum of Cultural History, University of California.

DRUG ENFORCEMENT ADMINISTRATION

1993 Coca Cultivation and Cocaine Processing: an Overview. http://
www.druglibrary.org/schaffer/govpubs/cocccp.htm.

DUGGER, CELIA W.

2004 The Food Chain, Survival of the Biggest: Supermarket Giants Crush
Central American Farmers. *New York Times,* December 28.

DURAND, JOHN T.

1967 The Modern Expansion of World Population. *Proceedings of the
American Philosophical Society,* vol. 111.

ELLIOTT, LARRY; CHARLOTTE DENNY; AND DAVID MUNK

2003 Blow to World Economy as Trade Talks Collapse. *The Guardian,*
http://www.guardian.co.uk/print/0,3858,4753641–103635,00.html,
September 15.

FAVRE, HENRI   *Bibliography*

1984 Perú: Sendero Luminoso y horizontes ocultos. *Quehacer* 31–32
(September–October):25–35. (Also published as Pérou: Sentier Lu-
mineux et Horizons Obscurs, *Problèmes d'Amérique Latine* 72:3–27
[1984]).

FERNANDEZ, JAMES W.

1990 Tolerance in a Repugnant World and Other Dilemmas in the Cultural
Relativism of Melville J. Herskovits. *Ethos* 18(2):140–164.

FERNÁNDEZ SALVATTECI, MAJ. JOSÉ (RET.)

1986 *Terrorismo y guerra sucia en el Perú.* Lima: Editorial Fernández
Salvatteci.

FERRONI, M. A.

1980 The Urban Bias of Peruvian Food Policy: Consequences and Alternatives. PhD diss., Cornell University.

FIGUEROA, ADOLFO

1983 Mito y realidad de la economía campesina. In *La cuestión rural en el
Perú,* ed. J. Iguñiz. Lima: Fondo Editorial, Pontificia Universidad
Católica del Perú.

1999 Social Exclusion and Rural Underdevelopment. Paper prepared for
the World Bank Conference on Evaluation and Poverty Reduction,
Washington, DC, June 14–15.

2001 Social Exclusion as Distribution Theory. In *Social Exclusion and Poverty Reduction in Latin America,* ed. C. S. E. Gacitúa and S. Davis.
Washington, DC: World Bank.

FINANCIAL TIMES

2004 Editorial: Sickly Sugar, May 21.

FORERO, JUAN

2003 Ex-Generals and Others Protest Peru Report on Rebel Conflict. *New
York Times,* September 8.

2004 Colombia: Payments in Cluster Bombing. *New York Times,* May 27.

2005 Free Trade Proposal Splits Bolivian City. *New York Times,* March 9.

FRANK, ANDRE GUNDER

1998 *Reorient: Global Economy in the Asian Age.* Berkeley & Los Angeles:
University of California Press.

FRANKLIN, DAVID, ET AL.

1985   *Consumption Effects of Agricultural Policies: Peru: Trade Policy, Agricultural Prices and Food Consumption: An Economy Wide Perspective.* Raleigh, NC: Sigma One Corp. (USAID/PERU).

FRIEDLANDER, JUDITH

1975   *Being Indian in Hueyapan: A Study of Forced Identity.* New York: St. Martin's Press.

FUMERTON, MARIO

2002   *From Victims to Heroes: Peasant Counter-Rebellion and Civil War in Ayacucho, Peru, 1980–2000.* PhD diss., University of Utrecht. http://www.library.uu.nl/digiarchief/dip/diss/2002–1211–101726/inhoud.htm (distributed in U.S. by Purdue University Press).

GARCILASO DE LA VEGA, EL INCA

1966   [1609] *Royal Commentaries of the Incas and General History of Peru [1616–1617],* trans. H. V. Livermore. Austin: U. of Texas Press.

GILL, LESLIE

1997   Creating Citizens, Making Men: The Military and Masculinity in Bolivia. *Cultural Anthropology* 12(4):527–550.

2000   *Teetering on the Rim: Global Restructuring, Daily Life, and the Armed Retreat of the Bolivian State.* New York: Columbia University Press.

2004   *The School of the Americas: Military Training and Political Violence in the Americas.* Durham, NC: Duke University Press.

GLASS, D. V., AND D. E. C. EVERSLEY

1965   *Population in History.* Chicago: Aldine.

GONZÁLEZ-CUEVA, EDUARDO

2000   Conscription and Violence in Peru. *Latin American Perspectives* 27(3):88–102.

GONZALES DE OLARTE, EFRAÍN

1987   *Inflación y campesinado: Comunidades y microrregiones frente a la crisis.* Lima: Instituto de Estudios Peruanos.

GORRITI, GUSTAVO

1990   *Sendero: Historia de la guerra milenaria del Perú.* Lima: Editorial Apoyo.

1999   *The Shining Path: A History of the Millenarian War in Peru.* Trans., intro. R. Kirk. Chapel Hill: University of North Carolina Press.

GUARDIAN, THE

2005   The Global Remittance Rip-off. March 30. http://www.guardian.co.uk/international/story/0,3604,1449026,00.html.

HAMANN, A. JAVIER, AND C. PAREDES

1991   The Peruvian Economy: Characteristics and Trends. In *Peru's Path to Recovery: A Plan for Economic Stabilization and Growth,* ed. C. E. Paredes and J. D. Sachs. Washington, DC: Brookings Institution.

HANDWERKER, W. PENN

1986   Culture and Reproduction: Exploring Micro/Macro Linkages. In *Culture and Reproduction: An Anthropological Critique of Demographic Transition Theory,* ed. W. P. Handwerker. Boulder, CO: Westview Press.

HANDWERKER, W. PENN, ED.

1986   *Culture and Reproduction: An Anthropological Critique of Demographic Transition Theory.* Boulder, CO: Westview Press.

1987   *Death, Sex and Fertility: Population Regulation in Preindustrial and Developing Societies.* New York: Columbia University Press.

HARRIS, OLIVIA

1978   Complementarity and Conflict: An Andean View of Women and Men. In *Sex and Age as Principles of Social Differentiation,* ed. J. S. L. Fontaine. London: Academic Press.

1994   Condor and Bull: The Ambiguities of Masculinity in Northern Potosí. In *Sex and Violence: Issues in Representation and Experience,* ed. P. Harvey and P. Gow. New York: Routledge.

HARVEY, PENELOPE

1994   Domestic Violence in the Peruvian Andes. In *Sex and Violence: Issues in Representation and Experience,* ed. P. Harvey and P. Gow. New York: Routledge.

HUBER, LUDVIG

1995   *Después de Dios y la Virgen está la ronda: Las rondas campesinas de Piura.* Lima: Instituto de Estudios Peruanos/Instituto Francés de Estudios Andinos.

HUNT, SHANE

1996   Peru: The Current Economic Situation in Long-term Perspective. In *The Peruvian Economy and Structural Adjustment: Past, Present and Future,* ed. E. Gonzales de Olarte. Coral Gables, FL: North-South Center, University of Miami.

IGUÍÑIZ ECHEVERRÍA, JAVIER

1996   The Difficult Moments of the Fujimori Economic Strategy. In *The Peruvian Economy and Structural Adjustment: Past, Present and Future,* ed. E. Gonzales de Olarte. Coral Gables, FL: North-South Center, University of Miami.

ISBELL, BILLIE JEAN

1978   *To Defend Ourselves: Ecology and Ritual in an Andean Village.* Austin: University of Texas Press.

JACKSON, JEAN AND KAY WARREN

2005   Indigenous Movements in Latin America, 1992–2004. *Annual Review of Anthropology* 34:549–573.

KANDIYOTI, DENIZ

1988   Bargaining with Patriarchy. *Gender and Society* 2(3):274–290.

KAUFMAN KANTOR, GLENDA, AND JANA L. JASINSKI

1998   Dynamics and Risk Factors in Partner Violence. In *Partner Violence: A Comprehensive Review of 20 Years of Research,* ed. J. L. Jasinski, L. Finkelhor, and D. Finkelhor. Thousand Oaks, CA: Sage.

KAWELL, JO ANN

1995   The Cocaine Economy. In *The Peru Reader: History, Culture, Politics,* ed. O. Starn, C. I. Degregori, and R. Kirk. Durham: Duke U.P.

KIRK, ROBIN

1991   *The Decade of Chaqwa: Peru's Internal Refugees.* Washington, DC: U.S. Committee for Refugees.

1993   *Grabado en piedra: Las mujeres de Sendero Luminoso.* Lima: Instituto de Estudios Peruanos.

1995   Chaqwa. In *The Peru Reader: History, Culture, Politics,* ed. O. Starn, C. I. Degregori, and R. Kirk. Durham, NC: Duke University Press.

1997   *The Monkey's Paw: New Chronicles from Peru.* Amherst: University of Massachusetts Press.

Bibliography

KUNITZ, STEPHEN J.

1983 *Disease Change and the Role of Medicine: The Navaho Experience.* Princeton, NJ: Princeton University Press.

LATIN AMERICAN AND CARIBBEAN COMMITTEE FOR THE DEFENSE OF WOMEN'S RIGHTS (CRLP) AND CENTER FOR REPRODUCTIVE LAW AND POLICY (CLADEM).

2003 *Silence and Complicity: Violence against Women in Peruvian Public Health Facilities.* New York: CLADEM and CRLP.

LIFTON, ROBERT JAY

1986 *The Nazi Doctors: Medical Killing and the Psychology of Genocide.* New York: Basic Books.

LOBO, SUSAN

1982 *A House of My Own: Social Organization in the Squatter Settlements of Lima, Peru.* Tucson: University of Arizona Press.

LONG, NORMAN, AND BRYAN R. ROBERTS

1984 *Miners, Peasants, and Entrepreneurs: Regional Development in the Central Highlands of Peru.* Cambridge: Cambridge University Press.

LYONS, BARRY J.

2002 "To Act Like a Man": Masculinity, Resistance, and Authority in the Ecuadorian Andes. In *Gender's Place: Feminist Anthropologies of Latin America,* ed. R. Montoya, L. J. Frazier, and J. Hurig. New York: Palgrave Macmillan.

MALCOLM, JANET

1990 *The Journalist and the Murderer.* New York: Knopf/Random House.

MANRIQUE, NELSON

1998 The War for the Central Sierra. In *Shining and Other Paths: War and Society in Peru, 1980–1995,* ed. S. J. Stern. Durham, NC: Duke University Press.

MARIÁTEGUI, JOSÉ CARLOS

1959 [1928] *Siete ensayos de interpretación de la realidad peruana.* Lima: Empresa Editora Amauta.

1971 *Seven Interpretive Essays on Peruvian Reality.* Austin: University of Texas Press.

MARX, KARL

1869 [1852] *The Eighteenth Brumaire of Louis Napoleon.* Chaps. 1 & 7, trans. S. K. Padover from German edition of 1869; chaps. 2–6 based on 3rd ed., prep. Engels (1885), trans. & pub. Progress Publishers, Moscow, 1937. Full text available online at http://www.marxists.org/archive/marx/works/1852/18th-brumaire/ch01.htm.

MATOS MAR, JOSÉ

1984 *Desborde popular y crisis del estado.* Lima: Instituto de Estudios Peruanos.

MAYER, ENRIQUE

1991 Peru in Deep Trouble: Mario Vargas Llosa's "Inquest in the Andes" Reexamined. *Cultural Anthropology* 6(4):466–504.

1994 Patterns of Violence in the Andes. *Latin American Research Review* 29(2):141–171.

2002 *The Articulated Peasant: Household Economies in the Andes.* Boulder, CO: Westview Press.

1981   *Maidens, Meal and Money: Capitalism and the Domestic Community.*
        New York: Cambridge University Press.

MENCHÚ, RIGOBERTA, AND ELISABETH BURGOS-DEBRAY
1983   *Me llamo Rigoberta Menchú y así me nació la conciencia.* Barcelona:
        Ediciones Gallimard.
1984   *I, Rigoberta Menchú: An Indian Woman in Guatemala.* London:
        Verso.

MILLONES, LUIS, AND MARY LOUISE PRATT
1990   *Amor Brujo: Images and Culture of Love in the Andes.* Syracuse, NY:
        Syracuse University, Maxwell School of Citizenship and Public Affairs.

MITCHELL, WILLIAM P.
1976   Irrigation and Community in the Central Peruvian Highlands. *American Anthropologist* 78:25–44.
1979   Inconsistencia de status social y dimensiones de rango en los Andes
        centrales del Perú. *Estudios Andinos* 15:21–31.
1991a   Some Are More Equal Than Others: Labor Supply, Reciprocity, and
        Redistribution in the Andes. *Research in Economic Anthropology*
        13:191–219.
1991b   *Peasants on the Edge: Crop, Cult, and Crisis in the Andes.* Austin: University of Texas Press.
1994   Dam the Water: The Ecology and Political Economy of Irrigation in
        the Ayacucho Valley, Peru. In *Irrigation at High Altitudes: The Social
        Organization of Water Control Systems in the Andes,* ed. W. P. Mitchell
        and D. Guillet. Washington, DC: American Anthropological Association, Publication Series of the Society for Latin American Anthropology, vol. 12.
1997   Pressures on Peasant Production and the Transformation of Regional
        and National Identities. In *Migrants, Regional Identities, and Latin
        American Cities,* ed. T. Altamirano and L. Hirabayashi. Washington,
        DC: American Anthropological Association, Publication Series of the
        Society for Latin American Anthropology, vol. 13.
1999   Detour onto the Shining Path: Obscuring the Social Revolution in
        the Andes. In *Deadly Developments: Capitalism, States and War,* ed.
        S. P. Reyna and R. E. Downs. Amsterdam: Gordon & Breach.
2001   Stolen Glory: David Stoll and Rigoberta Menchú. Invited paper presented at colloquium on Rigoberta Menchú, George Mason University, April 25.

MITCHELL, WILLIAM P., AND DAVID GUILLET, EDS.
1994   *Irrigation at High Altitudes: The Social Organization of Water Control
        Systems in the Andes.* Washington, DC: American Anthropological
        Association, Publication Series of the Society for Latin American Anthropology, vol. 12.

MITCHELL, WINIFRED L.
1994   Women's Hierarchies of Age and Suffering in an Andean Community.
        Journal of Cross-Cultural Gerontology 9:179–191.

MONTAGU, ASHLEY
1942   *Man's Most Dangerous Myth: The Fallacy of Race.* New York: Columbia University Press.

1980 *Capitalismo y no capitalismo en el Perú: Un estudio histórico de su articulación en un eje regional.* Lima: Mosca Azul Editores.

MYERS, STEVEN LEE
1996 Old U.S. Army Manuals for Latin Officers Urged Rights Abuses. *New York Times,* September 22.

NASH, JUNE
1979 *We Eat the Mines and the Mines Eat Us: Dependency and Exploitation in Bolivian Tin Mines.* New York: Columbia University Press.
1992a *I Spent My Life in the Mines: The Story of Juan Rojas, Bolivian Tin Miner.* New York: Columbia University Press.
1992b Interpreting Social Movements: Bolivian Resistance to Economic Conditions Imposed by the International Monetary Fund. *American Ethnologist* 19(2):275–293.
1994 Global Integration and Subsistence Insecurity. *American Anthropologist* 96(1):7–30.

NATIONAL CATHOLIC REPORTER
2001 Peru's New Cardinal Known for Standing with the Powerful—Juan Luis Cipriani. *National Catholic Reporter,* March 23. http://www.findarticles.com/p/articles/mi_m1141/is_21_37/ai_729 60577.

NENCEL, LORRAINE
1996 Pacharacas, Putas and Chicas de Su Casa: Labelling, Femininity and Men's Sexual Selves in Lima, Peru. In *Machos, Mistresses, Madonnas: Contesting the Power of Latin American Gender Imagery,* ed. M. Melhuus and K. A. Stølen. New York: Verso.

NEW JERSEY DEPARTMENT OF HEALTH AND SENIOR SERVICES
2001 Hazardous Substance Fact Sheet: Lead Arsenate. http://www.state.nj.us/health/eoh/rtkweb/1098.pdf.

NEW YORK TIMES
2003a Editorial: The Rigged Trade Game, July 20.
2003b Editorial: America's Sugar Daddies, November 29.
2004 Editorial: Trading on Subsidies, July 30.

NOEL MORAL, BRIG. GEN. CLEMENTE
1989 *Testimonio de un soldado.* Lima: Publinor.

NORTH AMERICAN CONGRESS ON LATIN AMERICA (NACLA)
2002 Cleaning up after Fujimori: Peruvian Panel Probes "Economic Crimes" Linked to Privatization: An Interview with Investigator Óscar Ugarteche. *NACLA Report on the Americas* 35(4).

OBANDO, ENRIQUE
1998 Civil-Military Relations in Peru, 1980–1996: How to Control and Coopt the Military (and the Consequences of Doing So). In *Shining and Other Paths: War and Society in Peru, 1980–1995,* ed. S. J. Stern. Durham, NC: Duke University Press.

ORLOVE, BENJAMIN
1988 A Stranger in Her Father's House. In *Lucha: The Struggles of Latin American Women,* ed. C. Weil. Minnesota Latin American series, no. 2. Minneapolis: Prisma Institute.

PALMER, DAVID SCOTT, ED.
1992 *Shining Path of Peru.* New York: St. Martin's Press.

PAREDES, CARLOS E., AND JEFFREY D. SACHS, EDS.
1991 *Peru's Path to Recovery: A Plan for Economic Stabilization and Growth.* Washington, DC: Brookings Institution.

PASTOR, MANUEL, AND CAROL WISE
1992 Peruvian Economic Policy in the 1980s: From Orthodoxy to Heterodoxy and Back. *Latin American Research Review* 27(2):83–117.

POOLE, DEBORAH, AND GERARDO RÉNIQUE
1991 The New Chroniclers of Peru: U.S. Scholars and Their "Shining Path" of Peasant Rebellion. *Bulletin of Latin American Research* 10(1): 133–191.
1992 *Peru: Time of Fear.* London: Latin America Bureau (Monthly Review Press).

PORTES, ALEJANDRO, AND KELLY HOFFMAN
2003 Latin American Class Structures: Their Composition and Change during the Neoliberal Era. *Latin American Research Review* 38(1): 41–84.

Bibliography

PORTOCARRERO, GONZALO
1998 *Razones de sangre: Aproximaciones a la violencia política.* Lima: Fondo Editorial, Pontificia Universidad Católica del Perú.

POTTER, GEORGE ANN
2000 *Deeper Than Debt: Economic Globalisation and the Poor.* London: Latin America Bureau (Monthly Review Press).

PRESTON, SAMUEL H.
1985 Mortality in Childhood: Lessons from WFS. In *Reproductive Change in Developing Countries: Insights from the World Fertility Survey,* ed. J. Cleland and J. Hobcraft. Oxford: Oxford University Press.

REID, MICHAEL
1985 *Peru: Paths to Poverty.* London: Latin America/Third World Publications Bureau.

RISEN, JAMES, AND CHRISTOPHER MARQUIS
2001 Officials Long Debated Risks of Anti-Drug Patrol in Peru. *New York Times,* May 22.

ROSS, ERIC
2003 Malthusianism, Capitalist Agriculture, and the Fate of Peasants in the Making of the Modern World Food System. *Review of Radical Political Economics* 35(4):437–461.

RUDOLF, GLORIA
1999 *Panama's Poor: Victims, Agents, and Historymakers.* Gainesville: University Presses of Florida.

SABOGAL DIÉGUEZ, JOSÉ
1952 *El "kero," vaso de libaciones cuzqueño de madera pintada.* Lima: Ministerio de Educación Pública, Museo de la Cultura Peruana.

SABOGAL WEISSE, JOSÉ R.
1989 *El "kero."* Lima: Biblioteca Nacional del Perú.

SCHACTER, DANIEL L.
2001 *The Seven Sins of Memory: How the Mind Forgets and Remembers.* Boston: Houghton Mifflin.

SELIGMANN, LINDA J.
1995 *Between Reform and Revolution: Political Struggles in the Peruvian Andes, 1969–1991.* Stanford, CA: Stanford University Press.

2004   *Peruvian Street Lives: Culture, Power, and Economy among Market Women of Cuzco.* Urbana: University of Illinois Press.

SENGUPTA, SOMINI

2005   Vigilantes May Be Nepal's Secret Weapon against Rebels. *New York Times,* April 11.

SHEAHAN, JOHN

1999   *Searching for a Better Society: The Peruvian Economy from 1950.* University Park: Pennsylvania State University Press.

SILVERBLATT, IRENE

1987   *Moon, Sun, and Witches: Gender Ideologies and Class in Inca and Colonial Peru.* Princeton, NJ: Princeton University Press.

SILVERSTEIN, KEN

2001   Mercenary, Inc. *Washington Business Forward,* April 26.

SINGER, PETER W.

2003   *Corporate Warriors: The Rise of the Privatized Military Industry.* Ithaca, NY: Cornell University Press.

STARN, ORIN

1991   Missing the Revolution: Anthropologists and the War in Peru. *Cultural Anthropology* 6(1):63–91.

1992   "I Dreamed of Foxes and Hawks": Reflections on Peasant Protest, New Social Movements, and the Rondas Campesinas of Northern Peru. In *The Making of Social Movements in Latin America: Identity, Strategy and Democracy,* ed. A. Escobar and S. Álvarez. Boulder, CO: Westview Press.

1994   Rethinking the Politics of Anthropology: The Case of the Andes. *Current Anthropology* 35(1):13–38.

1995   Nightwatch. In *The Peru Reader: History, Culture, Politics,* eds. O. Starn, C. I. Degregori, and R. Kirk. Durham, NC: Duke University Press.

1997   Villagers at Arms: War and Counterrevolution in the Central-South Andes. In *Between Resistance and Revolution: Cultural Politics and Social Protest,* eds. R. Fox and O. Starn. New Brunswick, NJ: Rutgers University Press.

1998   Villagers at Arms: War and Counterrevolution in the Central-South Andes. In *Shining and Other Paths: War and Society in Peru, 1980–1995,* ed. S. J. Stern. Durham, NC: Duke University Press.

1999   *Nightwatch: The Making of a Movement in the Peruvian Andes.* Durham, NC: Duke University Press.

STARN, ORIN, ED.

1993   *Hablan los ronderos: La búsqueda por la paz en los Andes.* Lima: Instituto de Estudios Peruanos.

STARN, ORIN; CARLOS I. DEGREGORI; AND ROBIN KIRK, EDS.

1995   *The Peru Reader: History, Culture, Politics.* Durham, NC: Duke University Press.

STERN, STEVE J., ED.

1998   *Shining and Other Paths: War and Society in Peru, 1980–1995.* Durham, NC: Duke University Press.

STIGLITZ, JOSEPH E.

2003   *Globalization and Its Discontents.* New York: W. W. Norton.

STØLEN, KRISTI ANNE

1987   *A media voz: Ser mujer campesina en la sierra ecuatoriana.* Quito, Ecuador: Ceplaes.

STOLL, DAVID

1993   *Between Two Armies in the Ixil Towns of Guatemala.* New York: Columbia University Press.

1999   *Rigoberta Menchú and the Story of All Poor Guatemalans.* Boulder, CO: Westview Press.

TAPIA, CARLOS

1997   *Las fuerzas armadas y Sendero Luminoso.* Lima: Instituto de Estudios Peruanos.

THORP, ROSEMARY

1996   A Long-Run Perspective on Short-Run Stabilization: The Experience of Peru. In *The Peruvian Economy and Structural Adjustment: Past, Present and Future,* ed. E. Gonzales de Olarte. Coral Gables, FL: North-South Center, University of Miami.

THORP, ROSEMARY, AND G. BERTRAM

1978   *Peru: 1890–1977: Growth and Policy in an Open Economy.* New York: Columbia University Press.

TOKAR, BRIAN, ED.

2004   *Gene Traders: Biotechnology, World Trade, and the Globalization of Hunger.* Burlington, VT: Toward Freedom.

TOURÉ, AMADOU TOUMANI, AND BLAISE COMPAORÉ

2003   Your Farm Subsidies Are Strangling Us. *New York Times,* July 7.

UGARTECHE, ÓSCAR

1998   *La arqueología de la modernidad: El Perú entre la globalización y la exclusión.* Lima: Desco.

2000   *The False Dilemma: Globalization: Opportunity or Threat?* New York: Zed Books.

UNITED NATIONS POPULATION DIVISION

1953   *The Determinants and Consequences of Population Trends.* New York: United Nations.

UNITED STATES, DEPARTMENT OF STATE

N.d.   *Reported Human Health Effects from Glyphosate: Executive Summary.* United States Embassy, Colombia. http://usembassy.state.gov/colombia/wwwfuc1e.pdf.

URTON, GARY

1993   Moieties and Ceremonialism in the Andes: The Ritual Battles of the Carnival Season in Southern Peru. In *El mundo ceremonial andino,* ed. L. Millones and Y. Onuki. Senri Ethnological Studies, no. 37. Osaka, Japan: National Museum of Ethnology.

VAN DONGEN, RACHEL

2003   U.S.'s "Private Army" Grows. *Christian Science Monitor,* September 6.

VAN VLEET, KRISTA

N.d.   Transnational Spectacle: Situated Performance: Narrating Agency and Negotiating Identity in Andean "Ritual Battles" (manuscript).

2002   The Intimacies of Power: Rethinking Violence and Affinity in the Bolivian Andes. *American Ethnologist* 29(3):567–601.

Bibliography

1983   *Informe de la comisión investigadora de los sucesos de Uchuraccay.* Lima: Editoria Perú.

VECCHIO, RICK

2000   Trashy Shows Entertain, Distract during Election Year. *Holland Sentinel* (Holland, MI), March 15.

2004a   Enmeshed in Peru's Corruption Wars, TV Queen Crusades for the Poor from a Studio-Turned-Prison. *Associated Press,* September 21. http://ap.tbo.com/ap/breaking/MGBQEDCFLZD.html.

2004b   Peruvian Telemundo Host Says She's Being Held for Supporting Fujimori. *Associated Press,* August 23.

VIDAL, JOHN

2003   Farmer Commits Suicide at Protests. *The Guardian,* September 11. http://www.guardian.co.uk/international/story/0,3604,1039650,00.html.

2005   Global Poverty Targeted as 100,000 Gather in Brazil; Activists Join Presidents as Annual World Social Forum Gets Under Way in Porto Alegre. *The Guardian,* January 26. http://www.guardian.co.uk/globalisation/story/0,7369,1398435,00.html.

WADE, SHAWN M.

1997   Terrorism and Democracy: The "Defeat" of Sendero Luminoso and the Suspension of Civilian Rule in Peru. In *Peru beyond the Reforms: 1996 PromPerú Summer Internship Program,* ed. K. McTigue. Lima: PromPerú.

WAHL, JENNY B.

1996   *Oil Slickers: How Petroleum Benefits at the Taxpayer's Expense.* Institute for Self-Reliance. http://www.ilsr.org/carbo/costs/truecostes.html.

WEBB, RICHARD, AND G. FERNÁNDEZ BACA

1990   *Almanaque estadístico: Perú en números, 1990.* Lima: Cuánto.

2002   *Anuario estadístico: Perú en números.* Lima: Instituto Cuánto.

WEISMANTEL, MARY

1997   White Cannibals: Fantasies of Racial Violence in the Andes. *Identities* 4(1):9–43.

1988   *Food, Gender, and Poverty in the Ecuadorian Andes.* Philadelphia: University of Pennsylvania Press.

1998   Race in the Andes: Global Movements and Popular Ontologies. *Bulletin of Latin American Research* 17(2):121–142.

2001   *Cholas and Pishtacos: Stories of Race and Sex in the Andes.* Chicago: University of Chicago Press.

WEST, CANDACE, AND DON H. ZIMMERMAN

1987   Doing Gender. *Gender and Society* 1(2):125–151.

WISE, CAROL

2003   *Reinventing the State: Economic Strategy and Institutional Change in Peru.* Ann Arbor: University of Michigan Press.

WORLD WILDLIFE FUND

2001   *Letter from World Wildlife Fund Regarding Herbicide Spraying in Colombia,* November 21. http://www.ciponline.org/colombia/112101.htm.

WRIGHT, ANGUS

1990   *The Death of Ramón González: The Modern Agricultural Dilemma.* Austin: University of Texas Press.

Index

vision of land among children), 16, 100; by Horacio and Benjamina, 71; *interés* (inherited land), 99–101, 122, 224n.2; by Martín, 88, 91–92; by Pablo and Claudia, 19–20; and SINAMOS, 92; and Valentina and Roberto, 99–101, 121, 122; by women, 46. *See also* Land reform

Land reform, 90, 92–93, 101, 160, 179. *See also* Land ownership

Leva (military levy), 39, 71

Lifton, Robert Jay, 168

Lima: crime in, 3; electricity and electrical blackouts in, 204, 209; homes in, 113–114, 202–203; migrants in, 2, 3, 65, 66, 72–73, 82, 84, 113–114, 138, 162; Mitchell in, 7, 202–204; population of, 2; poverty in, 3, 202; and Shining Path war, 204, 205; Triga in, 138; Valentina in, 103–104; wealth in, 202–204. *See also* Artisans

Literacy. *See* Education

Lost development decade, 210–211

Machista (masculine): Roberto as, 100–101. *See also* Gender

Maize, 14, 19, 20, 22–25, 24, 42, 65, 174, 208

Maize beer (*chicha*). *See* Alcohol use

Malcolm, Janet, 68–69, 168

Manchachico (dead spirit), 18, 101, 107, 186–187, 224n.3; digging for buried treasure of, 101

Manrique, Nelson, 137, 159

Mariátegui, José Carlos, 224–225n.1

Marlowe, Christopher, 10

Marriage: Benjamina's relationship with Horacio, 44–45, 46; civil and Catholic weddings, 42, 43, 98, 110; courtship and marriage of Benjamina and Horacio, 42–43, 46; destruction of Valentina's store by husband, 114–115; extra-marital sexual relationships of Horacio, 43–44; and family responsibilities, 120–122; of Martín and Fortunata, 83–88, 90; and multiple families, 86–87; parents' opposition to, 42–43, 104–111;

of Roberto and Valentina, 104–117; separation during, due to economic reasons, 83–88, 112; and shared patronyms, 43–44; and tension between natal and conjugal families, 109–110; trial marriage, 19, 42, 43; of Triga, 141; *warmi qurquy* (marriage by capture), 43, 46, 107–110; women's use of maiden names after, 37. *See also* Child support; Childbirth and pregnancy; Kin networks; Wife beating

Martín. *See* Velarde, Martín

Marx, Karl, 217

Masculinity. *See* Gender

Masonry, 85

Mates. See Gourds

Matos Mar, José, 206

Matronym, 43–44

Men. *See* Gender; and specific men

Menchú, Rigoberta, 199–200

Mercenaries (in Shining Path war), 129–131, 133–134, 136, 195–196

Mestizos. See Race and ethnicity

Mexico, 71, 82, 216

Migrants: clubs for, 89–90, 94; conversion of, to Protestantism, 94; education of, 82–83; as farm workers, 80–82, 81, 84–85, 90; international migrants from Peru, 214; land ownership by, 91–92; in Lima, 3, 65, 66, 72–73, 82, 83, 113–114, 138, 162; odd jobs for, 87; poverty of Martín, as, 78–96; in Punta Madera, 77–96; salary for, 84, 85; squatter settlements of, 77, 78, 79, 224n.1; Triga's migration to Lima, 138; Valentina in United States, 98, 118–119, 122. *See also Desplazados;* Poverty; Resettlement policy; Rodriguez, Valentina; Triga; Velarde, Martín

Military. *See* Peasant militias; Shining Path war; Sinchis

Militias. *See* Peasant militias

Minka (festive work party), 22–23, 52

Mitchell, Daphna, 175

Mitchell, William P.: adoption of, by Pablo and Claudia, 15–16, 59,